A New Orleans Cookbook From Momma's Kitchen

New Orleans and Louisiana
Creole, Cajun and Family
Recipes and Memories,
Past and Present

by

Eulalie Miscenich Poll

A New Orleans Cookbook
From Momma's Kitchen
by Eulalie Miscenich Poll
Edited by Jonathan K. Poll

A Cornerstone Book
Published by Cornerstone Book Publishers
Copyright © 2010 by Eulalie Miscenich Poll

All rights reserved under International and Pan-American Copyright Conventions. No part of this book may be reproduced in any manner without permission in writing from the copyright holder, except by a reviewer, who may quote brief passages in a review.

Cornerstone Book Publishers
Hot Springs Village, AR

First Cornerstone Edition - 2010
Second Cornerstone Edition - 2015
Third Cornerstone Edition - 2021
Fourth Cornerstone Edition - 2025

www.cornerstonepublishers.com

ISBN: 978-1-61342-249-6

Eulalie Miscenich Poll

Illustrations

"Magazine St. Grocery" by Weldon Miscenich .... Cover

"Cafe du Monde" by Jenny Byers xviii

"T-Boy's Estate" by Weldon Miscenich 22

"Bourbon St. Grocery" by Weldon Miscenich 42

"St. Charles Streetcar" by Weldon Miscenich 68

"The Lakefront" by Jenny Byers 94

"Lee Circle Bar" by Weldon Miscenich 116

"Lake Pontchartrain Lighthouse" by Weldon Miscenich 132

"City Park Walk" by Jenny Byers 150

"The Alley" by John Miscenich 174

"Boat Rentals at City Park" by John Miscenich 196

"St. Louis Cathedral" by Jenny Byers 222

"City Park Boathouse" by Jenny Byers 238

"Magazine St. Grocery" by Weldon Miscenich 248

"City Park View" by John Miscenich 282

"Family Tree" by John Miscenich 334

"The Captain's House" by John Miscenich 350

All art under copyright by the artists and used by permission.

Eulalie Miscenich Poll

Dedication

    This book is in memory of my Momma. Well Mom, here's our book. And to my Mamere, who made the best gumbo in the world. And to a very Special Friend of mine, with Love.

    Also, to my own beloved Children, Mike, Laurie and Johnny, my lovely Daughter-in-law Eve, and my dear little Grandchildren, Matt, Jenny, Bobby and Jonny, with a heart full of Love. May they never forget their heritage.

E.M.P.

Acknowledgments

This book is in memory of my Mom, my mentor, my role model, my Dearest Friend, and the finest cook I have ever known. For the love she had for and the faith she had in me. Mom taught me that you can do anything you want in this life, as long as you believe you can do it, and then to have the courage to work at it. So, Mom, here's our book.

To my three children, Mike, Laurie and Johnny. My son Mike, my brave guinea pig, my sampler who encouraged me, along with his wife Eve, with everything he sampled, no matter how it tasted, and urged me on. Who assisted me in putting the book together and getting it ready to go, and then publishing it for me through his own Publishing Company. My daughter Laurie, who was so determined that I finish the book that she set up an office for me in our home, with everything I needed, including one of my most prized possession, my computer. Who brought food to her office for her co-workers to willingly, or unwillingly, try. And who helped me in editing the recipes. My little son John left us many years ago to go to God, but in my heart I feel Johnny close to me, and feel his love every time I sit down to type.

To my two oldest grandchildren Matt and Jenny, for their patience, love and support in trying to teach me the intricacy and mysteries of the computer. Matt took care of the technical end, and Jenny for trying to teach me, (or doing it for me) the design and layout of the book. If it were not for the invaluable help and advice of these two young people, I would have given up long ago. The technical advice of Matt, this young Webmaster, and for some of the photographs taken by my Photographer Granddaughter Jenny that I proudly used in this book, and her assistance with the layout of the book have helped me more than anything else. Thank goodness we all live in the same house, for I call on one or the other of them almost daily to help me out with problems I have on this scary machine. And to my two little grandsons Bobby and Jonny, who bolster my ego by telling me, "Mamere, you're a good cooker."

To my Artist brother Weldon Miscenich, a lover of food, for the many conversations we have had on food, and for the many recipes he has sent me. But most important, for allowing me to use copies of some of his beautiful paintings in my book. And to his lovely wife Barbara, who also shares her recipes with me. To my cousins,

Helene Ware Wagner and Vivian Ware Dawkins, for the encouragement they gave me and the faith they expressed in me in the writing of this book, and who also shared their recipes with me, And to the rest of my family and friends who has suffered through the trials and failures in my cooking.

And especially to a Very Dear Friend, for the kindness and gentle encouragement given that means so much to me.

Eulalie Miscenich Poll

Table of Contents

Beverages 1

Appetizers 21

Gumbo and Soups 41

Salads and Dressings 67

Sauces 93

Beans, Rice, and Jambalaya 115

Seafood 131

Poultry 149

Meat 173

Vegetables 195

Casseroles 221

Pasta 237

Bread and Sandwiches 247

Cakes, Cookies, and Desserts 281

Lagniappe 333

Index 349

A New Orleans Cookbook from Momma's Kitchen

Forward

    Cooking is a way of life for many Southerners. In hard times the Southern cook spent much time inventing good, tasty meals with low-cost items. This is Southern Cooking. Making the best of what you have. I hope you enjoy these recipes.

Eulalie Miscenich Poll

Introduction

We have come home! We are once again living in Louisiana. For nine years we were living in the foothills of the beautiful Blue Ridge Mountains of Virginia. Nestled in the countryside, we were living minutes from Charlottesville, in a little community called Earlysville, and about a 20 minute drive from Skyline Drive on the Blue Ridge Parkway. Our home was comfortable and the scenery was breathtakingly beautiful. We were new to Virginia. My son and his family, my daughter and her children, our dogs and I had moved to Virginia, and the warm loving people of that peaceful community welcomed us with open arms. They are special people, those people of Virginia, kind, warm, generous, loving, and with hearts as big as the magnificent mountains that surround them. We were happy there, but my heritage – and my heart and soul – is in the city of my birth, New Orleans. I missed home. How could I not, it is where I was born, grew up, married, raised a family and lived until moving to Virginia.

But when hurricane Katrina ravaged New Orleans, we could not stay away, we wanted to come back home. We came back to unbelievable devastation. But in just the short time that we have been back, I have seen the indomitable spirit and unshakable faith and the resiliency of the people of my beloved city, who are determined to take back the city that the storm tried to claim. This city is called the "Big Easy," the "City that care forgot," a city that is known for partying, for laying back and having a good time. But it has been a sleeping tiger. It has awakened from its indolence, and my people here have rolled up their sleeves and are working to make their beautiful city as good, and even better, than it has ever been. I am so very proud to call this home.

But some things have not changed. The people are still as warm and caring and fun loving as they always were, the familiarity of the climate, and the comforting feeling of walking into a supermarket and finding the shelves and coolers filled with the items we have missed for so long. Things like pickled pork, Creole cream cheese, the Creole and Cajun herbs and spices, long loaves of crispy Po'boy bread, the strong chicory coffees, Camellia dried red beans, etc. And the seafood! We can't seem to get enough of it. It is so good to once again sit on the shore of beautiful Lake Pontchartrain, and to feed stale bread to the ducks at West End, and to walk through beautiful Audubon Park. The zoo, the aquarium, the two impressively beautiful Universities, Loyola and Tulane, on lovely St. Charles Avenue, The Riverfront, Dueling oaks and the beautiful Art Museum and the Celebration in the Oaks at Christmas time in City Park. And then there is Mardi Gras and the masking and the balls! The Spring Fiesta in the French Quarter

– so many special events and days like All Saints Day, St. Joseph's day and the St. Joseph Alters, the Jazz Fest, the Greek Festival on Robert E. Lee Blvd. – St. Patrick's day and the Irish and Italian parades, and the incomparable Mardi Gras parades - the parades - parades for any and all events - so many places – so many things to do and see. There truly is no place like home.

My Daughter, my Granddaughter and I are the third, fourth and fifth generation of women in our family to be born in New Orleans, and the seventh, eighth and ninth born in Louisiana. My Mother and my Grandmother were born in New Orleans, and my Great-Grandmother moved to New Orleans as a bride during the Civil War when she was fifteen years old. Marie, my Great-Grandmother, was born on a plantation in Vacherie, a town in southeast Louisiana on the River Road, on the West Bank of the Mississippi River. My Great-Great Grandmother's family were living on the East bank of the Mississippi River when she was born, and her Mother and Grandmother were also born there. Cesaire, my Great-Great Grandmother, became Mistress of the plantation in Vacherie when she went there as a bride. So, the customs of Southern Louisiana, and in particular, the culture and "Joie de vivre" of this beautiful old city of New Orleans is deeply ingrained in my soul.

My Grandmother Eulalie's ancestors, on her Paternal side, came from Bordeaux and Marseilles, France. On her Maternal side, her ancestors were known as Acadians, migrating from the Black Forests of Bavaria, Switzerland, and Alsace-Lorraine, France to Nova Scotia. From there they went to the village of Jeremie in Santo Domingo. They then settled on the West Bank of the Mississippi River on the River Road in La Paroisse St. Jacques (St. James Parish). The area was known as the settlement of Kabahannossé by the earliest settlers. Kabahannossé, or as it was later known, Cabanocey, is a Choctaw Indian word meaning mallard's roost. Hakhoba – mallards –anosi – to sleep there- roost. Today the area is called Vacherie. It is just a little corner of southeast Louisiana, but an incredible story lies behind its quiet serenity. It was the first exile of the Acadians and, much later, the Gold Coast of the wealthiest Sugar Barons of Louisiana. Rich in history, this land of my ancestors has sheltered Paupers and entertained Princes. It was the land of sugar cane, tobacco, rice, and cotton. The land of small farms and great plantations. Of mosquitoes, pirogues and great River boats, Fais-do-do's and grand balls. Of hurricanes and unbearable heat, damp cold that chilled to the very bones, plagues, floods, parties and pleasant times. Spanish moss hanging from live oak trees, magnolias, camellias, and unbelievably beautiful days and evenings. Of proud people with a unique sense of values characterized by a sunny outlook on life and strong family ties. Strong, enduring men and women with hope and optimism in their hearts, great love for their families, and courage to wrest a life out of an unknown land.

Their food was from the land, sky, and water. Influenced as they were by their French and German ways of cooking in their homelands, and the different ingredients they used, the first settlers had difficulties in adjusting to cooking in this new land. So, in desperation they turned to the Indians, who showed them how to use the abundant seafood, fresh fruit and vegetables that grew all year long, and the fowl and wildlife that were so plentiful.

The bottom of Louisiana (the most southern part) is a rare and strange mixture of ecologies. Between the Mississippi River and the Atchafalaya River where the waters empties into the Gulf, the mixture of fresh and salt water creates one of America's last great wetland wildernesses, and is the home of the Pelicans (Louisiana, the Pelican State) The products of this land where the first Acadians settled were pigs, which later on were used for sausages like andouille and boudin, free ranging chickens, ducks, and geese. Game, like armadillo, possum, rabbit, 'coon, squirrel, black bear and deer. Wildfowl like bobolink, bobwhite, coot, mallard, mourning doves, partridge, pintail ducks, quail, snipes, teal, and woodcocks. And from the waters, crabs, crawfish, oysters, shrimp, black drum, catfish, croaker, garfish, mullet, pompano, redfish, red snapper, sac-a-lait, sheepshead, Spanish mackerel, speckled trout, alligator, frogs, turtles, and many other unnamed fish. And to name a few of the plants, corn, eggplant, a variety of greens, onions, large tomatoes (now called Creole tomatoes), yams, blueberries, strawberries and a many other berries, and many fruit trees such as fig, mulberry, peach, pear, pecan and orange, trees. There were also cotton, rice, sugarcane, tobacco, and peppers, from the mild sweet green peppers to a variety of hot ones, and these settlers learned to use it all.

So, these French and German descent Acadians landed in the middle of this fertile land and made it their own. Their endurance and spiritual strength was their salvation, and their thrifty and unique style of cooking made, through the coming generations, their way of preparing food famous.

My Great-Grandmother Marie Selma was Acadian, or as they became known, Cajun. But my Grandmother Eulalie was a true Creole cook. Born and raised in New Orleans, her cooking was influenced not only by the Cajun ways, but by the French, Italian, African, and Spanish cultures in New Orleans. There is a difference in the Cajun cooking of the country and the Creole cooking of the city. The Creole cooking tends to be more light and disciplined, Cajun cooking more robust and highly seasoned. It is said that the Cajun food explodes the palate, the Creole food titillates it. The dishes are often the same, but depending on where the cook lives, the difference lies in the techniques used when the dish is prepared, a little more or less of the same ingredients. The results are wonderful, but never quite predictable, for every cook adds their own touch.

New Orleans's love affair with food "goes way back" as the saying goes, and this love affair is now Internationally known and acclaimed. But visitors to our city often get the wrong impression of New Orleans cuisine. That it is all French, highly seasoned, difficult to prepare, and expensive. But some of the best of our dishes are simple, thrifty, and designed to use whatever is available. This is New Orleans cooking. Making do with what you have. In a good Southern kitchen, food is never thrown away. Learning to make something good out of whatever you have on hand is the basis of Creole cooking.

As I said earlier, my Mamere (Grandmother) was a wonderful cook. So was my Mother, although she did not cook in the true Creole way. My Father was born in a beautiful little mountainous town in northern Yugoslavia on the coast of the Adriatic Sea. So, my Mother toned down her cooking because he wasn't accustomed to highly seasoned food. But she was still the best cook I have ever known in my life. My Father's family had grape vineyards in his homeland, and they made, and sold, wine. He brought to his adopted country a knowledge and love of fine wines, which he passed on to his wife and children. So, between the two of them we had the best of both worlds. My Mamere made the best gumbo I have ever tasted. I remember, as a little girl, going to her home and sitting with her while we ate her gumbo. She had a little wood stove in her kitchen and in the winter we would sit with our feet on the bottom of the little stove and eat her gumbo. My mouth would feel as if it was on fire and the tears would run down my face from the hot pepper, but Oh, it was so delicious. As we ate, she would tell me stories of our family of the past, and of when she was young, and what it was like to be a young girl growing up on lovely Esplanade Ave, by the river, on the edge of the Vieux Carre (The French Quarter) shortly after the Civil War.

New Orleans is a melting pot for all cultures and their methods of cooking. The French for their ability to create haute cuisine from anything edible. The Spanish, for their spicy dishes. The African Americans of New Orleans, who are among the city's best cooks. The Indian's gifts of herbs and spices such as the sassafras leaves called "File", so important in Gumbo File. The Italians, who shared their tomato gravies, pasta, and one of the city's specialties, the Muffulatta sandwich. The Irish, the Germans, and on and on.

The people, the music, the great restaurants, the food, and the way of life in New Orleans are incomparable, as many visitors to the Crescent City will attest. New Orleanians love to cook, to eat, and to talk about food. But many of the traditional dishes prepared in local homes are disappearing, as often they haven't been written down. So please accept some of my family's recipes. Try them, add your own touches to them (as every New Orleanian does). Enjoy them and "Laissez les Bons Temps Rouler" (Let the good times roll).

A New Orleans Cookbook
From Momma's Kitchen

A New Orleans Cookbook from Momma's Kitchen

Beverages

New Orleans Chicory Coffee 3
Café au Lait 4
Café Brulot 4
Café Parfait (Iced Coffee) 5
Irish Coffee 5
Ice Cream Sodas 6
Malts and Milkshakes 7
Super Chocolate Malt 7
Quick Chocolate Malt 7
Vanilla Malt 7
Strawberry Milkshake 7
Gelatin and Ice Cream Drink 8
Chocolate Sauce 8
Black Cow Shake 8
Breakfast Smoothie 9
Fruit Smoothie 9
Queasy Stomach Smoothie 9
Super Smoothie 10
Hot Cocoa 10
French Hot Chocolate 11
Ice Ring Mold
(Decorative) 11

Lemonade 12
Mint Iced Tea 12
Pink Tea Refresher 13
Iced Tea and Ginger Ale 13
Hurricane Punch 14
Spiced Cranberry Punch 14
Cranberry Punch 15
Planter's Punch 15
Laurie's Champagne Punch
(Wedding Punch) 16
Champagne Punch a La Creole 16
Mint Julep 17
Creole Mary
(The Designated Driver's Drink) 17
Mimosa 17
Ramos Gin Fizz
(New Orleans Gin Fizz) 18
Spanish Sangria
(Wine Punch) 18
Mulled Wine
(Bischof) 19

New Orleans Chicory Coffee

The first thing many New Orleanians do when they open their eyes in the morning is to reach for a cup of black coffee, or a "Petit Noir" (small black) as the old Creoles used to say. Then you have started the day right. The Creoles say that this early cup lengthens the life span. I don't know how true this is, but it really does tone you up for the day. The Creoles describe the coffee they drink as:

> Noir comme le Diable
> Fort comme la Mort
> Doux comme l'amour
> Et chaud comme l'enfer.

Translated, this means they like their coffee black as the devil, strong as death, sweet as love, and hot as Hades! Although black coffee is served to awaken you, after breakfast, after lunch, dinner, or at any time, the people of New Orleans usually drink café au lait, which is a combination of ½ cup boiling milk and ½ cup hot strong coffee, sweetened to taste. This is the coffee that is so popular in the Coffee Houses in the French Quarter. After an exhausting day of shopping at the River-walk mall at the Riverfront, or the lovely Esplanade mall on the outskirts of the city, the shoppers will stop at the coffee stand on the lower level of the mall and sit and relax with a steaming cup of café au lait and a small plate of hot beignets covered with powdered sugar. Or if they are at the Lakeside mall near beautiful Lake Pontchartrain, they will go to the coffee shop behind the mall to have their café au lait and beignets. Beignets are the small French Quarter donuts made famous at the big Coffee Houses in the French Market in the Vieux Carre. The people of New Orleans, and the visitors to our city, go to the Coffee Houses in the Vieux Carre on the Riverfront, and sit at the outdoor café tables under the canopy at all hours of the day or night. For breakfast, after lunch, to stop and rest, or at 2 or 3 A.M. they will be there. After parties, the Carnival Balls or the Opera or Ballet, the people of our city will wind up the day with a steaming cup of café au lait and a plate of beignets.

Café Brulot is served as a dramatic finale to an elegant dinner. There is Irish coffee, Kahlua coffee, Café Parfait, which is an iced coffee my Mother often served at lunch time in the summer (without the liquor.). Whatever way it is fixed, New Orleans has always had a love affair with its strong chicory coffee. My roots are deep in New Orleans. And there are some things I cannot do without. And my strong coffee is one of them. When my family and I were living in the beautiful countryside of the Blue Ridge Mountains of Virginia I had my strong chicory coffee shipped to my new home! It was one of the small pleasures from my old home, enjoyed in my new home.

Café au Lait
New Orleans favorite Creole coffee served at the French Market coffee houses
(And in many homes in New Orleans)

3 cups whole milk
½ cup breakfast cream
6 to 8 cups hot, strong New Orleans chicory coffee
Sugar to individual taste

    Combine milk and cream and heat just to boiling point. Remove from heat. Fill large mugs ⅓ full with coffee. Fill rest of mug with milk and cream mixture. Sweeten to taste. If desired, make the coffee darker or lighter by increasing the amount of coffee or milk.

Café Brulot
Prepared in the Traditional old New Orleans Style

¼ inch cinnamon stick
12 whole cloves
¼ cup thinly slivered orange peel
¼ cup thinly slivered lemon peel
1½ tablespoons sugar
2 ounces Cognac, preferably Courvoisier
1½ ounces orange curacao
4 cups very hot, strong, black coffee

    Combine the first five ingredients in a Brulot bowl or chafing dish. Knead the mixture with the ladle. Add the Cognac and the Curacao and stir well. Carefully ignite Cognac and keep stirring until sugar is dissolved. Slowly pour in the black coffee and continue to stir until the flame goes out. Serve at once in Brulot or Demitasse cups.

Café Parfait
(Iced Coffee)

1 quart dark roast coffee and chicory
1 quart milk
2 oz. Brandy or Cognac (optional)
Sugar to taste
Shaved ice

Mix all ingredients together. Serve in tall 10 ounce tumblers over shaved ice.

Variation: Iced coffee with vanilla ice cream

In place of milk, substitute 1 quart of vanilla ice cream. Pour coffee, half of ice cream, and Brandy or Cognac into a punch bowl. Beat with electric beater until mixture gets bubbly. Add remaining ice cream so that it floats in center. Serve in punch cups or old-fashioned glasses.

Irish Coffee

1 ounce Irish whiskey
1 tablespoon sugar
4 ounces hot coffee
Whipped cream

Combine Irish whiskey, sugar and coffee in a coffee cup or Irish coffee glass. Stir and cover the top with whipped cream. Makes one drink.

Ice Cream Sodas

Vary soda according to what flavor you want.

Ice Cream Soda
3 tablespoons chocolate syrup, fruit flavored pancake syrup, or cherry or pineapple sundae topping
¼ cup milk
1 cup club soda, chilled
1 or 2 scoops ice cream
Whipped cream and maraschino cherry (optional)

Add syrup and milk in a tall soda glass and stir. Put in scoops of ice cream and club soda. If you are using cream and cherry, add to top. Serve with a straw and iced teaspoon.

Strawberry Soda
1½ cups milk
1 10-ounce package sliced frozen strawberries, partially thawed
1 pint strawberry ice cream
1 16-ounce bottle club soda

Place milk and strawberries in blender, cover and process on high speed until well blended. Pour into 5 tall glasses. Add a scoop or two of ice cream to each glass, and slowly add club soda. Serve immediately with spoons and straws.

Tropical Cooler

Divide 2 cups cut-up mixed fresh or frozen, thawed, fruits of your choice (mixed berries, peaches, oranges, bananas, etc.) between 4 12-ounce glasses. To each glass add ¼ cup each pineapple and orange juice and a large scoop of vanilla ice cream. Slowly fill glasses with club soda.

Malts and Milkshakes

Super Chocolate Malt

1 cup vanilla ice cream
2 tablespoons chocolate sauce, see page 8
2 tablespoons malt powder
1 cup chilled heavy cream

Quick Chocolate Malt

¾ cup milk
3 tablespoons
chocolate syrup
2 tablespoons malt (optional)
1 pint chocolate ice cream

Vanilla Malt

1 cup vanilla ice cream
2 tablespoons malt (optional)
2 teaspoons vanilla extract
¼ cup chilled heavy cream or milk

Strawberry Milkshake

1-pint strawberry ice cream,
¼ cup chilled heavy cream,
2 tablespoons strawberry syrup.
Top with a fresh strawberry if desired

Place all ingredients in a blender, cover, and blend at high speed until smooth. Pour malts into chilled 12-ounce glasses. Serve with large straws.

Gelatin and Ice Cream Drink

2 cups cold milk
1 package Jell-O grape, strawberry, or cherry gelatin
2½ cups vanilla ice cream

Pour milk into blender. Add gelatin and ice cream. Blend at high speed until smooth, about 30 seconds. Pour into glasses and serve immediately.

Chocolate Sauce

2 ounces unsweetened chocolate
7 ounces semisweet chocolate
⅜ cup light corn syrup
½ cup hot water

In the top half of a double boiler over hot, not boiling water, melt chocolate with corn syrup, stirring constantly. Then whisk in the water. Whisk until smooth and shiny.

Black Cow Shake

½ of a 12 ounce can chilled root beer and a large scoop of vanilla ice cream. Serve in a tall chilled 10-ounce glass with a straw and iced-tea spoon.

Breakfast Smoothie

1 cup low fat vanilla yogurt
½ cup strawberry nectar
1 frozen banana, sliced
1 cup frozen strawberries or berry blend

Combine the yogurt and strawberry nectar in a blender. Add the banana and the berries and blend until smooth. Serves two.

Fruit Smoothie

½ ripe mango, peeled and seeded
½ ripe papaya, peeled and seeded
1 ripe banana
¼ cup freshly squeezed orange juice
½ cup skim milk
¼ cup nonfat yogurt
1 teaspoon honey
2 cups ice

Place all ingredients in blender and process until smooth.

Queasy Stomach Smoothie

1½ cups diced pears
½ cup low fat peach yogurt
½ cup pear nectar
1 teaspoon fresh lemon juice
¼ teaspoon grated fresh ginger
3 to 5 ice cubes, crushed

Combine all ingredients in a blender and blend until smooth.

Super Smoothie

1 cup ice cream, any flavor
½ cup plain yogurt
2 small frozen bananas
¼ cup shaved ice (optional)
1 cup milk
1 teaspoon vanilla extract
½ cup raspberries, blackberries, strawberries, or a combination of all
2 tablespoons soy protein powder (optional)
2 tablespoons Ovaltine (optional)

Place all ingredients in blender and blend until smooth.

Hot Cocoa

6 tablespoons cocoa
6 tablespoons sugar
⅛ teaspoon salt
½ cup water
6 cups milk
½ teaspoon vanilla extract
Whipped cream or marshmallows (optional)

In saucepan, mix cocoa, sugar, salt, and water. Bring to a boil over low heat and boil gently for 2 minutes, stirring. Add milk and heat slowly just to the boiling point. Add vanilla and beat with a whisk or beater until smooth and foamy. Pour into mugs and top with whipped cream or marshmallows, if you like. Serve immediately.

French Hot Chocolate

4 squares semisweet chocolate
¼ cup light corn syrup
Dash of salt
½ teaspoon vanilla extract
1 cup heavy whipping cream, whipped
4 cups hot milk

In a heavy saucepan over low heat, or in a double boiler over hot, not boiling, water, heat chocolate, corn syrup, and salt, stirring, until chocolate is melted and blended. Remove from heat and stir in vanilla. Cover and refrigerate for about 20 to 25 minutes, or until mixture is cool. When cooled and ready to serve, fold chocolate mixture into whipped cream. Place a large, well rounded tablespoon of chocolate and cream mixture into each serving cup. Gently add hot milk to fill each cup.

Ice Ring Mold
(Decorative)

6 cups water
5 or 6 large garden leaves - bay or lemon leaves, etc. (not holly) washed well.
Fruit - such as unpeeled lemon, lime or orange slices, pineapple chunks or rings, fresh strawberries, cherries, clusters of grapes, red and green, springs of mint or fruit of your choice.

Before filling ring mold set water on side in a bowl, stir it well several times during a 10 minute period to break up air bubbles. Otherwise, the ice mold will be cloudy instead of clear.

Select a decorative 6 cup ring mold. Fill with 3 cups of the water you set aside in bowl. Partially freeze. On top of slush-like layer of water arrange fruit of your choice in a pretty pattern. Carefully and slowly pour a small amount of water around fruit and leaves. Return to freezer until frozen. When frozen add more water to fill mold to the top. Allow the contents to become thoroughly frozen. The day before serving, unmold ice ring by dipping bottom of mold in cold water. Turn out on heavy foil. Wrap ring securely in foil and return to freezer. So, serve, unwrap and float ice ring fruit side up in punch bowl. Pour punch of your choice over it.

Make another ice ring and keep it in freezer to use if needed.

Lemonade

⅔ cup fresh lemon juice
¼ cup fresh orange juice
Simple syrup
2 cups water

Stir together juices, syrup, and water. Add to a pitcher partly filled with ice. Garnish with a sprig of mint. Makes about 4 cups

Simple Syrup

⅔ cup water
⅔ cup sugar

Place water and sugar in a small saucepan. Bring to a boil and, stirring continually, boil until sugar is dissolved. Cool before adding to lemonade.

Mint Iced Tea

1 quart water
4 family size tea bags (recommended, Luzianne tea bags)
2 cups sugar
2 cups water
1 bunch mint leaves
1 lemon, sliced for garnish

Bring the 1 quart of water to a boil. Remove from heat, add the tea bags and cover. Allow to steep for 20 minutes. Meanwhile, make a simple syrup by adding the 2 cups of sugar and 2 cups of water to a small pot. Bring to a boil and continue to boil, stirring until sugar dissolves. Pour the simple syrup into a large jug. When the tea has steeped, remove the lid and tea bags. Pour the tea over the simple syrup in the jug. Stir well and then place the tea bags back into the jug. Fill the jug with cold water to yield one gallon. Stir well To serve, pour tea over ice cubes in a tall glass and garnish with mint leaves and slices of lemon.

Pink Tea Refresher

3 cups boiling water
1 Lipton family size flow-thru tea bag
1 cup cranberry juice cocktail
6 tablespoons sugar
1 tablespoon lemon juice

In teapot, pour water over tea bag. Brew for 4 minutes and remove tea bag. Pour into pitcher and stir in cranberry juice, sugar and lemon juice. Serve over ice in tall glasses. Makes 6 servings. Recipe easily doubled.

Iced Tea and Ginger Ale

3 quarts tea (steep 3 family size tea bags in 3 quarts water)
½ cup sugar
1½ cups lemon juice (about 9 lemons) or 1 (12 oz.) can frozen lemonade concentrate
1 quart bottle ginger ale

Combine tea, sugar, and lemon juice. Just before serving stir in ginger ale and pour over crushed ice in glasses. A fresh mint sprig may be added to each glass. Serves 10.

Hurricane Punch

1 (46 oz.) can Hawaiian punch
1 (12 oz.) can frozen orange juice
1 (6 oz.) can frozen lemonade
¾ cup sugar (optional)
4 oz. amber rum per glass
Orange slices
Maraschino cherries

In a punch bowl or large pitcher combine the first four ingredients. Stir well. Add crushed ice to 16-ounce glasses and add 4 ounces rum per glass. Fill glasses with punch mixture. Garnish with orange slices and cherries.

Spiced Cranberry Punch
For Jenny

½ cup sugar
1 cup water
3 whole cinnamon sticks
3 cups cranberry juice
½ cup fresh lemon juice
1 cup fresh orange juice
1 quart chilled ginger ale
Whole cloves
Fresh lemon and orange slices
1/5 rum or vodka (optional)

Add the first four ingredients to a saucepan. Bring to boiling point and low boil for five minutes. Strain, cool, and then mix with fruit juices. When ready to serve pour into punch bowl over ice or decorative ice ring. Add ginger ale. Stud orange and lemon slices with cloves and add to punch bowl. If using liquor add rum or vodka. Easily doubled for a larger amount.

Cranberry Punch

½ to 1 cup sugar
1 cup water
2 cups frozen lemon juice
2 cups frozen orange juice
1 quart cranberry juice
2 quarts ginger ale
2 pints vodka (optional)

Make a simple syrup by boiling water and sugar for 5 minutes. Add frozen juices and cranberry juice and mix well. When ready to serve add ginger ale and, if using, vodka. Mix well and pour into a punch bowl. Add an ice ring.*

*Ice Ring - See page 11.

Planter's Punch

1½ oz. light rum
½ oz. lemon juice
½ oz. orange juice
⅓ oz. grenadine syrup
½ oz. dark rum
Slice of orange
Maraschino cherry

Fill a 12-ounce glass with shaved ice or ice cubes. Add the light rum, fruit juices and grenadine syrup. Stir well. Pour the dark rum on top and add orange slice twisted and a cherry on top.

Laurie's Champagne Punch
(Wedding Punch)

4 (6 oz.) cans frozen lemonade concentrate plus 4 cans water
4 (6 oz.) cans frozen pineapple juice plus 4 cans water
2 quarts ginger ale
1 quart sparkling water
1 quart Champagne
Fresh strawberries, washed and stems intact
Ice ring*

   Mix fruit juices, ginger ale, and sparkling water. When ready to serve, pour in Champagne. Pour over ring of ice in pretty punch bowl. Add whole strawberries.

*Ice Ring - See Page 11.

Champagne Punch a La Creole

1 quart white wine
2 quarts club soda
¼ cup curacao
2 cups lemon juice
2 cups sugar
6 ounce can crushed pineapple, undrained
6 ounce can pineapple rings, drained
3 dozen strawberries, washed but with stems remaining
1 quart Champagne
1 Ice ring*

   Put all ingredients except Champagne and ice ring into large punch bowl. Stir well. When ready to serve place ice ring in center and pour in Champagne. Serve in small cups. Will serve twenty-five people.

*Ice Ring - See page 11.

Mint Julep

2 oz. Bourbon
3 to 4 sprigs fresh mint
2 teaspoons sugar syrup (simple syrup)

Combine all ingredients into a tall glass. Fill with cracked ice and mix vigorously with a mixing spoon until the outside of the glass is coated with frost. Put an extra sprig of mint and a slice of orange on top before serving.

Creole Mary
(The Designated Driver's Drink)

8 ounces V8 vegetable juice
1 teaspoon taco sauce
½ teaspoon prepared white horseradish
½ teaspoon ground cumin
¼ teaspoon chili powder
Dash of Tabasco sauce

Mix all ingredients together and serve over ice. Easily doubled.

Mimosa

8 ounces chilled fresh orange juice
½ cup chilled cranberry juice
32 ounces chilled Champagne
8 slices orange

Combine orange and cranberry juices in a large pitcher. When ready to serve add Champagne. Serve in Champagne glasses with a slice of orange as garnish. Recipe easily doubled and may be served in a punch bowl.

Ramos Gin Fizz
(New Orleans Gin Fizz)

This is one of New Orleans' most famous drinks, invented in the 1800s by Henry Ramos.

1½ oz. gin
1 oz. lemon juice
1 egg white
1 drop vanilla
2 dashes orange flower water
2 teaspoons very fine granulated or powdered sugar
2 oz. half and half or milk
½ cup crushed ice
Soda

Combine all ingredients except soda in an electric blender, cover and blend for 1½ minutes or shake and shake until it is frothy, almost like whipped cream. Pour into an 8-ounce highball glass and fill with soda.

Spanish Sangria
(Wine Punch)

1 orange, thinly sliced
1 lemon, thinly sliced
½ lime, thinly sliced
2 good dashes of cinnamon
1 (27 oz.) bottle full bodied dry red wine
1 cup flavored liqueur (Grand Marnier or curacao)
1 cup simple syrup*
12 Maraschino cherries

In a punch bowl or a very large pitcher (about 4 quarts) place first four ingredients and mash together slightly. Add remaining ingredients and stir until well mixed, adding additional sugar if more sweetness is desired. Garnish glasses with more sliced fruit, fill with ice and punch.

*Simple syrup: Boil for 5 minutes, 1 part water to 2 parts sugar, or half as much water as sugar.

Mulled Wine
(Bischof)

A hot beverage very popular in France
and in other Northern European countries

1 cup sugar
Grated rind of 1 orange
Grated rind of 1 lemon
2 whole cloves
1 stick cinnamon
1½ cups of water
1 bottle of wine – Bordeaux or Burgundy – white or red, Rhine, Champagne, or any other wine

    Place all ingredients except wine into a saucepan. Make a simple syrup by stirring the ingredients well and cooking for 5 minutes over medium heat. Add one bottle of wine. Stir and heat until a light foam is formed on the surface. Strain through a fine strainer. Serve in a large pitcher or a punch bowl. A little Madeira, Sherry or Marsala wine is sometimes added to this drink to make it more stimulating.

Appetizers

Artichoke Balls 23	Savory Cheese Rounds 30
Party Artichokes 24	Marinated Cheese 30
Avocado Dip No. 1 24	Chicken Fingers with Dipping
Avocado Dip No. 2 25	Sauce 31
Avocado Pesto 25	Deviled Eggs 32
Classic Bleu Cheese and	Guacamole 32
Sautérne Dip 26	Party Chicken and Tomatoes 33
Blue Cheese Sautérne Dip 26	Hot Crab Dip 33
Blue Cheese Dip with Bacon ... 27	Stuffed Mushrooms Hors
Crudites and Dip 27	d'Oeuvres 34
Celery Stuffed with Blue Cheese 28	Oyster Patties 35
Cheese Ball No. 1 28	Roasted Spiced Pecans 36
Cheese Ball No. 2	Shrimp Scampi 36
(Made with 3 cheeses) 29	Tapenade 37
Cheese Drops or fingers 29	Welsh Rarebit 38

Artichoke Balls

This recipe was given to me by my
Sister-in-law, Barbara Duffy Miscenich

2 tablespoons olive oil
8 cloves finely minced garlic
2 cans (8 ounces each) artichoke hearts, drained and chopped or mashed well
2 eggs, slightly beaten
Juice of 1 lemon
¼ teaspoon dried thyme
¼ teaspoon parsley, chopped
¼ teaspoon oregano
Salt and Pepper to taste
6 tablespoons Parmesan cheese
2 cups Italian seasoned breadcrumbs

Sauté garlic in heated olive oil for about 1 minute. Add artichokes, eggs and rest of ingredients except cheese and breadcrumbs. Stir over low heat for about 3 minutes. Remove from heat, add breadcrumbs and Parmesan cheese and mix well. Mix together more cheese and breadcrumbs and put in a pie plate. Measuring about a teaspoonful at a time, form artichoke mixture into small balls and roll into breadcrumbs and cheese mixture, coating well. Place balls on paper towels on a large plate or cookie sheet and Chill until desired firmness. Freezes well.

Party Artichokes

12 Cocktail size patty shells
2 (3 ounce each) packs Philadelphia cream cheese, room temperature
2 eggs, lightly beaten
4 tablespoons butter, room temperature
⅛ teaspoon Tabasco sauce
Dash of garlic powder (optional)
1 teaspoon Worcestershire sauce
1 can artichoke hearts, coarsely chopped

Combine cream cheese with eggs, butter and seasonings. Beat well and then divide in half. With teaspoon, spoon half of mixture into bottom of patty shells. Spoon chopped artichoke hearts on top of cheese in shells and cover with remaining cheese mixture. Bake in a preheated 475 degrees oven until lightly brown on top, about 25 to 30 minutes. Serve immediately.

Avocado Dip No. 1

2 large avocados, peeled and mashed
1 tablespoon lime juice
½ teaspoon chili powder
1 clove garlic, minced fine
¼ teaspoon salt
⅓ cup mayonnaise
4 strips bacon, cooked crisp and crumbled

Mash avocados and add lime juice, chili powder, garlic and salt. Blend well and put into small bowl. Spread mayonnaise over top, covering the mixture completely to prevent darkening. Cover with saran wrap and chill for an hour or two. Before serving, stir mayonnaise into avocado mixture and check seasonings. Add more seasoning if needed, then garnish with crumbled bacon. Dip may be prepared the day before, but do not cook or add bacon until ready to serve. Corn chips are very good as dippers. Yield: about 2 cups. May be easily doubled.

Appetizers

Avocado Dip No. 2

1 avocado, peeled and mashed
1 (8 oz.) package softened cream cheese
2 tablespoons lemon juice
½ teaspoon Worcestershire sauce
1 clove garlic, minced fine
¾ teaspoon salt
¼ teaspoon chili powder

Blend avocado and cheese until smooth. Add other ingredients and blend well. Cover with Saran wrap and chill. Serve with corn chips. May be doubled.

This dip may be prepared the day before serving. Spread a thin layer of mayonnaise on the surface to prevent darkening, then stir it in just before serving.

Avocado Pesto

2 Medium garlic cloves
1 cup fresh basil leaves
¼ cup packed parsley leaves
2 tablespoons pine nuts
2 tablespoons freshly grated Parmesan cheese
1 large ripe avocado, preferably black skinned, pitted, peeled and sliced
6 tablespoons pure olive oil or avocado oil
Salt and pepper

Drop garlic cloves into food processor with blades turning until finely chopped. Add basil, parsley, pine nuts and cheese until mixture is finely chopped and well mixed. Drop avocado slices through feed tube and puree. Gradually add oil, Uncover machine, scrape down sides, season to taste with salt and pepper, and then continue to process until well blended. Transfer to bowl and refrigerate. Serve within 2 hours of preparing pesto. If you wish to make it ahead, puree avocado and blend with pesto shortly before serving. Pesto is delicious served as a dip surrounded by an assortment of crudites – cauliflower and broccoli florets, cucumber slices, celery and carrot sticks, and radishes, for example, and with potato or corn chips. You can also serve it as a spread on bread or for canape type appetizers, topped with baby shrimp. It is also, like other classic pesto, great with pasta.

For Avocado Pesto with Pasta, see page 239.

Classic Bleu Cheese and Sautérne Dip

½ pound blue cheese, crumbled
1 (3 ounce) package cream cheese, softened
1 cup sour cream
¼ cup Sautérne wine or ½ cup heavy cream
1 teaspoon Worcestershire sauce
2 teaspoons garlic puree
1 teaspoon salt
¼ teaspoon Tabasco sauce or cayenne pepper or to taste

Place all ingredients in blender and blend until smooth. Refrigerate. Remove from refrigerator about an hour before serving. Recipe easily doubled.

Note: This dip can also be used on grilled hamburgers.

Blue Cheese Sautérne Dip

½ pound blue cheese, crumbled
1 (3 ounce) package cream cheese
¼ cup Sautérne wine
1 teaspoon Worcestershire sauce
¼ teaspoon garlic salt
¼ cup chopped parsley

Place all ingredients in blender and blend until smooth. Refrigerate. Remove from refrigerator about an hour before serving. Recipe easily doubled.

Appetizers

Blue Cheese Dip with Bacon

½ cup sour cream
1 (4 ounce package crumbled blue cheese
1 (3 ounce) cream cheese, room temperature
⅛ teaspoon Tabasco sauce
2 tablespoons chopped green stuffed olives
4 slices bacon, cooked and crumbled

Add first 4 ingredients to a food processor or blender and blend until smooth, scraping down sides to process completely. Remove and stir in olives and half of the bacon. Cover and refrigerate for 2 or 3 hours until chilled. When ready to serve, stir in remaining bacon. Serve with crackers, melba toast rounds, raw vegetables or chips.

Note: Add a little milk and dip becomes a delicious salad dressing.

Crudites and Dip

Broccoli – Tiny florets
Cauliflower – Tiny florets
Carrots – Slivers or iced curls
Celery – Long slim pieces, slivers or iced curls
Cucumber – Peeled, long pieces or sliced
Radishes – Lengthwise quarters
Tomatoes – Cherry or tiny pear whole
Potato or corn chips (optional)

Place vegetables in a pattern on lazy Susan or serving platter. Put Bleu cheese dip in a small bowl in center of lazy Susan or platter. If using chips, serve in separate bowl.

Celery Stuffed with Blue Cheese

Celery, cut each rib into 3 inch pieces
4 ounces blue cheese, room temperature
6 ounces Philadelphia cream cheese, room temperature
Cream (only if needed)
Paprika

Wash and lightly salt celery. Beat cheeses in electric mixer until smooth. Add a touch of cream if you feel mixture needs to be thinned slightly, but be careful that it does not become too thin. Spread on celery and sprinkle with paprika.

Variation: A pinch of cayenne pepper may be added when beating cheeses.

Cheese Ball No. 1

½ pound (2 cups) shredded sharp Cheddar cheese
1 (8 ounces) pack Philadelphia cream cheese, (room temperature)
1 tablespoon chopped parsley
1 small garlic clove, finely minced or ¼ teaspoon garlic powder
¼ cup onion, finely chopped or ½ teaspoon onion powder
½ teaspoon salt or seasoned salt
1 teaspoon Worcestershire sauce
Dash Tabasco sauce
Chopped pecans, dried parsley, or mixture of half paprika and half chili powder

Blend Cheddar and cream cheeses in a large bowl or in a food processor. Add next six ingredients and mix until blended. Shape the mixture into a ball and roll in chopped pecans, dried parsley, or mixture of paprika and chili powder. May be refrigerated several days or wrapped in foil and frozen. If frozen, thaw in refrigerator overnight. Serve with bread rounds or crackers.

Note: This cheese ball would be perfect wrapped in netting, tied with a bow, and given as a gift during the Holiday season. May also be stored in small crocks and given as a gift.

Cheese Ball No. 2
(Made with 3 cheeses)

½ pound shredded sharp cheddar cheese
1 (8 oz.) package cream cheese (room temperature)
¼ pound Roquefort or blue cheese
1 clove garlic, crushed or ¼ teaspoon garlic powder
2 teaspoon grated onion, or ½ teaspoon onion powder (optional)
⅛ teaspoon cayenne pepper, (or to taste)
1 teaspoon Worcestershire sauce
1 cup finely minced parsley (divided)
1 cup chopped pecans (divided)

Place all ingredients except parsley and pecans into a food processor or blender and mix thoroughly. Add ½ cup each of chopped pecans and parsley to cheese mixture and blend well. Mix remaining pecans and parsley together and spread on a piece of aluminum foil or wax paper. Remove cheese mixture from blender or processor and form into a ball. Roll ball into parsley and chopped pecans. Refrigerate before using. Freezes very well. If frozen, thaw in refrigerator overnight before using.

As with recipe for other cheese ball, this cheese ball, also, wrapped in netting, would be a perfect holiday gift.

Cheese Drops or fingers

2 cups flour
½ to 1 teaspoon cayenne pepper
2 teaspoons baking powder
½ teaspoon salt
2 sticks (½ pound) butter, softened
½ pound grated sharp cheddar cheese, room temperature
2 teaspoons caraway seeds

Preheat oven to 350 degrees. Cream butter and cheese. Add sifted dry ingredients and fold in caraway seeds. Make small balls using 1 teaspoon dough. Shape into small, flattened balls or roll balls into finger length rolls. Bake on a greased baking sheet for 15 to 18 minutes, or until crisp and beginning to brown. Recipe easily doubled. Freezes well.

Savory Cheese Rounds

½ pound (2 sticks) butter or margarine, room temperature
1 pound sharp cheddar cheese, shredded, room temperature
4 cups all-purpose flour
½ teaspoon salt
½ to 1 teaspoon cayenne pepper (or to taste)
½ teaspoon paprika

Add butter and cheese to an electric mixer and beat until blended. Add remaining ingredients, mixing well until blended. Remove dough, wrap in plastic wrap and refrigerate until well chilled, about 2 hours. Remove dough and shape into 4 logs, each about 8 inches in length. Wrap again in plastic wrap and chill for about 8 hours or overnight. When ready to bake, preheat oven to 350 degrees. Cut logs into thin slices and place on ungreased cookie sheets. Bake for 15 minutes. Cool on wire racks and store in airtight containers. Nice served as appetizers.

Marinated Cheese

½ cup olive oil
½ cup white wine vinegar
1 (2 ounce) jar diced pimentos
3 tablespoons chopped fresh parsley
3 tablespoons minced green onions
3 cloves garlic, minced
1 teaspoon sugar
¼ teaspoon dried basil
½ teaspoon salt
½ teaspoon pepper
8 ounces sharp Cheddar cheese, cut into 1-inch cubes
8 ounces cream cheese, cut into 1-inch cubes

Combine all ingredients except cheeses in a jar and shake well. Arrange the Cheddar cheese cubes and cream cheese cubes alternately in a serving dish. Pour the marinade over the cheese. Marinate in the refrigerator for at least 8 hours. Provide toothpicks to serve. Serves 6 to 8. Recipe easily doubled or tripled.

Appetizers

Chicken Fingers with Dipping Sauce

8 Skinless and boneless chicken breast halves, each half cut into 4 strips
2 cups milk
1 teaspoon salt
½ teaspoon lemon pepper
½ teaspoon black pepper
⅛ teaspoon cayenne pepper
2 cups all-purpose flour
Vegetable oil

Combine chicken strips, milk, salt, lemon pepper, black pepper, and cayenne pepper in a large zip-loc plastic bag. Shake and marinate in refrigerator for about 4 hours. When ready to prepare, remove chicken from marinade and dredge chicken in flour. Fry chicken in a Dutch oven or electric fryer in about 2 inches of oil that has been heated to 350 degrees. Fry for about 5 minutes, or until golden. Drain on paper towels and serve as appetizers with dipping sauce below.

Dipping Sauce

1 cup mayonnaise
½ cup chili sauce
2 tablespoons water
4 teaspoons prepared mustard
⅛ teaspoon paprika
2 garlic cloves, minced fine

½ cup olive oil
¼ cup catsup
2 tablespoons Worcestershire sauce
2 teaspoons black pepper
¼ teaspoon tabasco sauce

Blend all ingredients in a food processor or blender. Pour into a bowl, cover and refrigerate for 1 hour before serving.

Deviled Eggs

8 eggs, hard boiled
3 ½ tablespoons mayonnaise
¾ teaspoon seasoned salt*
1 teaspoon yellow mustard
½ teaspoon lemon juice
⅛ teaspoon Tabasco sauce
Salt and pepper to taste*
Paprika

Shell and cut egg in half lengthwise. Remove and mash yolks with fork. Add rest of ingredients except paprika and mix well. Fill egg whites with mixture and sprinkle with paprika. Chill.

*Seasoned Salt – See page 341.
*Taste mixture before adding salt and pepper and season accordingly.

Guacamole

3 ripe avocados
1 tablespoons freshly squeezed lime juice
¼ cup finely minced red onion
½ Jalapeño, stemmed, seeded and minced or 1 Serrano Chile, minced
1 medium tomato, seeded and diced
¼ cup freshly chopped cilantro (preferably) or parsley leaves
Kosher salt
Freshly ground black pepper and dash of cayenne (optional)

Cut each avocado in half, remove pit, and scoop out the flesh with a spoon. Combine with lime juice and rest of the ingredients and mash with the back of a fork, keeping a chunky texture. Taste to see if more seasoning is needed. Prepare and refrigerate shortly before using. Use as a dip for tortilla chips or quesadillas, or as a garnish on everything from hamburgers to tacos.

Appetizers

Party Chicken and Tomatoes
This recipe was created by my 14 year old Grandson, Jonathan Klebert Poll.

4 boneless, skinless chicken breasts halves or chicken tenders
1 tablespoon cooking oil and 1 tablespoon butter
Creole Seasoning, (Preferably Tony Chachere)
Salt and black pepper
Parmesan cheese
4 fresh tomatoes, diced

Heat oil and butter in a frying pan. Season chicken breasts or tenders well with salt, pepper, and Creole seasoning. Sauté the chicken in the pan for 2 to 3 minutes each side, or until cooked through. Cut the chicken or tenders into bite size pieces and set aside. In the same pan place the diced tomatoes. Season with salt, pepper, and Tony Chachere seasoning. Stir continuously until tomatoes are soft and well cooked. Pour tomatoes into a food processor and process until they are a fine cream. Pour back into the frying pan, add the chicken and stir until well mixed and heated. Pour mixture into a shallow bowl. Sprinkle top liberally with Parmesan cheese. Stick a toothpick into each piece of chicken and you're ready to eat. Recipe easily doubled.

Hot Crab Dip
This recipe was given to me by my Cousin, Helene Ware Wagner

½ pound fresh, frozen or canned crab meat
8 oz. Cream cheese, softened
1 tablespoon milk
2 tablespoons grated onion
¼ teaspoon horseradish
¼ teaspoon salt
⅛ teaspoon white pepper
2 to 4 tablespoons mayonnaise
¼ cup grated parmesan cheese

Preheat oven to 350 degrees. Blend all ingredients to smooth consistency. Place in small baking dish and sprinkle top with parmesan cheese. Bake 15 minutes or until top bubbles. Serve on crackers of your choice, or French bread cut thin and toasted. Recipe easily doubled.

Stuffed Mushrooms Hors d'Oeuvres

24 fresh mushrooms, cleaned and drained (select large caps)
3 to 4 tablespoons butter or margarine, melted
4 tablespoons finely chopped green onions
1 clove garlic, minced
½ pound cooked crabmeat or ½ cup diced pepperoni sausage
2 eggs, lightly beaten
2 tablespoons Progresso Italian breadcrumbs
2 tablespoons mayonnaise
1 tablespoon chopped parsley, fresh or dried
1 teaspoon lemon juice
½ teaspoon salt
¼ teaspoon oregano
Black pepper to taste
Cayenne pepper to taste (optional)
Parmesan cheese

    Preheat oven to 400 degrees. Remove the stems from the mushrooms and chop the stems. Dip the caps in melted butter or margarine. In a skillet sauté the chopped stems with the chopped green onions and garlic remaining melted butter. Add the crabmeat or sausage, eggs, breadcrumbs, mayonnaise, parsley, lemon juice, and seasonings to the skillet. Stir well and simmer for a few minutes. Fill caps, not too full, and top with Parmesan cheese. Place in a well buttered shallow baking dish and bake for 10 to 15 minutes until mushrooms are tender and tops are brown. Serve at once.

Appetizers

Oyster Patties
This is a classic at New Orleans Cocktail Parties

Can be served in a chafing dish surrounded by small patty shells or as hors d'oeuvres by filling small patty shells with hot oyster mixture. Or fill large patty shells with hot oyster mixture and serve with a green salad for a luncheon or a Sunday night supper.

12 small or 6 large patty shells, reserve tops
2 dozen oysters and liquid
2 tablespoons butter and 2 tablespoons oil
3 tablespoons flour
1 bunch shallots (green onions) chopped
2 cloves garlic, minced fine
2 tablespoons fresh flat leaf parsley, chopped fine
1 teaspoon Worcestershire sauce
½ teaspoon salt
¼ teaspoon black pepper
⅛ teaspoon cayenne pepper (or to taste)
¼ teaspoon thyme leaves
Water

Place patty shells in a shallow baking dish or pan and set aside. Sauté oysters in their own liquid until edges curl. Drain, reserving liquid, and chop oysters into small pieces. Set oysters and liquid aside. Heat butter and oil in a heavy or cast iron skillet or saucepan over medium heat. Add flour and stir until blended and light brown. Add onions and garlic and keep cooking, stirring constantly until roux turns dark brown, being careful not to let it burn. Turn heat to a low simmer and add oyster liquid, parsley, Worcestershire sauce, salt, peppers, and thyme. Continue to stir constantly and add a little water if needed. Add oysters, stir well and remove from heat. Mixture should be thick. Divide the oyster mixture between the patty shells and replace patty shell tops. Bake in a 350 degree oven for about 15 minutes or until they are piping hot. Serve immediately.

Roasted Spiced Pecans

½ cup margarine
1 tablespoon Worcestershire sauce
1 teaspoon crushed dried thyme
¼ teaspoon cayenne pepper
3 cups shelled pecans
Seasoned salt to taste

Preheat oven to 275 degrees. Melt margarine in a bowl. Add Worcestershire sauce and pecans, coating pecans thoroughly. Mix seasonings and add to pecans. Toss well to coat and spread mixture in a shallow baking pan or on a cookie sheet. Roast for about 45 minutes or until desired crispness is reached. Stir pecans about every 15 minutes, being careful not to scorch them. Transfer pecans to paper towels and salt them. Serve warm or at room temperature. Recipe easily doubled or tripled. To store them place in an airtight container. Nice served at a Cocktail party or at a barbecue.

Shrimp Scampi

⅓ cup olive oil
8 to 12 cloves garlic, or to taste, minced fine, or 3 or 4 teaspoons garlic puree
2 pounds raw shrimp, peeled and deveined
½ cup dry white wine
3 tablespoons fresh lemon juice
1 teaspoon salt
½ teaspoon black pepper
3 tablespoons parsley, chopped, plus more for garnish

Heat the olive oil in a large pan. Add garlic and cook for 2 to 3 minutes, just until softened but do not let the garlic brown. Add the shrimp, wine, lemon juice, salt and pepper. Cook over moderate heat for 3 or 4 minutes, until shrimp are cooked through Add the parsley and stir well. Spoon into 4 plates, garnish with additional parsley and serve. May also be served over rice pilaf, plain rice, or 1 pound cooked and drained pasta.

Variation: 1 (11 ounce) package frozen artichokes, thawed and chopped, or 1 (14 ounce) can artichoke hearts, drained and chopped, may be added along with shrimp. Continue as directed.

Tapenade

A tangy sauce from Provence that can be used as a sauce or as a dip for raw vegetables. Its wonderful Mediterranean flavor gives a flair to anything from roast chicken, meats, fish, sandwiches, salads, or pizza.

1½ cups pitted and chopped Niçoise or Kalamata olives
1½ tablespoons capers
2 tablespoons anchovy paste or
12 anchovy fillets, or less, to taste, rinsed and chopped
4 garlic cloves, finely minced
½ teaspoon black or white pepper
½ teaspoon dried thyme
¼ teaspoon crushed red pepper (optional)
1 teaspoon minced lemon peel
2 teaspoons lemon juice
⅓ cup extra virgin olive oil
1 to 2 tablespoon Cognac or Brandy (optional)

    Put olives, garlic, capers, and a small amount of the olive oil in a food processor or blender. Process until smooth. Add the anchovy fillets and the rest of the ingredients to the container and blend to a thick puree. Taste for seasoning, and add more pepper or Cognac, if needed. Place in a bowl, cover and refrigerate overnight. Best if prepared a day before serving. 1 tablespoon Dijon mustard may be added to Tapenade, if desired. Tapenade will keep refrigerated for up to a week. Great on crusty bread slices, see page 267 for Crostini tapenade.

    Tapenade Mayonnaise. Mix half tapenade and half mayonnaise. Use as a dressing for vegetable salads.

    Tapenade with Avocado. Fill halved avocados with tapenade or add cold boiled shrimp to tapenade and fill avocado cavities.

    Tapenade stuffed cherry tomatoes. Cut tomatoes in half, scoop out pulp with a melon baller. Add a teaspoon of tapenade to each tomato half. Sprinkle with chopped parsley. Serve as an appetizer.

    Tapenade eggs. Place halved or quartered hard boiled eggs on salad greens. Spoon tapenade over eggs.

    Tapenade and fish. Spoon tapenade over broiled fish fillets.

    Tapenade and roast beef, sliced chicken, or pork sandwiches. Split rolls in half. Add beef, sliced chicken or pork and top with tapenade sauce. Lettuce and tomato slices may be added if desired.

Welsh Rarebit
An English melted cheese preparation
made in a Fondue pot or in double boiler

3 tablespoons butter
½ pound cheddar cheese, shredded
1 tablespoon Dijon mustard
2 teaspoon Worcestershire sauce
⅛ teaspoon cayenne pepper, or to taste
1 egg, slightly beaten
1 cup beer

Melt the butter in the top of a chafing dish or the top of a double boiler over boiling water. Add the cheese, mustard, Worcestershire sauce and cayenne pepper. Cook over low heat, stirring constantly with a wooden spoon until the cheese has melted. Add a little of the hot cheese mixture to the egg. Beat well and then return the egg and cheese mixture to the pan. Add the beer and cook for 1 or 2 more minutes, continuing to stir until it is very hot and smooth. But do not let the rarebit come to a boil Serve over buttered toast.

Variation: Cook in a fondue pot. Give guests long handled forks to spear bread cubes to be dipped into the creamy cheese fondue.

Gumbo and Soups

Gumbo Z'Herbes
(Green Gumbo) ... 43
Chicken and Sausage Gumbo
(Gumbo Ya Ya) ... 45
Seafood Gumbo Filé ... 47
Turkey and Sausage Gumbo ... 48
Chilled Avocado Soup ... 49
Avocado and Cucumber Soup ... 50
Cream of Broccoli Soup ... 50
Creamy Artichoke Soup ... 51
Cream of Asparagus Soup ... 52
Chicken Soup ... 53
Clam Chowder ... 54
Potato Soup ... 54
Corn and Crab Bisque ... 55

Gazpacho ... 56
Kale and Bean Soup ... 57
Cream of Leek and Potato
Soup ... 58
French Onion Soup
(Soupe a L'Oignon) ... 59
Soupe a l'Oignon Gratinée
(Onion Soup Gratineed with
Cheese) ... 60
Oyster Soup ... 60
Oyster and Artichoke Soup ... 61
Split Pea Soup ... 62
Tuscan White Bean Soup ... 63
Vegetable and Meat Soup
(Soupe en Jardinière et Bouilli) ... 64
Vichyssoise ... 64

Gumbo Z'Herbes
(Green Gumbo)

The first gumbo I will list is Gumbo Z'Herbes, the "gumbo of herbs" or as it is sometimes called, Gumbo Vert, (Green Gumbo). A dish that originated in New Orleans. This Creole Gumbo is called the "King of Gumbos." It was originally prepared without meat and served as a Lenten dish on Good Friday. No longer a Lenten dish, meat is now added to the recipe. Legend had it that you would make a new friend in the coming year for every green that was put into the gumbo. Greens, as many as are available, the more the better. I remember when I was small, going to the French Market with Momma to get the necessary greens for this unique gumbo. But nowadays I just use as many greens as I can find, fresh or frozen, at the local supermarket.

Roux Ingredients
1 cup vegetable oil or preferably, bacon drippings
1 cup flour
1 large or 2 medium onions, chopped
1 sweet pepper, chopped
3 ribs celery, chopped
4 cloves minced garlic
½ cup chopped parsley, fresh or dried
¾ cup chopped shallots (green onion) tops

Gumbo Ingredients
1 bunch each in any combination of greens - spinach, turnip, mustard, collard, kale, Swiss chard, etc. or 1 package each frozen greens, of as many frozen greens as you can find
1 small green or half of a large green cabbage, chopped
2 cups water
1 pound lean baked ham, cubed or, 2 meaty ham hocks, or slab bacon, cubed
4 bay leaves
1½ teaspoon dried thyme
1 teaspoon dried basil
2 tablespoons kosher salt
1 teaspoon cracked black pepper
1 teaspoon white pepper
¼ teaspoon cayenne pepper (or to taste)
1 tablespoon soy sauce
2 cans red kidney beans (optional)
5 tablespoons flour
¼ stick of butter (room temperature)
Steamed or boiled rice

(Continued Next Page)

Remove and discard all coarse stems and discolored outer leaves from greens. Wash all greens thoroughly and drain. Chop or shred greens finely. (This is the secret of this great gumbo). Put into a large pot with 2 cups water. (If you are using frozen greens, put frozen greens into the pot with water.) When the water in the bottom of the pot begins to boil cover the pot tightly, reduce heat to medium, and steam for 12 to 15 minutes, or until greens are wilted but not cooked. Drain greens in a colander over a large bowl and reserve water.

Meanwhile prepare the roux, either the Microwave or French Roux.* Add the vegetables listed as instructed in the roux recipes. When the roux is ready, heat a large 7 or 8 quart iron or heavy pot over high heat. Pour the roux into the pot, Add the cubed meat or ham hocks and stir well. Add greens, seasonings, and red kidney beans, if using. Add reserved water in which greens were steamed plus water to equal 2 quarts, stirring to mix thoroughly. Raise the heat to high, bring the gumbo to a boil, then lower the heat again, partially cover and simmer until it becomes thick, about 1 and a half hours or so. Stir well and adjust seasonings to taste. About 30 minutes before the gumbo is finished, put the 5 tablespoons flour in a small bowl, add the ¼ stick of butter and mix it into a paste until smooth. Taking a little at a time, add the paste to the pot, stirring well. The lumps will disappear as you stir. Serve gumbo over bowls of steamed or boiled rice. A dash or two of filé may be added to the bowls after serving, but do not add it to the pot, because once it is added, the gumbo must never be reheated. Heating the gumbo after the filé has been added will make the gumbo stringy and unfit to eat.

This gumbo is best if refrigerated overnight then reheated and served the next day. Any leftover gumbo may be frozen for future use.

When New Orleans cooks refer to "shallots," they mean green onions or scallions.

*For French Roux or Microwave Roux, see pages 95 & 96.

Gumbo and Soups

Chicken and Sausage Gumbo (Gumbo Ya Ya)
With Microwaved Roux
For my Daughter-in-law Eve

Chicken and Sausage Gumbo is the most popular Gumbo in Louisiana, as the ingredients are so readily available. This gumbo is quicker if you chop the vegetables and sausage and cook the chicken ahead of time, preferably the day before. See page 156 for the pre-prepared recipe for "Chicken, Cooked in Microwave."

Gumbo:

Pre-prepared microwaved roux with vegetables (see below)
1 pound Andouille sausage or polish Kielbasa sausage, thinly sliced or diced
1 (5 pound) "cooked" chicken, boned and cut in bite size pieces (see page 156)
Chicken stock or chicken stock and hot water to equal 3 quarts
1 pack frozen sliced okra, defrosted (optional)
1 tablespoon salt
½ teaspoon black pepper
¼ teaspoon cayenne pepper (or to taste)
1 bay leaf
2 teaspoons crushed thyme
1 tablespoon basil
Steam or Boiled Rice

Microwaved Roux: This amount of roux will thicken 3 quarts of liquid to a gumbo consistency.

1 cup oil
1 cup flour
2 cups chopped onions
2 cups chopped celery
1 cup chopped sweet pepper
2 cups shallots (green onions)
¼ cup chopped garlic
½ cup chopped parsley

Microwave Roux:

Mix oil and flour together in a large (6 cup) microwave safe measuring cup or bowl. Microwave uncovered on high for 7 to 10 minutes. Stir and continue to cook,

(Continued Next Page)

stirring about every 30 seconds to a minute, until roux reaches a very dark caramel color. The right shade should take about 15 to 18 minutes total. (Be sure you do not let the roux burn.) Carefully remove the hot roux from the microwave and stir onion, celery, green onions, and sweet pepper into roux, making sure you stir well, bringing the roux up from the bottom of bowl or measuring cup. Return to microwave and cook for 4 minutes. Remove roux again from microwave and stir in the garlic and parsley. Cook on high for 2 minutes.

Gumbo:

Remove roux mixture from microwave and pour into a large heavy pot (not iron) over medium heat. Add sausage and chicken to roux mixture. Lower heat and sauté about 6-7 minutes, stirring constantly. Slowly add chicken stock, okra, if using, and seasonings, stirring well. Bring to a full boil, stir well, then lower heat to a simmer. Cook, partially covered, for about 45 minutes to an hour, stirring occasionally. Serve over steamed or boiled rice.

Seafood Gumbo Filé
(Filé is pronounced "Fee-lay")

⅔ cup bacon drippings or oil
⅔ cup flour
2 onions, chopped
4 cloves garlic, minced
1 large, sweet pepper
2 ribs celery, chopped
½ cup shallots (green onions) chopped
⅓ cup parsley, chopped fine
½ pound slice raw ham, cut into cubes
2 quarts hot water
2 bay leaves
4 teaspoons salt
1 teaspoon black pepper
¼ teaspoon (or to taste) cayenne pepper
1 teaspoon thyme
1 tablespoon Worcestershire sauce
2 pounds large shrimp, peeled and deveined
1 pound fresh or frozen crab meat
1 quart oysters and oyster water
3 tablespoon file powder
Steamed rice

    In a large, heavy pot (preferably iron) make a roux by gradually adding flour to the oil, stirring constantly over low heat. When it is dark brown - the color of a pecan - quickly add onions, garlic, sweet pepper, shallots, celery, parsley and ham. Cook over low heat about 10 minutes more, stirring constantly. Then add one half cup of the water and the rest of the seasonings except the filé. Still keeping a very low heat, gradually add the rest of the water. Raise heat, and bring to a quick boil, continuing to stir. Again, reduce heat to low and cook for about 20 minutes. Add shrimp and crab meat and simmer for 20 minutes more, adding oysters and oyster water after 15 minutes. Remove pot from heat and let simmering stop. Let it sit for about 5 minutes. Add filé and stir, or preferably filé may be added to individual bowls when served, sprinkling liberally on top of gumbo in each bowl. The gumbo should never be reheated after adding filé, as the filé will get stringy. Serve over deep bowls of steaming rice.

Turkey and Sausage Gumbo
A traditional New Orleans Soup for using up
An "After Thanksgiving or Christmas" Turkey

1 turkey carcass
2 turkey legs or thighs
Water to cover carcass (about 3 to 4 quarts)
½ to 1 cup dry vermouth wine or one cup chicken stock
½ teaspoon salt, black pepper and cayenne pepper to taste
½ cup bacon grease
½ cup cooking oil
1 cup flour
8 ribs celery, chopped
2 large onions, chopped
1 sweet (green) pepper, chopped
2 cloves garlic, minced
½ cup chopped parsley
1 pound Andouille or smoked sausage, chopped
1 pound fresh or frozen okra, sliced
2 cans Rotel tomatoes, (10 ½ ounce size)
2 quarts of turkey stock and 2 quarts water
½ cup Worcestershire sauce
1 teaspoon Tabasco sauce, or to taste
1½ teaspoon salt
4 slices bacon, cut into 1 inch pieces
2 bay leaves
2 teaspoon dried thyme
1 teaspoon poultry seasoning
1 tablespoon lemon juice
1 pint oysters, with water (optional)
4 to 6 cups steamed rice

    Break up the turkey carcass into pieces and place, along with the legs, into a large soup pot with the water, vermouth wine and salt, black pepper and cayenne pepper to taste Bring to a boil and boil for 1 hour, or until turkey meat begins to fall off the bones. Remove turkey bones from water, place in a large bowl, and allow to cool enough to handle. Remove remaining meat from the bones, place in a large bowl and set meat aside. Discard the bones. Continue to simmer the stock until it is reduced in volume by about one-fourth. (This serves to concentrate the flavors of the finished Gumbo). Drain the stock and reserve.

(Continued Next Page)

Over medium heat make a roux with the bacon grease, oil and flour in a large Dutch oven, stirring constantly until a golden brown. Add the onion, garlic, sweet pepper, celery and parsley to the roux and cook for about 15 minutes, stirring constantly. Add the sausage and the okra and continue cooking for another 5 minutes. Add 2 quarts of the turkey stock and 2 quarts of water, Worcestershire sauce, Tabasco sauce, Rotel tomatoes, salt, bacon, thyme, poultry seasoning and bay leaves Cover and simmer, stirring occasionally, for about 2 to 2½ hours. Add the turkey meat and lemon juice and simmer for an additional 30 minutes. If you want to use the oysters, add them, along with the oyster water, about 10 minutes before serving, or until oysters curl. Do not overcook the oysters. Ladle the gumbo over bowls of hot rice, along with piping hot French bread.

Chilled Avocado Soup

4 ripe Avocados, peeled, seeded and chopped
2 cups heavy cream
2 cups sour cream
3 peeled shallots, chopped or 2 tablespoons fresh chives
2 (14½ oz.) cans clear chicken broth, undiluted
1 teaspoon salt
¼ teaspoon garlic powder
½ teaspoon Tabasco sauce
Juice of one lemon

Puree mixture in batches in food processor or blender. Transfer to serving bowl and chill. Serve with a simple lettuce and tomato salad with a light vinaigrette dressing for a refreshing summer lunch.

Avocado and Cucumber Soup

1 ripe California Avocado
1 ¾ cucumbers, (about 1½ pounds) cut into ½ inch pieces
1 (8 ounce) container plain low-fat yogurt
3 tablespoons chopped fresh chives
1 teaspoon lime juice
1 teaspoon salt, or to taste
Freshly ground black pepper
1 cup small ice cubes

Peel and pit avocado. Place all ingredients in a blender and blend until smooth, about 1 to 2 minutes. Refrigerate to chill. When ready to serve garnish with chopped avocado and chopped chives. Recipe easily doubled by pureeing in batches.

Cream of Broccoli Soup

2 tablespoons butter and 2 tablespoon vegetable oil
2 medium onions, chopped
3 cloves garlic, minced
2 (10 ounce) packages broccoli florets
3 medium potatoes (1 pound), peeled and cut into cubes
¼ cup chopped parsley
⅛ teaspoon ground nutmeg
4 tablespoons lemon juice
5 or 6 cups chicken stock
2 cups milk
Salt and pepper and cayenne pepper to taste

In a heavy, pot sauté onions in butter and oil until limp. Add garlic and cook for a half minute. Add the broccoli, potatoes, parsley, nutmeg, lemon juice and chicken stock and bring to a boil over moderate heat. Lower heat to simmer, cover and cook for about 20 minutes or until broccoli and potatoes are tender. Transfer the mixture to a food processor or blender, working in batches, and process until liquified. Return the blended mixture to the pan and add the milk and seasonings. Simmer for 5 minutes. Serve hot, garnished with chopped parsley.

Creamy Artichoke Soup

2 tablespoons olive oil
2 leeks, white part only, washed well and chopped
1 clove garlic, minced
1 small potato, peeled and chopped
1 (8 ounce) package frozen artichoke hearts, thawed
2 cups chicken stock
½ teaspoon salt
¼ teaspoon freshly ground black pepper
2 tablespoons plus ⅓ cup mascarpone cheese
2 tablespoons chopped, chives, for garnish

Heat olive oil in a heavy, large pot over medium heat. Add the leeks and the garlic and stir. Add the potatoes and cook for 5 minutes, stirring often. Add the artichokes, stock, salt, and pepper and cook until the vegetables are tender, about 25 minutes.

Using a handheld immersion blender, or in a blender in batches, puree the soup. Add the 2 tablespoons mascarpone and blend again to combine. In a small bowl, stir the remaining ⅓ cup mascarpone to soften. Ladle the soup into serving bowls. Dollop the top of each of the soups with a spoonful of the softened mascarpone cheese and top the cheese with chives.

When blending hot liquids: Remove liquid from the heat and allow to cool for at least 5 minutes. Transfer liquid to a blender or food processor and fill it no more than halfway. If using a blender, release one corner of the lid. This prevents the vacuum effect that creates heat explosions. Place a towel over the top of the machine, pulse a few times then process on high speed until smooth.

Cream of Asparagus Soup

3 cups chicken broth
1 pound fresh or frozen asparagus
1 potato, peeled and diced small
2 small ribs celery, sliced thin
Salt and white pepper to taste
1 teaspoon dried thyme
1 cup cream, half and half cream or milk
2 tablespoons butter
2 tablespoons flour

Rinse asparagus and snap off tough ends and discard the ends. Remove 1 inch off top tips of each spear and set aside, reserving middle part. Add chicken broth to a 3 to 5 quart pot over medium heat. Add middle parts of asparagus, diced potato, celery, thyme, salt and pepper. Cover and bring to a boil, turn heat to low and simmer for 12 to 15 minutes or until vegetables are soft. Remove from heat and let cool.

Place half of the soup at a time in a blender container or food processor. Cover and blend at high speed for 20 to 30 seconds or until very smooth. Return blended soup to the pot. Add reserved asparagus tips and cream, half and half cream or milk and heat thoroughly. If soup seems too thin, in a small pot add 1 tablespoons butter. When melted stir in 1 tablespoon flour. Add a little milk, stir and add to soup. If soup seems too thick, a little more milk may be added. Easily doubled.

Note: 2 percent milk or half and half cream may be used in place of the cream, although it won't taste quite as rich and delicious. Be sure to adjust seasoning after you add the cream or milk. This soup may be served either hot or cold.

Chicken Soup

1 large chicken, (And additional pieces, if desired) cut up
3 celery ribs, chopped
3 carrots, chopped (optional)
2 medium or 1 large onion, chopped fine
4 cloves garlic, minced
2 bay leaves
½ cup chopped parsley
1 tablespoon crushed dried thyme
1 tablespoon salt
1 teaspoon coarse ground black pepper
1 to 2 cups Sautérne or dry Vermouth wine (optional)
6 to 8 quarts water (about)
½ cup Barley (optional)
Noodles or Vermicelli
*Mojo Topping (optional)

Put all ingredients except egg noodles or vermicelli and Mojo topping in a large soup pot, about 8 quarts. Bring to a boil, lower heat to simmer, partially cover and simmer for 4½ to 5 hours. Remove the chicken from the pot, debone and chop the chicken into bite size pieces. Add as much of the chopped chicken to the broth as you wish (depending on how rich you want the soup to be.) The remaining chicken pieces can be set aside for other uses. Return the fire to low and then stir in 3 to 4 cups egg noodles or vermicelli, cooking until noodles or vermicelli are tender, approximately 15 minutes. Season with additional salt and pepper if needed. Stir and serve, adding Mojo sauce if desired.

Chicken Vegetable Soup. Add noodles or cooked rice and diced chicken along with any number of vegetables. Some finely shredded cabbage, peas and mushrooms, or chopped spinach leaves may be added for a richer, much more filling soup.

Note: Using a very large pot, recipe may be doubled, and soup can be frozen in 1 quart containers for future use.

*Mojo Topping: See page 339. A Healthful addition to a bowl of Soup, especially if you have a cold or flu.

Clam Chowder
This recipe was given to me by my brother,
Weldon Miscenich

¼ pound butter
1 onion, chopped
2 ribs celery, chopped
3 cans clams, with juice
3 cans potato soup
1 pound small seafood boiled potatoes or 1 pound tiny
New potatoes, peeled and quartered
2 soup cans of half & half cream
1 tablespoon parsley flakes
1 bay leaf
Salt and pepper to taste

Sauté onion and celery in butter until soft. Add clams and juice, potato soup (undiluted) and boiled potatoes. Add half and half, parsley flakes, salt, bay leaf and pepper. Bring to a slow simmer. Serve at once.

Potato Soup

4 cups potatoes, peeled and diced into small cubes
6 shallots (green onions) or 1 onion, finely chopped
1 clove garlic, finely minced
1 cup finely chopped celery
6 slices bacon, cooked and crumbled
1 tablespoon flour
2 quarts milk, scalded
1 teaspoon salt
¼ teaspoon white pepper
1 tablespoon butter
2 tablespoons parsley

Cook potatoes in enough salted water to cover. Meanwhile, fry bacon until crisp, crumble and set aside. To bacon fat add onion, garlic and celery and cook until limp. Remove from pot and set aside with bacon. Add flour to remaining fat and stir quickly. Add some of milk and bring to simmer, stirring continuously. Add the rest of milk and the potatoes which should now be done. Add bacon, onion, garlic, celery, salt and pepper. Heat all and adjust seasoning to taste. Add parsley and butter, stir and serve.

Corn and Crab Bisque

1 tablespoon olive oil
1 bunch chopped shallots (green onions)
2 ribs celery, chopped fine
3 garlic cloves, minced fine
2 teaspoons salt
½ teaspoon white pepper
¼ to ½ cayenne pepper (to taste)
1 teaspoon dried thyme flakes
¼ cup chopped parsley
Corn kernels from 2 or 3 ears of corn, about 1 cup, or 1½ cups frozen corn
2 cups seafood stock, chicken stock, or water
4 cups heavy cream, or 2 cups cream and 2 cup milk or 4 cups half and half
3 tablespoons blond roux*
½ teaspoon Worcestershire Sauce
1 pound cooked white crab meat, or 2 cans crab meat

    Heat the oil in a large pot over medium heat. Add the shallots, celery, garlic, salt, white pepper, cayenne pepper, thyme flakes, parsley and corn. Sauté, stirring, about a minute or two, Add the seafood or chicken stock and bring to a boil. Lower heat to simmer, and slowly add the cream, or the milk and cream and using a slotted spoon or whisk, mix well to combine the mixture. Bring mixture back to a boil and then reduce the heat to simmer and simmer, uncovered, for 7 to 10 minutes, stirring occasionally. Stir in the roux, 1 tablespoon at a time. Reduce the heat to low and continue to cook, whisking until the mixture thickens. Stir in the crab meat and Worcestershire sauce and simmer for about 5 to 10 minutes. The bisque should have the consistency of melted ice cream. Taste to adjust seasoning. Serve hot, ladled into soup bowls. Serve immediately. Recipe easily doubled.

    Variation: 1 pound crawfish tails, peeled and cleaned, may be used in place of crab meat.

*Blond Roux – See page 95.

Gazpacho

A chilled Spanish soup, Gazpacho was originally a Gypsy Soup from eastern Europe. It is the most refreshing of soups.

2 cups tomato juice
2 tablespoon extra-virgin olive oil
¼ cup fresh lemon juice
1 tablespoon red wine vinegar
3 cloves garlic, minced
1 cup croutons
6 large ripe tomatoes, seeded and chopped, or 1 can (28 ounces) whole tomatoes, chopped
1 small red onion, chopped
1 sweet pepper, (green pepper) chopped
2 ribs celery chopped
4 shallots (Green onions) chopped
1 medium cucumber, chopped
⅓ cup minced fresh Parsley or cilantro
1 teaspoon Kosher salt
¼ to ½ teaspoon cayenne pepper (or to your taste)
Freshly ground coarse black pepper
1 teaspoon ground cumin (optional)
1 tablespoon Worcestershire sauce
2 Tablespoons dry Vermouth or dry white wine of your choice (optional)
2 Avocados, peeled and diced
Garnish: (optional) 6 radishes, finely sliced and celery stalks.

Place tomato juice, oil, lemon juice, vinegar, garlic and croutons in blender or food processor. Cover and blend for a few seconds. Add remaining ingredients except avocado and blend well. Taste, and correct seasonings if needed. Chill at least 4 hours.

The soup can be made to this point and refrigerated the day before serving.

When ready to serve, stir in Avocado. To serve in the traditional Spanish manner, spoon Gazpacho into chilled bowls. Serve with separate bowls of chopped cucumber, chopped sweet pepper, chopped tomatoes, minced green onions, and croutons. Any or all of these condiments may be added to individual soup bowls. The bowl of soup

(Continued Next Page)

may be topped with a spoonful of Guacamole. Or, if desired, float radish slices in each bowl and garnish with celery stalks. For a nice summer luncheon or a light supper, serve Gazpacho with spicy cheese toast sandwiches.*

Variation: Gazpacho with shrimp. Add about 24 cold, cooked, and peeled shrimp to Gazpacho. Mix and serve.

* Spicy Cheese Toast - See page 276.

Kale and Bean Soup

½ cup olive oil
3 large onions, finely diced
5 garlic cloves, minced
¼ cup chopped parsley
10 cups vegetable or chicken stock
1 (16 ounce) can diced tomatoes
1 (15 ounce) can kidney beans, drained and rinsed, or 1½ cup freshly cooked beans
1 pound kale, leaves torn from stems and finely chopped (10 cups leaves)
3 medium size red-skinned potatoes, unpeeled and cut into ½ inch dice
2 teaspoons paprika
¼ teaspoon red pepper flakes
1 teaspoon salt
¼ teaspoon black pepper
2 bay leaves
¼ teaspoon dried thyme

Heat the oil in a large stock pot over medium heat. Sauté onions and garlic until onions are tender, about 10 minutes. Raise heat to high and add the rest of the ingredients, stirring well. Bring to a boil, lower heat to simmer and cook for 30 minutes, or until soup has thickened. Remove and discard bay leaves Put about 2 cups of the soup in a blender or food processor and blend. Return it to the soup and stir well. May be made a few days in advance, as the flavor will intensify with time. Double the amount of soup may be made and frozen.

Cream of Leek and Potato Soup
For my Grand-daughter Jenny

Leeks are especially prone to catching large amounts of grit and sand between their layers. You should completely remove any grit by thoroughly rinsing the leeks under running water. The water should be run over the leek, while pulling the layers back so that all of the grit can be flushed out.

3 cups sliced leeks, white and tender green parts, split open and washed very well before slicing
3 to 4 cups peeled and diced baking potatoes, (about 1½ pounds)
3 cups chicken stock and 3 cups water
1 teaspoon minced garlic
1 to 3 tablespoons butter (optional)
1½ teaspoon salt
¼ teaspoon white pepper
½ cup heavy (whipping) cream
½ cup sour cream
⅓ cup minced parsley

In a large heavy saucepan, bring the leeks, potatoes, chicken stock and water, garlic, butter, if using, salt and pepper to a boil over high heat. Cover partially, reduce heat and simmer for 30 to 45 minutes, or until the vegetables are tender. Puree with a handheld immersion blender, or in batches in a food processor until smooth. Whisk in the heavy cream and sour cream. Taste for seasoning and add salt and pepper if needed. Reheat before serving. Top each serving with a sprinkling of fresh parsley or parmesan cheese. For a soup with more body, remove some of the potatoes before pureeing and then return them from the pot. Recipe easily doubled.

Variation: For a different flavor, add one cup of drained and chopped, bottled roasted red peppers and 1 sprig of fresh thyme along with the potatoes, leeks, garlic, water and salt. The leeks and red pepper make a wonderful combination. Continue as above. Remove and discard the thyme before pureeing.

French Onion Soup
(Soupe a L'Oignon)

The onions for an onion soup need to be cooked long and slowly in butter and oil or bacon drippings and a long simmering in stock to develop the deep rich flavor which characterizes an ideal onion soup. Only the cooking in butter and oil or bacon drippings requires watching. The rest of the simmering can go unattended.

5 cups of yellow onions, roughly chopped
3 tablespoons butter and 1 tablespoon oil or
⅓ cup bacon drippings
1 teaspoon salt
¼ teaspoon sugar (to help the onions to brown)
3 tablespoons flour
2 quarts boiling brown stock, canned beef broth, or
1 quart boiling water and 1 quart stock or broth
½ cup dry white wine or dry white vermouth
Salt and white pepper to taste
3 tablespoons Brandy or Cognac
12 to 16 rounds of hard toasted French bread
¾ cup each of grated Swiss and Parmesan cheese, mixed together

Heat butter and oil or bacon drippings in a heavy bottomed 5 or 6 quart Dutch oven or soup pot. Add onions and cook slowly, covered, on a very low fire, stirring often, until they are golden brown, about 15 minutes. About halfway through browning the onions, stir in the salt and sugar. Continue to cook, stirring frequently, until onions have turned a deep golden brown. Add the flour and stir for about 2 minutes. Add the liquid and wine, season to taste. Lower the heat, partially cover, and simmer gently for 30 to 40 minutes more. Just before serving, stir in the Cognac. Pour the soup into a soup tureen or soup bowls over rounds of French bread. Pass the cheese separately to sprinkle on top of soup.

Soupe a l'Oignon Gratinée
(Onion Soup Gratineed with Cheese)

Preheat oven to 325 degrees. Place the rounds of bread in one layer in a roasting pan or on a cookie sheet and bake for about 30 minutes, until the bread is thoroughly dried out and lightly browned. Halfway through the baking, remove pan from oven and rub each side of bread rounds with cut clove of garlic. With a pastry brush baste each side with olive oil. Or if you prefer, baste each side with garlic butter. Continue baking. Bring soup to a boil and pour into oven proof tureen or individual oven-proof bowls. Float the bread rounds on top of soup and sprinkle heavily with the grated mixed cheese. Bake for 20 minutes in the oven, then place for a minute or two under a pre-heated broiler to brown the top lightly. Serve immediately.

Oyster Soup
A delicious old-fashioned soup
As good today as it was in the past.

3 dozen oysters, chopped
Oyster liquid plus water to make 2 cups liquid
8 tablespoon butter or margarine
6 shallots (green onions) chopped fine
2 ribs celery, chopped fine
4 tablespoons flour
2 cups milk and 2 cups half and half cream (heat but do not boil)
Salt and pepper to taste
2 tablespoon parsley, minced fine

Simmer oysters and their liquid over medium heat until the edges of the oysters curl. Meanwhile in another pot sauté shallots and celery in butter until very soft. Add flour and stir until smooth. Gradually add heated milk. Cook over medium heat until slightly thickened. Add the oysters and the liquid to the sauce and salt and pepper to taste. Simmer for about 5 minutes, stir in parsley, and serve at once with oyster crackers or crusty French bread.

Oyster and Artichoke Soup

½ cup butter (1 stick)
2 bunch shallots (green onions) chopped fine
2 ribs celery, chopped fine
3 cloves garlic, minced fine
2 (14 ounce) cans artichoke hearts, drained and chopped
3 tablespoons flour
1 to 1½ quarts chicken stock
½ teaspoon red pepper flakes
1 teaspoon salt
1 Tablespoon Worcestershire sauce
¼ teaspoon thyme
1 quart oysters, drained and chopped, reserve liquid
½ cup Vermouth wine (optional)
2 tablespoons chopped fresh parsley
1 cup half and half cream

In a heavy 4 quart pot sauté shallots, garlic and celery in butter until soft. Add the artichoke hearts and sprinkle in the flour, stirring quickly. Do not let the flour brown. Gradually add the chicken stock, stirring constantly. Add the red pepper flakes, salt, Worcestershire sauce and thyme. Stir well, lower heat to simmer, cover the pot and simmer for 15 minutes. Add the oysters and oyster liquid, Vermouth wine, if using, and parsley to the artichoke mixture, and simmer for about 10 minutes. Do not boil. Stir in the cream and milk. Cool and refrigerate for at least 8 hours so flavors can blend before heating and serving.

Split Pea Soup

2 pounds dried split green peas
1 pound Ham or Canadian bacon, cubed, or 2 ham hocks
1 pound Kielbasa or smoked sausage, sliced (optional)
2 onions, chopped
3 cloves garlic, minced
3 ribs celery, chopped
2 medium carrots, chopped (optional)
1 tablespoon thyme
1 teaspoon black pepper
¼ teaspoon red pepper flakes (or more if desired)
2 tablespoons chopped parsley
2 teaspoons kosher salt
1 tablespoon Worcestershire sauce
16 cups chicken stock or water (or half of each)
4 red potatoes, peeled and cubed small, or ½ cup pearl barley (optional)

Wash and drain peas and add to a large pot along with rest of ingredients except potatoes. If using barley, it may be added at this time. Bring to a boiling point, then lower to simmer. Partially cover pot and simmer, stirring occasionally, for about 2 to 3 hours. As you stir, mash some of the peas with the back of the spoon The more mashing, the creamier the soup. Add potatoes and continue to cook until tender. At the end of cooking time, remove ham hocks from soup, cut ham from the bone and add the ham to the soup. Potatoes or barley make a heartier soup, but on occasion omit for a lighter soup. Adjust seasoning and serve with saltine crackers and butter or crispy French bread and butter.

Tuscan White Bean Soup

2 tablespoons butter
1 tablespoon olive oil
1 bunch green onions, chopped
2 (15 ounce) cans cannelloni beans, drained and rinsed
4 cups chicken broth
4 cloves garlic, cut in half
½ cup heavy cream
½ teaspoon freshly ground black pepper

Place a medium, heavy soup pot over medium heat. Add the butter, olive oil and green onions. Cook, stirring occasionally, until the onions are softened, about 5 minutes. Add the beans and stir to combine. Add the broth and bring the mixture to a simmer. Add the garlic and simmer until the garlic is softened, about 10 minutes. Pour the soup into a large bowl. Carefully ladle ⅓ to ½ of the soup into a blender and puree until smooth. Be careful to hold the top of the blender tightly, as hot liquids expand when they are blended. Pour the blended soup back into the soup pot. Puree the remaining soup. Once all the soup is blended and back in the soup pot, add the cream and the pepper. Keep warm, covered, over very low heat. Recipe easily doubled. Serve soup with warm poor boy bread or garlic bread.

Vegetable and Meat Soup
(Soupe en Jardinière et Bouilli)

I was a child of the Depression years, so Momma often made inexpensive pots of food, red beans and rice, stews, gumbos, etc. and her delicious and healthy vegetable soup made in her tremendous soup pot was one of my favorites. Momma used meaty soup bones for the meat, which was often given as Lagniappe by the neighborhood butcher shops. The vegetables were often homegrown, or bought from local farmers who would ride down the streets with their horse and wagon, the wagon loaded down with fruit and vegetables of all kinds, grown on their truck farms. As they passed, they would call out what they had in the wagons, and the housewives would hurry out with their baskets and choose the fruit and vegetables of their choice. I have inherited Momma's big soup pot and her recipe for her vegetable soup. Unfortunately, we can no longer find those tasty, meaty soup bones, so I use beef brisket. For the vegetables, I now use fresh from the Supermarket or frozen vegetables.

6 to 8 pounds beef brisket or chuck roast
3 large Creole tomatoes, chopped, or 1 large (28 ounce) can whole tomatoes, chopped
4 to 6 large carrots, sliced
2 large white onions, chopped
4 cloves garlic, minced fine
4 ribs celery, sliced
⅓ cup celery leaves, chopped
1 large, sweet pepper, chopped
3 small turnips, peeled and chopped
½ small cabbage, shredded
1 pound snap (green) beans, quartered
2 potatoes, peeled and cut up
1 pack frozen green peas
1 small bag frozen corn (optional)
1 tablespoon Worcestershire sauce
Water, enough to cover
6 sprigs parsley, chopped
2 tablespoons salt
1 teaspoon black pepper
1 teaspoon thyme
¼ teaspoon cayenne pepper
3 bay leaves
Vermicelli

In a large (about 10 quart) soup pot put all ingredients except seasonings and vermicelli. Add water, enough to cover generously, and bring to boil. Lower heat to simmer, keeping pot partially covered. After pot has been simmering for about 10 minutes, skim top of soup and then add seasonings. Continue to simmer for about 4 to 5 hours. Vermicelli may be added to soup during the last 20 minutes of cooking. When soup is done, remove meat. Cut off about two-thirds of the meat and set it aside. Cut

(Continued Next Page)

the remaining meat into small pieces and return to soup. Soup easily frozen.

Note: Steam or boil 4 to 6 peeled, whole white potatoes. After serving soup as a first course, slice meat that was set aside and serve along with a large sliced red onion and the steamed potatoes, as an entree. Serve with Creole tomato horseradish sauce* If you prefer, warm French bread can replace the potatoes.

*Creole Tomato Horseradish Sauce - see page 109.

Vichyssoise
A warm weather creamy-rich cold potato soup

3 tablespoon butter or margarine
1 medium size onion, chopped
2 cups sliced leek (white part only) or shallots (green onions, white part only)
1 quart chicken stock or broth
½ cup dry vermouth wine
4 or 5 russet potatoes, (about 2 pounds) peeled and diced
1 tablespoon salt (or to taste)
White pepper to taste
½ teaspoon celery salt (optional)
2 cups milk
2 cups half and half
2 cups heavy cream
Minced chives

Sauté onion and leeks in butter on medium heat only until tender (about 4 to 5 minutes). Do not brown. Add stock, wine and potatoes. Bring to a boil, lower to simmer, and simmer for about 30 to 40 minutes or until potatoes are soft. Pour half at a time into food processor or blender. Cover and blend until smooth. Return mixture to pot. Season to taste with salt, pepper, and celery salt. Stir in the milk and half and half. Heat until mixture comes to a boil. Remove from heat and put the soup into a large bowl and chill well in the refrigerator. When ready to serve, stir in the heavy cream, mixing well. garnish with minced chives.

Salads and Dressings

Classic French Dressing	69
Creamy Fruit Salad Dressing	69
Vinaigrette Dressing	69
Honey-Poppy Seed Salad Dressing	70
Italian Dressing	70
Lemon and Oil Salad Dressing	71
Lemon Vinaigrette	71
Roquefort or Blue Cheese Dressing No. 1	72
Roquefort or Blue Cheese Dressing No. 2	72
Spiced Fruit Compote	72
Bean Salad	73
Aspic Ring for Salad	74
Momma's Cole Slaw	74
Chicken Salad	75
Momma's Fruit Salad	75
Layered Fruit Salad	76
Chopped Salad	77
Cobb Salad	78
Spinach Salad	78
Copper Pennies (Marinated Carrots)	79
Molded Cranberry Salad	80
Egg Salad	80
Five Cup Salad	81
German Potato Salad	81
Greek Salad	82
Green Bean Salad	83
Marinated Tomatoes	83
Okra and Tomato Salad	84
Olive Salad (Salade d'Olive Italienne)	84
Pasta Salad	85
Shrimp Salad	85
Momma's Potato Salad	86
Salade Niçoise	87
Shrimp Salad with Sea Salt and Dressing	88
Waldorf Salad	88
Sicilian Salad	89
Shrimp Stuffed Avocado	90

Classic French Dressing

¾ cup olive or salad oil
¾ teaspoon salt
⅛ teaspoon black pepper
¼ cup wine or cider vinegar

In bowl or covered jar measure all ingredients. Blend or shake until thoroughly mixed. Chill well and shake or mix before serving.

Creamy Fruit Salad Dressing

½ cup heavy whipping cream
1 tablespoon powdered sugar
½ tablespoon grated lemon peel

Place a small bowl and the beaters of electric mixer in the freezer for a few minutes to chill. Beat ingredients on high speed until soft peaks form. If more dressing is needed, easily doubled. Delicious over any fruit salad.

Vinaigrette Dressing

½ teaspoon salt
¼ teaspoon white pepper
½ teaspoon dry powdered mustard
1 cup olive oil
⅓ cup vinegar

Blend or shake in a covered jar until thoroughly mixed. Store at room temperature. Makes 1½ cups.

Honey-Poppy Seed Salad Dressing

½ cup vegetable oil
⅓ cup honey
¼ cup lemon juice
1 tablespoon poppy seeds

    Place honey and lemon juice in electric blender, mixing well. Slowly add oil until well blended. Add poppy seeds and mix well. Place in covered container and chill. Recipe may be doubled and kept in refrigerator for weeks. Serve over chicken salad, salad greens or fruit salad. Stir before using.

Italian Dressing

½ cup olive oil
2 tablespoons white wine vinegar
2 teaspoons lemon juice
2 teaspoons garlic, minced fine
½ teaspoon black pepper
1 tablespoon sliced shallots
¼ teaspoon dried basil
¼ teaspoon oregano
½ teaspoon salt

    Combine all ingredients in a small bowl. Mix well with a whisk and let stand at room temperature for an hour or two. Mix again vigorously with whisk before pouring it over the salad.

Lemon and Oil Salad Dressing

Juice of 2 lemons
½ cup olive oil
1 clove finely minced garlic, or ½ teaspoon garlic powder
Salt

Combine all ingredients. Beat vigorously until creamy. Serve over lettuce, cooked broccoli, spinach, cauliflower, or brussels sprouts. Store in refrigerator. Makes one cup.

Variation: To make a Greek dressing, omit garlic and add ¼ teaspoon oregano

Lemon Vinaigrette

½ cup olive or vegetable oil
¼ cup lemon juice
1 tablespoon red wine vinegar
1½ teaspoons sugar
½ teaspoon salt
½ teaspoon dry ground mustard
½ teaspoon Worcestershire sauce
¼ teaspoon black pepper
¼ teaspoon garlic salt

Place all ingredients in a glass jar, cover tightly and shake well. Refrigerate for an hour or so to blend flavors. Shake before serving.

Roquefort or Blue Cheese Dressing No. 1

Prepared as Classic French dressing (page 73) but add ¾ cup crumbled Roquefort or blue cheese.

Roquefort or Blue Cheese Dressing No. 2

1 (6 oz.) package Roquefort or blue cheese, room temperature and crumbled
1 cup mayonnaise
2 garlic cloves, pressed through garlic press
Juice of 2 lemons
Salt, pepper and cayenne pepper to taste

Mix well together. Refrigerate

Spiced Fruit Compote

1 (17 oz.) can apricot halves
1 (16 oz.) can peach halves
2 (8 ½ oz.) cans pear halves
1 (15 ¼ oz.) can pineapple chunks
1 (6 oz.) jar maraschino cherries
1 cup orange juice
⅓ cup firmly packed brown sugar
1 tablespoon lemon juice
Skin of one lemon, cut into strips
1 (3 inch) stick cinnamon
4 whole cloves
⅛ cup mace

Drain fruit, reserving syrup for ice cubes. Cut apricot, peach, and pear halves in half. Combine fruit in a rectangular baking dish. Combine orange juice and remaining ingredients in a saucepan; bring to a boil, reduce heat, and simmer 2 minutes. Pour over fruit and bake uncovered at 350 degrees for 30 minutes. Cool. Cover and refrigerate up to 2 days. Remove cinnamon stick and cloves before serving. Serve hot or cold. Yield: 8 to 10 servings.

Bean Salad

1 (16 ounce) can navy beans or other white beans, rinsed and drained
1 (16 ounce) can Garbanzo peas, rinsed and drained
1 cup finely diced carrots
¼ cup finely diced celery
½ sweet (green) pepper, sliced into thin rings, then into fourths
½ sweet (red) pepper, sliced into thin rings, then in fourths
¼ cup minced shallots (green onions) green part only
2 tablespoons minced fresh parsley
Salt and pepper to taste

Combine beans and rest of ingredients in a large bowl. Add ½ cup (or more if needed) of the salad dressing, tossing until well blended. Cover and chill before serving. May be used as a side dish in place of a vegetable at a meal, or as a luncheon salad.

Dressing

1½ cup water
1 teaspoon cornstarch
¼ cup balsamic vinegar
2 tablespoons olive oil
Seasoned salt to taste*

Whisk water and cornstarch together in a small saucepan until cornstarch dissolves. Bring to a boil and stir constantly for one minute. Cool. Add remaining ingredients and mix thoroughly. Chill before adding to salad.

*Seasoned Salt – See page 341.

Aspic Ring for Salad

For a main dish salad that's cool, pretty and filling, serve the salad in a tangy aspic ring. Chicken, shrimp, tuna or crab or a number of other salads are delicious served this way.

1 (3 oz.) package lemon flavored gelatin
1 cup boiling water
1 (8 oz.) can tomato sauce
¼ cup cold water
Salt and pepper to taste
½ cup stuffed olives, sliced
¼ cup finely chopped celery
Lettuce leaves
Salad of your choice

Combine gelatin and boiling water, stirring until gelatin dissolves. Allow to cool. Add tomato sauce, cold water, salt and pepper to gelatin. Mix well and chill until slightly thickened. Stir in olives and celery. Spoon gelatin mixture into a 6 cup ring mold and chill until firm. Place lettuce leaves on a pretty serving plate, unmold aspic on top of lettuce leaves, and fill with salad of your choice.

Momma's Cole Slaw

4 cups finely shredded cabbage
3 cups grated carrots
1 cup mayonnaise
¼ cup lemon juice or vinegar
2 teaspoons salt (or to taste)
¼ teaspoon black pepper

Mix lemon juice, salt and pepper with mayonnaise. Toss shredded cabbage and carrots with dressing. Refrigerate.

Salads and Dressings

Chicken Salad
(Old fashioned chicken salad with chicken cooked in microwave)

Recipe for "Chicken Cooked in Microwave" plus

1 cup sliced celery
1 cup chopped green sweet pepper (optional)
⅔ cup mayonnaise, or more according to taste
1½ teaspoon salt
¼ teaspoon black pepper
2 teaspoons fresh lemon juice, or to taste

Follow recipe for "Chicken Cooked in Microwave." When finished, cool and marinate in refrigerator overnight. Next day remove chicken to bowl, dispose of onion and celery, strain and freeze chicken stock for future use. Cut the chicken into bite size pieces. Add the rest of the ingredients and mix well. Chill and serve on bed of lettuce.

Note: If you are in a hurry, use 4 cups of cut up store bought roasted chicken. Proceed as above.

Recipe for "Chicken, Cooked in Microwave" – see page 156.

Momma's Fruit Salad

7 large oranges
5 medium bananas
3 large apples, peeled and shredded
1½ cup orange juice
¼ cup sifted powdered sugar

Mix orange juice and powdered sugar. Stir well and pour into a large bowl. Shred apples and slice bananas and immediately add to juice to keep apples and bananas from browning. Mix well with slotted spoon. Peel oranges and cut oranges crosswise, slicing each section in half. Cut slices and add to bowl. Mix well and chill before serving.

Layered Fruit Salad

1 pound grapes
2 bananas
1 can (16 oz.) sliced peaches
1 pint fresh raspberries
2 oranges
3 kiwis
Juice from 2 oranges or ½ frozen orange juice
2 to 4 tablespoons powdered sugar (optional)

Rinse grapes, cut in half and remove seeds. Place in bottom of a glass serving bowl or trifle bowl. Peel and slice bananas. Place over grapes. Drain peaches well. Cut into smaller pieces. Distribute on top of bananas. Carefully rinse raspberries. Sprinkle on top of peaches. Peel oranges. Remove the white skin. Slice and cut into smaller pieces. Place on top of raspberries. Peel and slice kiwis. Garnish salad. Pour orange juice over top of salad and sprinkle with powdered sugar, if using. Keep salad refrigerated until ready to serve.

Good served with: Macaroons or crispy oatmeal cookies, wafers, or pound cake and coffee or dessert wine, as desired.

Variation: Any fruit of your choice may be added, such as canned pineapple chunks, 1 or 2 peeled and shredded apples, strawberries, sliced or cut in fourths, melons, scooped with melon baller, etc. Instead of layering, fruit may be all mixed together before putting into trifle bowl or large glass bowl.

Note: May be served with Honey-Poppy Seed Dressing instead of powdered sugar. See page 70 for Honey-Poppy Seed Dressing recipe.

Chopped Salad

4 teaspoons red wine vinegar
¼ teaspoon salt, plus more for seasoning
⅛ teaspoon freshly ground black pepper, plus more for seasoning
3 tablespoons olive oil
2 cups finely chopped romaine lettuce (½ head)
2 cups finely chopped radicchio (from ½ large head)
2 avocados, peeled and sliced
8 oil-packed sun-dried tomato halves, drained and chopped or
small cherry tomatoes

Whisk the vinegar, salt, and pepper in a large bowl to blend. Gradually whisk in the oil to blend. Add the lettuce, radicchio, avocado, and sun-dried tomatoes. Toss to coat. Season the salad to taste, with more salt and pepper, and serve.

Variation: *Lemon Vinaigrette*:

¼ cup freshly squeezed lemon juice (2 lemons)
½ cup olive oil
½ teaspoon kosher salt
¼ teaspoon freshly ground black pepper

In a small bowl whisk all ingredients together

Cobb Salad

1 head lettuce, shredded fine
2 cups cut up or diagonally sliced grilled chicken breasts
2 medium tomatoes, chopped
1 or 2 ripe avocados, peeled and cubed small
½ cup thinly sliced celery
¼ to ½ cup (1 to 2 ounces) crumbled blue cheese (optional)
5 slices bacon, crisply cooked and crumbled
2 hard boiled eggs, each quartered
Lemon Vinaigrette Dressing (See page 71)

Mix salad ingredients in a large salad bowl. Pour vinaigrette dressing over salad and toss well. Or, for a very pretty presentation, place shredded lettuce on a large oval platter. Arrange chicken, avocado, celery, and tomatoes in rows on lettuce. Sprinkle blue cheese and bacon overall. Just before serving spoon well-mixed dressing over salad.

Garnish with egg quarters. Salad serves four. But for extra servings, salad and dressing easily doubled.

Spinach Salad

1 pound fresh spinach
½ head lettuce
½ pound sliced fresh mushrooms (optional)
8 sliced bacon, cooked and crumbled
½ cup broken pecans (optional)

Vinaigrette Dressing – see page 69.

Remove stems from spinach. Wash lettuce and spinach leaves thoroughly and pat or spin dry. Tear into bite size pieces. Combine all ingredients. Toss with vinaigrette dressing until well coated. Season with salt and pepper. Croutons may be added.

Copper Pennies
(Marinated Carrots)

This golden oldie is a cool option for warm weather meals or barbecues

6 cups sliced carrots, fresh or frozen, boiled just until tender
1 medium red onion, sliced very thin
1 medium sweet pepper, sliced thin
2 cloves garlic, minced fine or ½ teaspoon garlic granules or powder
1 (10 ¾ ounce) can tomato soup, undiluted
½ cup salad oil
½ cup sugar
¾ cup vinegar (cider)
1 teaspoon dry mustard
1 teaspoon Worcestershire sauce
1 teaspoon salt
1 teaspoon black pepper

Place boiled and drained carrots in a large casserole and mix with sliced onion and sweet pepper. (Canned carrots in equivalent amount may be used if you don't want to take the time to cook them.) Place rest of ingredients in a blender and blend well, or ingredients can be put in a covered jar and shaken until well mixed. Heat the sauce in a small pot, stirring well, until sugar is completely dissolved. Pour sauce over carrot mixture. Marinate in refrigerator overnight, or for at least 6 hours. Drain to serve. Serve on salad plates atop a crisp lettuce leaf or shredded lettuce.

Molded Cranberry Salad

This recipe was given to me by my Cousin, Helene Ware Wagner. She said she uses it every year at Thanksgiving and Christmas. I can understand why. It is a very special addition to a holiday meal.

1 cup chopped cranberries
1 orange, chopped well including half of skin
1 cup chopped celery
1 (8 oz.) can crushed pineapple, drained, reserve syrup
¾ cups chopped pecans
Large package cherry flavored Jell-O
1 cup hot water
1 cup sugar
1 tablespoon lemon juice
1 cup reserved pineapple syrup

Chop cranberries, orange, celery and pecans. (Helene says she uses her food processor to grind all ingredients. It is so much faster and easier.) Dissolve Jell-O in hot water. Add sugar, lemon juice and pineapple syrup. Do not add more liquid than called for in recipe. Chill. When partially set mix in remaining ingredients. Pour into mold and chill until firm. Serve on small plates lined with lettuce leaves.

Egg Salad

6 hard boiled eggs
1 rib celery, chopped fine
¼ cup mayonnaise
1 teaspoon Dijon mustard
Juice of half a lemon
½ teaspoon salt
¼ teaspoon black pepper
Dash of cayenne pepper or Tabasco sauce

Chop up eggs well, add rest of ingredients. Mix well, taste and if needed, adjust seasonings to your own taste. Serve with crackers or on a sandwich with lettuce or finely chopped watercress, tomatoes, and sliced avocado.

Variation: 3 tablespoons soft Roquefort or blue cheese may be added.

Five Cup Salad

My cousin, Vivian Ware Dawkins, served this salad at a Thanksgiving dinner. It was so delicious that I told Vivian I had to have the recipe. Vivian said she received the recipe from her Mother-in-law and friend, Mrs. Ruth Webb Dawkins. Mrs. Dawkins always prepared it at Christmas holidays.

1 cup mandarin orange slices, drained
1 cup pineapple chunks, drained
1 cup maraschino cherries, cut in half
1 cup miniature marshmallows
1 cup shredded or flaked coconut
1 cup sour cream

Mix well and chill before serving. Recipe easily doubled.

German Potato Salad

8 medium white potatoes
6 slices bacon
½ cup onion, chopped
1 tablespoon all-purpose flour
2 teaspoon sugar
2 teaspoon salt
¼ teaspoon black pepper
¼ teaspoon celery seed
4 tablespoon wine vinegar
½ cup water
1 tablespoon minced parsley

Steam or boil potatoes until tender. Peel and cut into bite size pieces. Fry bacon until crisp. Remove and crumble, reserving 1 tablespoon bacon fat. Add flour, sugar, celery seed, salt, and pepper. Cook, stirring continually, until lightly brown. Stir in vinegar and water and cook until lightly thickened. Add bacon and parsley. Stir in potatoes and heat, stirring gently to coat potatoes. Potatoes should look creamy. Sprinkle with more parsley. May be served hot, cold, or at room temperature.

Greek Salad
*In memory of Anita Caterina Miscenich,
My Father's Greek Grandmother*

The Dressing:

¼ cup red wine vinegar or 6 tablespoons freshly squeezed lemon juice
2 teaspoons kosher salt, plus more to taste
½ teaspoon freshly ground black pepper
¾ to 1 cup extra virgin olive oil, preferable Greek
1 tablespoon chopped fresh oregano leaves or
1 teaspoon dried oregano

The Salad:

8 cups salad greens mix
1 cup peeled cucumber, sliced thin
½ cup thinly sliced red onion
¾ pound cherry tomatoes, halved or 2 tomatoes, coarsely chopped
4 radishes, sliced (optional)
1 green pepper, seeded and diced
1 cup Kalamata olives
½ pound feta cheese, crumbled
Anchovy fillets (optional)

Tear greens into bite size pieces and toss with next 5 ingredients in a large bowl. Add olives, feta cheese, and anchovy fillets, if using.

In a blender combine vinegar, salt and pepper and blend. With motor running, slowly pour in a steady stream of olive oil to make a smooth dressing. Transfer to a small bowl and stir in oregano, mixing well. Taste and season with more salt and pepper, if needed. Just before serving, add dressing to salad and toss well. Serve immediately. For a luncheon, serve in large portions with crusty rolls.

Salads and Dressings

Green Bean Salad

This very French salad is especially good made with very tender and young green beans that have been blanched and refreshed in cold water to set their color. But if fresh beans are not available, canned beans work very well, either the cut green beans or the green beans cut French style

3 cups green beans
2 ounce jar pimento, drained
1 cup red onion, sliced (optional)
1 cup sliced celery
Vinaigrette dressing*

If using fresh beans, blanch for 5 to 8 minutes or until tender. Refresh in cold water. Blend together the beans, pimento, onion, and celery. Pour vinaigrette dressing over mixture, mixing well. Marinate overnight in refrigerator.

Variation: For a salad in a hurry, use drained, canned beans and a good bottled French or Italian dressing, Mix and refrigerate while you prepare the rest of your dinner. When very pressed for time, we have often used the beans without the rest of the vegetables.

*Vinaigrette dressing – see page 69.

Marinated Tomatoes

4 Creole or large tomatoes
¼ cup basil leaves, chopped
3 tablespoons olive oil
2 tablespoons lemon juice
½ teaspoon sugar
Salt and pepper to taste

Cut tomatoes in slices ½ inch thick. Arrange slices on large plate or platter in single layer, slices slightly overlapping. Sprinkle with basil leaves. Mix remaining ingredients together in a small bowl, whisking well. Pour over tomatoes. Cover and let stand at room temperature for about an hour before serving.

Okra and Tomato Salad

2 pounds small fresh or frozen okra
2 tomatoes, each cut into eighths
Classic French Dressing*
Lettuce
1 hard boiled egg, chopped fine (optional)

Place okra in salted water. Bring water to a boil, lower heat and simmer for 15 to 20 minutes, or until tender. (If using frozen okra, follow directions on package) Remove from heat and drain in a colander. Refresh under cold water and drain. Trim off the stem ends and tips and slice the okra. Pour dressing over okra and tomatoes, tossing gently to coat. Marinate for about an hour. When ready to serve, arrange salad greens on a salad plate. Toss okra and tomatoes lightly and arrange on top of lettuce. Season to taste with salt and pepper. Garnish with chopped hard boiled egg before serving.

*Classic French Dressing – see page 69.

Olive Salad
(Salade d'Olive Italienne)

1½ cup olive oil
2 cloves garlic, minced fine
¼ teaspoon black pepper
¼ cup chopped parsley
1 tablespoon dried oregano leaves
2 anchovy fillets, mashed (optional)
4 cups prepared pickled Italian vegetables salad mix
1 cup celery, chopped fine
¾ cup chopped Greek or ripe olives

Wisk together the olive oil, oregano, garlic, anchovies, parsley and pepper in a bowl. Stir in remaining ingredients and mix well. Cover and refrigerate at least 8 hours or overnight. Delicious served on Muffuletta sandwiches or over a salad.

Pasta Salad

4 cups rotini rainbow macaroni or elbow macaroni
1 jar marinated artichoke hearts, drained and chopped, reserve oil
¾ cup bottled Italian dressing, plus reserved oil from artichoke hearts
2 tomatoes, chopped
1 sweet pepper, cut in julienne strips
1 cucumber, sliced (optional)
7 radishes, sliced (optional)
1 cup salad olives
1 teaspoon salt
1½ teaspoon Creole seasonings (Tony Chachere)
2 tablespoons chopped fresh parsley
2 teaspoon Dijon mustard
1 large can salmon or tuna fish, or 2 cups cooked chicken, turkey or ham, diced
Lettuce

Boil macaroni, rinse in cold water. Drain and mix with rest of ingredients except lettuce. Toss gently, mixing well. Cover and chill completely. When ready to serve, toss again and serve on lettuce lined plates.

Shrimp Salad

8 cups boiled shrimp, peeled and deveined
2 cups chopped celery
1 cup chopped sweet pepper (optional)
2 tablespoons lemon juice
1 cup mayonnaise
1 teaspoon salt
⅛ teaspoon cayenne pepper (or to taste)

Blend mayonnaise, lemon juice, salt, and pepper in bowl. Add shrimp, celery and sweet pepper and toss lightly. Refrigerate. Serve on lettuce lined plate. Garnish with hard boiled egg wedges, olives, and cherry tomatoes.

Shrimp salad with avocado. Add 1 cup or more diced avocado to the shrimp salad. Two or three tablespoons sliced stuffed olives may also be added.

Momma's Potato Salad

My heart is filled with memories whenever I think of my Mom's potato salad. I remember with love the many times she would prepare a big bowl of it for potluck dinners at my Dad's lodge meetings, or for family gatherings, or just for family meals. I miss sneaking a taste from the bowl when she made it for all of us. Now, one or the other of my kids who are there when I make it has to have a taste "just to make sure it's O.K." as they tell me. Potato salad is great with fried or broiled chicken, fish, or meat. But often in the summer, Mom would serve it just with hot dogs or deli cold cuts and sliced cheese. Potato salad should be made with waxy potatoes that can stand up to boiling or steaming. They must not be overcooked, and Momma always said you need to add the cut up potatoes to the rest of the ingredients while they are still warm, so the potatoes will absorb all of the flavors.

5 pounds potatoes, Yukon gold or red
6 eggs, hard boiled
2 cups chopped celery (about 4 long ribs)
1 cup chopped sweet peppers (about 1 large)
4 large sour pickles, chopped
½ cup stuffed green olives, sliced (optional)
2 cups mayonnaise
½ cup vinegar (preferably white distilled)
2 tablespoons salt
1 teaspoon black pepper
½ teaspoon dry mustard (optional)
Chopped parsley, for garnish (optional)
Tomato wedges and/or canned asparagus spears, for garnish (optional)

Steam or boil potatoes until fork tender. If boiling, place the potatoes in a medium size pot. Add cold water to cover and about a teaspoonful of salt. Bring to a boil over medium high heat. Reduce the heat to low and simmer, covered, until the potatoes are barely tender and easily pierced with a fork, about 15 to 20 minutes. Potatoes continue to cook as they cool, so be careful not to overcook them. Meanwhile, peel and chop hard boiled eggs and put into a large mixing bowl. Add rest of ingredients including potatoes that have been peeled and cut into bite sized pieces and mix well. If steaming the potatoes, steam until fork tender. Peel potatoes while still warm and cut into bite size pieces. (about 1 inch cubes.) Add to the rest of the ingredients in the large bowl. Mix well but very gently so potatoes are not mashed. Refrigerate, covered, preferably overnight to marinate, so flavors will blend. If desired, for a festive touch, garnish with finely chopped parsley and add tomato and/or asparagus next to salad on lettuce lined serving plates.

Salade Niçoise

½ cup sauce vinaigrette (see page 69)
3 cups peeled and sliced potatoes, cooked to fork tender
⅓ cup chicken stock, fresh or canned
1 large head lettuce, or combination of greens of your choice, separated, washed and dried
1 (16 oz.) can French cut green beans, drained
3 hard boiled eggs, cooled, peeled and quartered
3 tomatoes, quartered
1 cup canned tuna chunks, drained, or 1½ cups cold, cooked sliced chicken breast
1 (2 oz.) can rolled anchovy filet with capers, drained and each cut in half
1 cup pitted black olives, each cut in half
4 canned artichoke hearts, quartered
2 tablespoons each parsley and tarragon

    Prepare vinaigrette and set aside. Place sliced, cooked potatoes in a serving bowl. Heat chicken stock and pour over the still warm potatoes (done immediately after peeling and slicing potatoes so the warm potatoes can absorb the stock). Toss gently several times and let stand for several minutes until stock is completely absorbed. Refrigerate to cool. When ready to serve, lightly season green beans and tomatoes with dressing, then place the lettuce leaves around edge of salad bowl. Mound the cold potatoes on bottom of the bowl. Arrange the tuna or chicken, artichoke hearts, green beans, tomato and egg quarters in an attractive pattern of your choice over potatoes. Sprinkle olives and anchovies over top, then parsley and tarragon. Remaining salad dressing may be poured over top or passed to be served separately.

    Variation: Salad may be arranged and served on individual salad plates. Slices of avocado may be added around side of plate.

Shrimp Salad with Sea Salt and Dressing

3 pounds cooked and shelled shrimp, medium or large size
2 pints cherry tomatoes, halved
½ cup black Kalamata olives, seeded
½ cup green olives, seeded
1 can hearts of palm
¾ cup coarsely chopped fresh flat-leafed parsley
½ cup chopped chives (optional)
¾ cup extra-virgin olive oil
¼ cup lemon juice
Coarse sea salt to taste, plus additional if needed when serving
¼ Teaspoon white pepper
1 lemon, sliced thin for garnish (optional)

Combine shrimp, tomatoes, olives, and hearts of palm and mix lightly but well. Combine herbs, lemon juice, salt, and pepper in a bowl. Whisk in olive oil and toss with shrimp salad. Serve on lettuce lined plates.

Waldorf Salad

2 cups peeled red apple, diced, or 1 cup each apple and canned pineapple chunks
2 tablespoons lemon juice
½ cup mayonnaise
1 cup thinly sliced celery
½ cup broken walnuts or pecans
½ cup raisins (optional)

Toss fruit with lemon juice and 1 tablespoon mayonnaise. Just before serving, add celery, walnuts or pecans, raisins, rest of mayonnaise, and toss well. Serve on salad plate lined with lettuce. Pour a little bit of French dressing over top.

Sicilian Salad

Italian Salad was once affectionately called Wop Salad by New Orleanians, including those of Italian descent and was served not only in Italian and Creole restaurants but in restaurants all over New Orleans, including the big Seafood restaurants at "West End" on the Lakefront of Lake Pontchartrain. It combines fresh greens, ripe Creole tomatoes, and a mélange of extra ingredients.

2 cups assorted lettuce, (Iceberg, Butter, Red leaf, Green leaf)
2 cups arugula or spinach leaves
2 Creole tomatoes, cut into wedges
½ cup pitted kalamata olives
6 sliced black olives
Small jar olive salad mix, undrained
1 small jar marinated artichoke hearts, undrained but chopped
½ of a small green (sweet) pepper, cut into strips
2 ribs celery, sliced
2 to 3 radishes, sliced (optional)
1 large cucumber, sliced
1 large or 2 small dill pickles, minced
16 to 18 flat anchovies
1 cup extra virgin olive oil
⅓ cup of red wine vinegar
1 tablespoon Worcestershire sauce
1 tablespoon Sicilian seasoning
Salt and pepper to taste
Large cooked or canned asparagus spears
Hard boiled eggs, quartered
Grated Romano or Parmesan cheese

Toss all of the torn, washed, and dried greens together in a large bowl, and set aside. In a separate bowl, combine the next 11 ingredients together and mix well. Combine with the salad greens and gently toss to mix well. Whisk together the salad dressing and drizzle over the mixed salad and toss very well so that all of the salad and greens are glistening with the dressing. Divide the salad on salad plates and place two crossed anchovies on top of each serving plate Place an asparagus spear on top of each salad, and place hard boiled egg wedges around the salad on the plates. Sprinkle the top of the salads with the grated cheese and serve immediately.

Shrimp Stuffed Avocado

2 to 3 cups peeled, boiled shrimp, if shrimp are large, cut in two
½ cup celery, diced small
2 tablespoons lemon juice
½ cup mayonnaise
Salt and pepper to taste
Dash cayenne pepper (optional)
Dash paprika
3 large avocados
Lettuce leaves
Tomato wedges
Hard boiled eggs, peeled and quartered
Pitted green Spanish olives

    Combine first seven ingredients in a large bowl and mix gently but well. Cover and marinate in refrigerator for several hours. When ready to serve cut Avocados in half lengthwise. Mound the shrimp salad into the avocado halves. Place on lettuce covered salad plates and arrange tomato wedges, hard boiled eggs, and olives around avocados. Nice served for a summer luncheon.

A New Orleans Cookbook from Momma's Kitchen

Sauces

The French Roux	95
Blond Roux (White Roux)	95
Microwave Roux	96
Creole Alfredo Sauce	97
Marinade Sauce for Pork or Steak	98
Artichoke Butter Sauce	98
Bechamel Sauce (White Sauce)	99
Mornay Sauce (Cheese Sauce)	99
Bordelaise Sauce	100
Whiskey or Brandy Sauce	100
Butter and Wine Sauce	101
Chocolate Fudge Sauce	101
Speedy Chocolate Fudge Sauce	101
Microwaved Hot Fudge Sauce	102
Cranberry Butter	102
Grilled Chicken Sauce	103
Hollandaise Sauce	103
Lemon Sauce	104
Mango Sauce	104
Meuniere Sauce	104
Marinara Sauce	105
Orange Sauce	106
Peach and Strawberry Sauce	106
Pesto Sauce	107
Raspberry and Blueberry Sauce	107
Le Salse Alla Puttanesca (Puttanesca Sauce)	108
Red Eye Gravy	109
Creole Tomato Horseradish Sauce	109
Remoulade Sauce	110
New Orleans Tartar Sauce	111
Seasoned Butter	111
Honey Butter	111
Raspberry Butter	111
Herb and Seasoned Butter	112
Parsley or Cilantro-Lime Butter	112
Creole Tomato Sauce	113

The French Roux
"First, You make a Roux"

To the Creole cook this is the foundation and success of all fine sauces. In making a brown roux equal parts of flour and butter or flour and oil are used, and this rule must be followed. Never let it become over-browned or burnt. It has always been customary to make a roux in a heavy pot. Very few Creole kitchens were without a big iron pot in which Gumbos and roux based dishes were cooked (and also dishes where a roux was not required). Slowly heat the oil or butter and gradually add the flour, stirring constantly until it is a golden brown or dark brown, the color varying according to the particular dish you are preparing. This is a slow process, taking about 20 minutes to a half hour. The key lies in the gradual introduction of ingredients. This begins the cooking of the desired dish. When adding water to the roux be sure the water is hot or it will separate the oil and flour.

A white roux is made by blending butter and flour together and slowly adding hot milk. You must never allow a white roux to brown. I like to make a white roux in a double boiler. Do not let the water boil beneath your sauce. Keep it at a simmer. Also, the water must not touch the bottom of the upper pan of the double boiler.

Blond Roux
(White Roux)

4 tablespoons pan drippings and or butter
6 tablespoons flour

Heat fat over medium high heat. Add flour all at once whisking vigorously. When mixture thins and starts to bubble, reduce heat to low and cut back on the whisking. Cook until you smell a toasty aroma then cook 2 minutes more, stirring occasionally.

Roux can be used immediately to thicken a liquid that is at or below room temperature. To thicken a hot liquid, allow to cool to room temperature, or refrigerate.

Tightly wrapped, roux can be refrigerated for up to a month. Simply break off pieces and use as needed.

Microwave Roux
(Now my favorite way of making roux)

1 cup oil
1 cup flour
1 large, chopped onion, (2 cups)
1 cup chopped celery
1 chopped sweet pepper (1 cup)
4 cloves garlic, minced
½ cup chopped parsley
¼ cup chopped shallots (green onions)
Approximately ¼ cup hot water

Mix oil and flour together in a 4 cup (or larger) Pyrex measuring cup. Whisk until all lumps disappear. Microwave uncovered on high for about 6 or 7 minutes. Stir and cook 3 minutes or so longer. Continue to cook, checking every 3 minutes until roux is the color of a pecan or caramel. You should have a perfect dark brown roux in 12 to 18 minutes, depending on the wattage of your particular microwave. When it is the color you desire, carefully remove hot roux from microwave and stir onion, celery and sweet pepper into the roux, mixing very well, especially at the bottom. Return to microwave and cook on high for 3 minutes. Add garlic, parsley and green onions to roux, stir (be very careful when stirring, as roux will be very hot) and return to microwave. Cook on high for 2 more minutes. Take out of microwave and pour off any oil that has risen to top. Slowly add enough hot tap water to bring roux to the 4-cup mark. Stir well and use immediately or freeze for future use in whatever recipe calls for a roux.

Creole Alfredo Sauce
(Fettuccine Alfredo made our way)

1 pound Fettuccine, linguine, or spaghetti
6 tablespoons butter or margarine
16 ounces (2 cups) half and half cream
½ teaspoon salt
¼ teaspoon white pepper
½ teaspoon red pepper flakes
½ teaspoon garlic powder
⅛ teaspoon (pinch) of cayenne pepper or Creole seasoning (optional)
½ cup or to taste chopped sun dried tomatoes (optional)
1 cup shredded Parmesan cheese
About ¼ cup pasta water, if needed
Fresh chopped parsley

Cook and drain pasta as directed on package. While pasta is cooking, melt butter or margarine in a saucepan or large skillet over medium heat. Add half and half cream, salt, pepper, garlic powder, and cayenne pepper or Creole seasoning, and heat to boiling. Boil about one minute, stirring with a wire whisk. Remove from heat, add sun dried tomatoes, if using, and whisk in cheese. Pour over cooked pasta and toss well. If sauce seems a little thick, add a little pasta water. More cheese may be added if desired. Top with a sprinkling of fresh parsley. May be served as a side dish with meat or poultry or as a meatless dish with green peas or a green vegetable of your choice and a mixed salad. Recipe easily doubled, if needed.

Variation: Mix ½ cup Italian dressing and 1 tablespoon Italian seasoning in a large glass or plastic bowl. Add 1 pound chicken tenders or 1 pound boneless chicken breasts cut into 1 inch pieces, turning to coat. Marinate in refrigerator for about 20 minutes. Prepare Alfredo sauce as directed. Cook and drain pasta as directed on package. While pasta is cooking, spray a 10 inch skillet with nonstick cooking spray. Remove chicken from marinate and sauté chicken in skillet over medium heat for 5 to 7 minutes, or until chicken is no longer pink in center. Stir in Alfredo sauce. Toss pasta and chicken mixture, or place pasta on a serving platter. Top with chicken and sauce and sprinkle with Parmesan cheese and about 2 tablespoons chopped fresh parsley.

Marinade Sauce for Pork or Steak

¼ teaspoon pepper
¼ teaspoon Tabasco Sauce
1 teaspoon ground ginger
1½ teaspoons curry powder
3 garlic cloves, crushed
2 tablespoons ketchup
¼ cup soy sauce
½ cup vegetable oil
½ cup red wine

Pour marinade sauce over Pork or Steak. Cover and refrigerate 24 hours before serving, stirring once or twice. Broil or grill about 5 or 10 minutes on each side or until cooked. Baste meat when cooking with marinade sauce.

Artichoke Butter Sauce
(To be served over Fish or Chicken)

½ cup butter
2 shallots (green onions) chopped fine (optional)
2 tablespoons chopped parsley
3 cloves garlic, minced fine
1 tablespoon lemon juice
1 (14 oz.) can artichoke hearts, drained and chopped
1 teaspoon salt
¼ teaspoon cayenne pepper (or to taste)

Place butter, green onions, parsley and garlic in a 4 cup microwave safe measuring cup. Microwave on high 2 minutes. Add rest of ingredients and microwave on high 4½ or 5 minutes longer, stirring halfway through. Pour over baked, broiled or microwaved fish fillets or chicken before serving. Delicious served over sautéed boneless chicken breasts. Pour sauce into pan chicken was sautéed in and stir and scrape bottom of pan. Pour over chicken breasts before serving.

Bechamel Sauce
(White Sauce)

4 tablespoons butter
4 tablespoons flour
2 cups hot milk
1 teaspoon salt
½ teaspoon Tabasco sauce
¼ teaspoon ground nutmeg

Melt butter in a heavy saucepan. Add flour slowly, stirring constantly to keep mixture smooth. Gradually whisk in milk, whisking constantly over medium heat until sauce is smooth and thickened. Remove from heat and whisk in salt, Tabasco sauce and nutmeg. Blend thoroughly.

Mornay Sauce
(Cheese Sauce)

To make a Mornay Sauce simply melt ½ to 1 cup shredded cheddar cheese to the Bechamel and cook slowly until the cheese is melted.

Variation: Bechamel or Mornay Sauces are easily made in a microwave. Heat milk in a 4 cup measure for 4 minutes on high heat. Add flour, salt, Tabasco sauce and nutmeg and slowly blend into milk. Microwave on high for 3 minutes, stirring at 1 minute intervals. For Mornay Sauce, Add cheese along with seasonings and proceed as above.

Bordelaise Sauce

¼ cup butter
2 tablespoons olive oil
5 cloves garlic, peeled and mashed or coarsely chopped
½ teaspoon salt
½ teaspoon white pepper
1 tablespoon red pepper flakes, (optional)
¼ cup chopped Italian flat leaf parsley
1 tablespoon chopped basil (optional)

Melt the butter in a heavy sauté pan over low heat. Add the olive oil and heat for about 3 minutes over the low heat. Add the garlic, salt, pepper, and continue to cook. Do not let the garlic burn or it will become bitter. As the garlic begins to brown, remove it from the sauce with a slotted spoon or skimmer. Add the red pepper flakes, if you are using, and sauté for 1 minute. Add the parsley and, if you are using, the basil, and mix. Good served over pasta and meat. Also good as a dipping sauce for shrimp or lobster.

Whiskey or Brandy Sauce

4 egg yolks
¼ cup sugar
2 tablespoons butter, melted
1 tablespoon flour
⅛ teaspoon ground cloves
¼ teaspoon salt
1 cup milk and 1 cup heavy cream heated to scalding point
4 tablespoons Brandy or Bourbon
4 tablespoons Grand Marnier

In bowl, beat egg yolks. Add sugar, butter, flour, cloves and salt and continue beating until light. Add hot milk and cream very slowly, stirring constantly. Put mixture in double boiler over hot, not boiling water, stirring constantly. Continue to cook until sauce has thickened to consistency of heavy cream. Immediately pour into cool bowl. Add Brandy and Grand Marnier. Stir and cover. Refrigerate until chilled. Serve over bread pudding, fruit compote, plain cake, gelatin, etc.

If custard should curdle, set bowl of custard in pan of ice water and beat vigorously with hand or electric beater. This will restore smoothness.

Butter and Wine Sauce
(To be served over fish or chicken)

½ cup butter
2 shallots, chopped (green part only)
2 tablespoons chopped parsley
⅛ teaspoon cayenne
⅓ cup Sautérne or dry Vermouth wine

Place all ingredients in a 4 cup microwave safe measure and microwave on high 3 minutes. Spoon over fish or chicken before serving. Very good served over sautéed boneless chicken breasts. Pour sauce into pan chicken was sautéed in and stir and scrape bottom of pan. Pour over chicken.

Chocolate Fudge Sauce

2 (12 ounce) packages semi-sweet chocolate chips
1 cup sugar
⅛ teaspoon salt
1 cup water
1 cup half and half cream

Combine first four ingredients in a small heavy bottomed pot over low heat. Stir constantly until chocolate and sugar melts. Remove from heat and stir in half and half. Serve immediately over cream puffs, ice cream or dessert of your choice.

Speedy Chocolate Fudge Sauce

1 (6 ounce) package semi-sweet chocolate chips
⅓ cup whipping cream

Combine chocolate chips and whipping cream in a 4 cup glass measure. Cover with heavy duty plastic wrap and microwave at medium power for 3 to 4 minutes or until melted. Stir after every minute. This recipe yields one cup but recipe is easily doubled.

Microwaved Hot Fudge Sauce

2 cups sugar
½ cup cocoa
⅛ teaspoon salt
¼ cup light corn syrup
¾ cup evaporated milk
1 tablespoon butter
1 teaspoon vanilla

Mix first five ingredients in a large microwave bowl or an 8 cup measuring cup. Cook on high for 6 minutes, stirring every 2 minutes. Remove from microwave and add butter and vanilla. May be kept in refrigerator until ready to use. To return to original consistency, simply reheat in microwave.

Cranberry Butter

1 cup fresh or frozen cranberries, thawed
1 cup sifted powdered sugar
½ cup unsalted butter, softened
1 tablespoon lemon juice

Blend all ingredients in the bowl of a food processor or blender until finely minced and smooth, scraping sides of bowl occasionally to be sure all is blended well. Transfer to a bowl and chill until firm. May be served from the bowl or mixture may be frozen for future use. To freeze, form into small disks, 1 tablespoon each, and place disks in a resealable plastic bag. Freeze and remove from bag as needed. Great on toast, raisin bread, waffles or pancakes. Recipe easily doubled.

Grilled Chicken Sauce

½ cup distilled vinegar
½ cup lemon juice
½ cup corn oil
1 tablespoon salt
¼ teaspoon ground black pepper
1½ tablespoon dry mustard
Sprinkle cayenne pepper

Preheat grill. In a bowl, mix all ingredients together. Pour mixed ingredients into a small saucepan. Over medium heat, bring sauce to a boil, stirring frequently. Remove saucepan from heat. While the chicken is grilling, use a pastry brush to apply sauce onto each piece of chicken.

Hollandaise Sauce
(Made quick and easy in a Microwave)

½ cup butter
3 egg yolks
1 tablespoon lemon juice
¼ teaspoon salt
½ teaspoon dry mustard
Dash of cayenne
Dash of paprika
2 tablespoons half and half cream

Place butter in a 2 cup microwave safe measure and microwave on high until melted, about 1 minute. Stir in rest of ingredients and microwave on high for 1 minute, stirring every 15 seconds. Remove from microwave and whisk until smooth. If sauce needs to be reheated, microwave on high for 1 minute.

Lemon Sauce

1 tablespoon cornstarch
½ cup sugar
Pinch salt
½ cup water
2½ tablespoons lemon juice
2 tablespoons butter

    In a small pot combine sugar, cornstarch and salt. Gradually stir in water, stirring constantly. Add rest of ingredients, still stirring boil until sauce thickens, about 4 or 5 minutes.

Mango Sauce

2 mangoes, peeled and cut into chunks (3 cups)
4 tablespoons fresh lime juice
2 tablespoons sugar
4 tablespoons orange liqueur (recommended: Cointreau)
½ cup fresh mint leaves (optional)

    In a blender or food processor, puree the mangoes with the lime juice, sugar and Cointreau until smooth. Spoon the sauce over slices of Angel Food cake, pound cake, or ice cream. If desired, garnish with mint leaves before serving.

Meuniere Sauce
New Orleans Butter sauce used with fish, shellfish, meat and poultry

8 tablespoons (1 stick) butter
1 teaspoon black pepper
1 tablespoon Worcestershire sauce
Juice of ½ lemon
3 tablespoon minced parsley

    Melt butter slowly over low heat in a small heavy saucepan, and continue to cook until butter turns a light brown. Remove from heat and add the rest of the ingredients. Return the pan to low heat for about a minute, stirring thoroughly. Then remove from heat and serve over the seafood, meat or poultry you are serving.

Marinara Sauce

½ cup olive oil
1 onion, finely chopped
3 cloves garlic, minced
1 carrot, chopped
1 rib celery, finely chopped
1 teaspoon salt, or to taste (preferably sea salt)
½ teaspoon black pepper
Pinch of Cayenne pepper (optional)
2 (28 ounce) cans whole or crushed tomatoes, chopped
1 tablespoon Worcestershire sauce
4 to 6 basil leaves
2 dried bay leaves
4 tablespoons unsalted butter, optional

In a large heavy pot, heat the oil over a medium flame. Add the onion, garlic, carrot, and celery, season with salt and pepper, and sauté until the vegetables are soft, about 5 minutes. Add tomatoes, Worcestershire sauce, basil and bay leaves. Simmer, covered and on low heat, stirring occasionally, until sauce thickens, for 1 hour. Remove and discard the bay leaves. Add sauce, one half at a time to a food processor. Process until smooth. Season the sauce with more salt and pepper to taste. The sauce can be made 1 day ahead. Cool, then cover and refrigerate. Rewarm in microwave or over medium heat before using. Recipe can be doubled and half of the sauce frozen for future use. Pour 1 to 2 cup portions into plastic freezer bags. This will freeze up to 6 months.

Variation: Add 1 pound raw peeled shrimp. Simmer for about 5 more minutes or until shrimp turns pink. Serve over pasta.

Orange Sauce
Delicious served over slices of plain cake

1 cup sugar
2 egg yolks
1 tablespoon flour
1 large orange, juiced,
Rind of the orange, grated or zested
1½ cups whipping cream

 Whisk together the first 3 ingredients. Add orange juice and rind and continue to whisk until well blended. Cook over low heat until it thickens then set aside until cool. Place the bowl and beaters of an electric mixer in freezer for 5 to 10 minutes. (Cream whips better in a cold bowl.) Remove bowl and beaters and whip the cream. Blend into the orange mixture. Place the sauce in refrigerator until well cooled. When ready to serve, spoon over slices of cake.

Peach and Strawberry Sauce

1 can (15 ounces) sliced peaches in juice
¼ cup sugar
1 tablespoon cornstarch
½ teaspoon almond flavoring
4 to 6 large fresh strawberries, sliced

 Drain juice from peaches into a saucepan. Combine sugar and cornstarch. Stir in juice. Cook over medium-low heat until thickened. Add almond flavoring, reserved peach slices, and sliced strawberries. Heat through. Serve over pound cake, sponge cake, or angel food cake.

 Note: If you want to use fresh peaches, use about 1½ cups and substitute peach nectar or juice for the canned peach juice.

Pesto Sauce

2 cups firmly packed fresh basil leaves with stems removed
¼ cup pine nuts (pignoli) or walnuts
2 cloves peeled garlic
½ cup grated Parmesan cheese
2 tablespoons grated Pecorino or Romano cheese
½ cup olive oil

Place basil, pine nuts and garlic in blender or food processor and process until finely chopped. Add cheeses and blend well. Slowly pour in olive oil, blending until fine paste forms. Makes 2 cups. Pesto will keep in refrigerator for about 3 days. May also be frozen in 1 cup portions in small freezer bags. Recipe easily doubled.

Raspberry and Blueberry Sauce
For Angel Food or Pound cake, and
Over ice cream

2 cups fresh or unsweetened frozen raspberries
⅓ cup raspberry preserves or jam
⅓ cup water
2 tablespoons granulated sugar
1 cup fresh or frozen small blueberries

Add one cup of the raspberries, the preserves, water and sugar in a heavy, medium size saucepan. Bring to a boil, mashing the raspberries with a wooden spoon. Boil one minute and remove from heat. Strain the mixture through a fine strainer over a bowl. Stirring and pressing down on the raspberries to release the juice. Discard remaining seeds in strainer. Stir the remaining cup of raspberries and the one cup blueberries into the hot syrup. Cover and refrigerate until ready to use. When ready to use, spoon over slices of cake or over ice cream.

Le Salse Alla Puttanesca
(Puttanesca Sauce)

This delicious and aromatic pasta dish, which originated in Naples, Italy, has a unique name and interesting history. Loosely translated, the name means "Harlot's Sauce." Apparently the "Ladies of the Evening" would, after preparing the sauce, place it on their windowsills, and the piquant aroma served to attract clients in off the streets. Whatever the name, it is one of the most savory of sauces. The anchovies, capers, olives and garlic result in a mysterious Italian taste experience even anchovy haters seem to like.

¼ cup olive oil
4 to 6 cloves of garlic, minced fine or garlic puree to equal 4 to 6 cloves
1 (28 oz.) can Italian peeled tomatoes, roughly chopped, with juice
1 (2 oz.) can anchovies or ½ to 1 tube of anchovy paste
2 tablespoon drained capers, rinsed
1 tightly packed cup black Greek or Kalamata olives, pitted and roughly chopped (do not use canned olives)
¼ cup chopped flat leaf Italian Parsley
¼ teaspoon dried oregano
¼ teaspoon red pepper flakes
1 pound pasta*
Additional chopped parsley for garnish
Parmesan Cheese (optional)

Heat olive oil in a heavy skillet or saucepan over medium heat. Sauté the garlic for a few seconds, being careful not to brown it. Add tomatoes and rest of ingredients except pasta, parsley, and cheese. Bring to a boil, cover, and reduce heat to a slow simmer. Simmer for 20 minutes, stirring occasionally. Set aside to marinate at room temperature for several hours so flavor will intensify. When ready to serve, may be reheated in microwave. Pour over cooked pasta, mixing well. Top with chopped parsley to garnish. Pass grated Parmesan cheese, if desired.

*May be used over any type of pasta, but penne or shell pasta is best, because it catches the sauce, which tastes so good you will want a lot of it.

Red Eye Gravy
(Served with Ham)

1 cup drippings from ham
2 tablespoons margarine or butter
⅓ cup strong freshly brewed coffee
½ cup boiling water
2 tablespoons paprika
Hot pepper sauce to taste
Salt and black pepper to taste

Heat ham drippings in a heavy skillet or frying pan until very hot (If using the same pan in which you fried a ham steak, be sure to scrape all the "fry" from the bottom of the pan to add to the gravy). Add margarine. Using a whisk, mix well and then add rest of ingredients. Bring mixture to a boil, continuing to whisk until mixture forms a thick glaze in the pan. When gravy is thoroughly blended into a smooth consistency, add salt and pepper to taste. Serve piping hot with baked ham or ham steak, spoon bread, or grits.

Creole Tomato Horseradish Sauce

½ cup catsup
2 teaspoons horseradish (hot or plain, to your taste)
½ teaspoon Creole mustard
1 teaspoon vinegar
¼ teaspoon salt

Mix well and chill. To be used with boiled beef brisket Double or triple as needed.

Remoulade Sauce
For Shrimp

1½ teaspoons salt
¼ teaspoon black pepper
¼ teaspoon white pepper
¼ teaspoon cayenne pepper
2 tablespoons paprika
2 tablespoons finely chopped parsley
1 tablespoon finely minced garlic
1½ tablespoons hot horseradish
2 tablespoons Creole mustard
2 tablespoons catsup
1 tablespoon Worcestershire sauce
2 tablespoons white vinegar
2 tablespoons lemon juice
4 tablespoons olive oil
2 ribs finely chopped celery
2 finely chopped shallots (green onions)
1 pound peeled and deveined boiled shrimp

In a blender or food processor combine all ingredients except oil, celery, shallots, and shrimp. Slowly add oil, blending thoroughly. Stir in celery and shallots. When well mixed pour into a bowl, cover, and refrigerate overnight so flavors will blend. When ready to serve, place shrimp on a bed of shredded lettuce on individual salad plates. Spoon sauce over, covering the shrimp completely. Garnish each salad with hard boiled eggs, tomato wedges and black olives. Easily doubled for larger portions.

Variation: Halve and peel avocado. Place shrimp in avocado. Spoon sauce over shrimp and avocado. Nice served with chilled asparagus spears, beets and hard boiled egg wedges.

New Orleans Tartar Sauce

4 dill pickles, chopped
1 tablespoon finely chopped parsley,
½ teaspoon garlic salt
1 tablespoon capers, drained and finely chopped
Dash cayenne pepper (optional)
¼ teaspoon white pepper
1 teaspoon lemon juice or ½ teaspoon tarragon vinegar
1½ cups mayonnaise

Mix all ingredients well. Chill for several hours before serving with fish or shellfish.

Seasoned Butter

These garnishes are tasty and simple to make. It is important to use fresh, and preferably unsalted butter. Allow about 1 tablespoon butter per serving. Seasoned butters may be frozen for a few weeks, but they should not be refrigerated longer than 24 hours, as the herbs deteriorate quickly.

Honey Butter

¼ cup honey
2 tablespoons softened butter
2 tablespoons whipping cream

Raspberry Butter

¼ pound (1 stick) unsalted butter, room temperature
½ cup raspberry preserves
⅛ teaspoon kosher salt

Fit electric mixer with paddle attachment. Mix ingredients until well blended. Serve at room temperature.

Herb and Seasoned Butter

¼ cup butter
Addition to the butter may be chosen from one or more of the following:
2 tablespoons parsley
2 tablespoons chives
2 tablespoons thyme
2 tablespoons rosemary
¼ cup grated Parmesan or Romano cheese
½ teaspoon lemon juice
½ teaspoon Worcestershire sauce or ½ teaspoon dry mustard
½ teaspoon lemon rind
1 tablespoon Anchovy paste
1 tablespoon horseradish

Beat the butter until soft. Add other ingredients gradually. Chill, form into little disks containing 1 tablespoon each of the mixture. Freeze in resealable bag and use as needed.

Recipe easily doubled or tripled. Honey butter is delicious on pancakes, toast, raisin bread, etc. Herbed butter is wonderful on vegetables, meats, seafood, etc.

Parsley or Cilantro-Lime Butter

2 sticks butter, room temperature
3 tablespoons finely chopped parsley or cilantro leaves
1 lime, juiced and zested, or 1 lemon, juiced and zested

Beat butter until soft. Still beating, gradually add rest of ingredients. Transfer butter to a large piece of plastic wrap. Roll butter in plastic wrap, forming a log, or follow directions above. Use as needed, cutting off 1 tablespoon at a time. Recipe easily doubled.

Sauces

Creole Tomato Sauce
(New Orleans Own Red Gravy)

⅓ cup bacon drippings, olive or vegetable oil
1 large onion, chopped
1 sweet (green) pepper, chopped
3 cloves garlic, minced
1 small can tomato paste
½ cup parsley, chopped fine (or ½ cup dried parsley)
3 teaspoons salt
½ teaspoon black pepper
¼ teaspoon (or to taste) cayenne pepper
¼ teaspoon basil
½ teaspoon oregano
½ teaspoon sugar
1 tablespoons Worcestershire sauce
1 large can (28 ounce) Progresso Italian tomatoes, chopped
1 large can sliced mushrooms (optional)
1 or 2 cups water
½ cup Parmesan cheese

Heat oil in a large Dutch oven and sauté onions, sweet pepper and garlic. When soft add tomato paste, rinsing can with about ½ can water and add to pot. Brown slightly, stirring quickly and well. Add seasonings, Worcestershire sauce, tomatoes, mushrooms and water. Stir well and then add ½ cup Parmesan cheese. Raise heat, bring to a boil, then lower heat. Partially cover and simmer slowly for about 45 minutes, stirring often. If gravy seems too watery, cook a little longer and thicken by adding a little more cheese as needed. Freezes well.

This gravy is delicious served simply over spaghetti and sprinkled with Parmesan cheese for a meatless meal. For Chicken Spaghetti, sauté chicken until lightly brown. When chicken is browned, add to gravy and cook for 30 minutes.

For Shrimp Spaghetti: When gravy is done, add 3 pounds cleaned, peeled and deveined raw shrimp and simmer for 30 minutes. Pour over spaghetti.

If you are making meatballs and spaghetti, add the meatballs after gravy has simmered for about 30 to 45 minutes and let the meatballs simmer in gravy for another 30 to 45 minutes. Serve the meatballs and gravy over cooked spaghetti and top with grated Italian cheese.

Meatball – See page 192 for recipe.

For Meat Sauce – See page 243 for recipe.

Beans, Rice, and Jambalaya

Preparing dried beans for cooking	117
Rice	118
Red Beans and Rice	119
Black-Eyed Peas and Rice	121
Black-Eyed Peas Side Dish	122
Black-Eyed Peas with Wine	122
Navy Beans (White Beans) and Rice	123
Green Beans and Ham	124
Mediterranean Rice Pilaf	124
Rice Pilaf	125
Mardi Gras Rice	125
Calas (Rice Cakes)	126
Riz au Lait (Rice and Milk)	127
Riz Persillé (Parsley Rice)	127
Hoppin' John Jambalaya	128
Chicken and Sausage Jambalaya L'Acadien	129

Preparing dried beans for cooking

Packaged dried beans should be rinsed under cold running water, discarding broken or defective beans. Dried beans should be soaked before cooking. There are two methods.

For the old-fashioned method, measure the beans in a cup measure and place them in a deep bowl. Add 3 cups water for each cup of beans. Cover and soak overnight. If possible, use the nutritious soaking water for cooking the beans.

For the quick method, measure beans in a cup measure and place in a deep pot. Add 3 cups water for each cup of beans, bring to the boiling point, and boil for 2 minutes. Remove from heat, cover pot and let stand at room temperature for 1 to 2 hours. Then proceed to cook beans according to your recipe.

Cover beans when cooking. Do not cook beans quickly or over high heat because this breaks their skins. Simmer over low heat, being careful not to overcook. Salt beans only when cooked. Salt slows their cooking because it toughens them. Acid like wine or tomatoes also slow down the softening process. Add them only when the beans are almost cooked. Beans freeze well.

Rice

Rice is a staple in Southern cooking. In cooking rice, 1 cup of raw rice equals 3 cups of cooked rice. My Momma never boiled rice. She steamed it in a pan held over boiling water by a rack filled with holes that fit over a large pot of water, and then cover the pan with another pot. That contraption is now mine and it is the only way I cook rice. The rice is never sticky. It is soft, but every grain falls separately. For firmer rice, use less water and steam for a shorter time. For softer rice, use more water (about ½ cup more) and steam for a longer time. Do not lift lid while cooking (the steam cooks the rice).

To steam, add equal amount of rice and water, usually 3 cups rice and 3 cups water. One to two teaspoons salt (or to taste). Mix well and steam over boiling water until rice is tender.

To cook rice on top of the stove use 1 cup of rice to 2¼ cups water, salt to taste, and 2 teaspoons butter (optional). Bring water to a boil. Add butter and salt. Stir in rice. Reduce heat, cover, and simmer for 20 minutes. Remove from heat and let stand covered 5 minutes or until water is absorbed. Fluff with a fork and serve.

To microwave rice, for 4 servings, use 2 cups hot water, 1 cup rice, and 1 teaspoon salt. Combine rice and water in a microwavable bowl or casserole. Add butter and salt. Cover and cook on high for 8 minutes. Stir, then reduce to medium (50 percent power) and cook for 20 minutes. Remove from microwave and let stand covered 5 minutes or until water is absorbed. Fluff with fork and serve

Rice freezes very well. I usually cook 2 or 3 times the amount I need and divide and freeze the remaining rice in plastic freezer bags. It defrosts quickly in the microwave.

It is a Southern joke that many New Orleans women get up in the morning, and the first thing they do is to put on a pot of rice, whether they need it that day or not. Actually, if I am spending time in the kitchen cooking, I will often steam a pan of rice while I am doing other things in the kitchen. I will then put it in freezer bags to be used at a later date. It saves time when I am in a hurry for rice.

Red Beans and Rice
(One of the most popular dishes of Old New Orleans)

Traditionally, Monday was always washday for Momma, and for most New Orleans women when I was a little girl. It was a tedious job. First, the clothes had to be washed. I remember, when I was a tiny little girl, on the washboard. Then the clothes were rinsed by hand in a large tub, and then some of the clothes had to be starched; so, they were dipped in a tub of thick sticky starch before being hung out on clotheslines, and then the lines hoisted up with long clothes poles. So, it was the custom to put on a pot of red beans early on a Monday morning, and they slowly cooked all day while the lady of the house tended her washing. The custom of eating red beans on Mondays remains to this day. Beans take to seasoning well, are inexpensive, and when served over rice are absolutely delicious. I remember the little girls singing as they skipped along to the grocery store to get the beans for their Mommas – "A nickel of beans, a nickel of rice, and a 15 cent pickled pork to make it taste nice." A pot of beans, along with rice (a complete meal) for 25 cents. This was the depression years. While it certainly costs more today, an incredibly rich old time version of creamy red beans cooked with a meaty ham bone, perhaps a slice of pickled pork, steeped in a rich natural gravy, and filling the whole house with a wonderful aroma, you never forget still endures today. You will find them in private homes, neighborhood restaurants, and in the kitchens of the grand restaurants of New Orleans. Red Beans and Rice is one of the favorite of the traditional dishes of Old New Orleans.

I remember when I was about 12 years old going swimming at beautiful Lake Pontchartrain with Daddy and some friends. We had missed lunch and came home ravenous. Momma sat Daddy and I at the kitchen table, put some rice on two plates, and covered the rice with some red beans from the pot that was simmering away on the stove. She added some pickled pork, thick slices of crispy buttered French bread, and two glasses of ice cold milk. She sat with us as we hungrily ate and talked about our swimming trip to Lake Pontchartrain. I don't think I have ever in my life tasted a meal quite as good as that one, and it is one of my special memories.

(Continued Next Page)

2 pounds dried red beans (or 6 or 7 cans red bean, preferably Van Camps New Orleans style canned Red Beans)
1 pound pickled pork and a ham bone or a large smoked ham hock
1 large or 2 medium onions, chopped fine
1 sweet (bell) pepper, chopped fine
5 cloves garlic, minced or 1 tablespoon garlic puree
1 tablespoon Worcestershire sauce
2 tablespoons chopped parsley
2 teaspoon salt (or to taste)
½ teaspoon black pepper
¼ teaspoon cayenne pepper or ¼ teaspoon crushed red pepper flakes (or to taste)
About 3 cups water
4 tablespoons (½ stick) butter (optional)
Steamed rice

Add dried beans that have been well rinsed and soaked overnight (or use quick method - see page 117) or canned red beans to a large iron or heavy pot. If using canned beans, rinse cans with some of the water, and add to pot along with remaining water and other ingredients, except rice. For dried beans, add soaking water to equal 3 or 4 cups, (or enough water to cover beans) along with all other ingredients, except rice. If you are using ham hock, rinse ham hock, Cut the heavy skin surrounding the ham hock open and add to pot. Bring to a boil, stir well, then lower heat, partially cover, and simmer for about 2 or 3 hours, or until beans are tender and gravy has thickened. Mash some of the beans against the side of the pot with a large spoon or ladle out about ⅓ cup of beans into a blender or to a food mill. Puree beans and return to the pot. This will make the beans richer and thicker. Add more water if needed. Stir often during the cooking to make sure the beans do not stick to the bottom of the pot. When beans are cooked, remove ham hock, cut off heavy skin and discard skin. Chop up ham pieces from ham hock and return pieces of ham to the pot. Add ½ to 1 stick of butter to the beans. Cook for an additional 10 minutes. Stir well and serve with steamed rice. If there are any left over, red beans freeze very well. Recipe easily doubled. I usually cook twice the amount, then freeze leftovers for another meal.

Note: leftover red beans can also be turned into a quick, delicious soup. A cup or so, depending on how much red beans are left, of boiled elbow macaroni can be added to the leftover beans, along with a dash or two of chili powder. Add a little water if needed and adjust seasoning. Heat and enjoy, along with perhaps a green salad. The Italians call this bean and pasta mixture Pasta e Fagioli. Momma just called it a quick bean soup.

Black-Eyed Peas and Rice

2 pounds dried black-eyed peas, soaked overnight in water, or
6 cans black-eyed peas, undrained.
1 large onion, chopped
1 sweet pepper, chopped
4 cloves garlic, minced
3 tablespoons chopped parsley
1 large ham bone or a 1 pound slice of pickled pork and 1 ham hock
1½ teaspoon salt (or to taste)
¾ teaspoon black pepper
½ teaspoon Tabasco sauce or ½ teaspoon crushed red pepper (or to taste)
3 bay leaves, halved
½ teaspoon dried thyme
½ teaspoon basil
1 cup dry Vermouth wine (optional)
1 quart water and 1 quart chicken stock, if using dried beans, or 2 cans water and 1 can chicken stock if using 6 cans undrained beans
Steamed rice

    Drain soaked beans and add to pot along with rest of ingredients except rice. (If using canned beans, add to pot undrained with rest of ingredients except rice). Bring to a boil over high heat, stir well, then lower heat and simmer for 2 to 2½ hours, or until beans are tender and a natural gravy has formed. Add water if necessary near end of cooking time if needed. Serve over steamed or boiled rice.

Black-Eyed Peas Side Dish

6 cups fresh black eyed peas or 2 pkg. 16 oz. Frozen
or 3 (16 oz.) cans
3 (14½ oz.) cans chicken broth
2 teaspoons Tony Chachere Creole seasoning
1 teaspoon olive oil
¼ teaspoon Tabasco sauce
Salt, to taste

Place black-eyed peas and rest of ingredients in a large heavy pot and bring to a boil. Partially cover and turn heat to low. Simmer for about 45 minutes or until peas are tender, stirring occasionally. Serve with a slotted spoon.

Variation: Navy beans may be substituted for black-eyed peas.

Black-Eyed Peas with Wine

3 (10 oz.) packs frozen or 4 cans black-eyed peas
1 large onion, chopped
3 cloves garlic, minced
½ teaspoon Tabasco sauce
1 cup Sauterne or Vermouth wine
2 cups water
½ pound bacon chopped, or ½ pound ham or Kielbasa sausage, cubed
Salt to taste

Sauté bacon in heavy pot until crisp. Remove bacon to a plate with a slotted spoon. Pour out all bacon grease but about 3 tablespoons. Add onions and garlic to pot and sauté until tender. Add beans, bacon, water, wine, and Tabasco sauce. Bring to a boil, lower heat, cover and simmer for about an hour or so or until beans are tender. Add salt just before the peas are done. Cook a few minutes longer, stir well, and serve with steamed rice. If you use ham or sausage, sauté in 3 tablespoons olive oil, then follow directions above.

Navy Beans (White Beans) and Rice

2 pounds dried navy beans, or 6 cans undrained navy Beans
1 large onion, chopped
1 large, sweet pepper, chopped
4 cloves garlic, finely minced
2 tablespoons chopped parsley
1 pound slice of pickle pork or 1 pound seasoning ham, cut into cubes
½ pound Polish Kielbasa sausage
1 teaspoon salt
½ teaspoon black pepper
⅛ teaspoon cayenne pepper (or more, according to taste)
2 bay leaves
3 or 4 cups water
Steamed rice

Add dried beans that have been soaked overnight (or use quick method - see page 117) or canned beans to a large iron or heavy pot. If using canned beans, rinse cans with some of the water and add to pot along with remaining water and other ingredients, except rice. For dried beans, add soaking water to equal 3 or 4 cups along with all other ingredients, except rice. Bring to a boil, stir well, then lower heat, partially cover, and simmer for about 2 or 3 hours, or until beans are tender and gravy has thickened. Mashing some beans against the side of the pot with a spoon will make the gravy richer and thicker. Add more water if needed. But if gravy seems a bit thin, 1 tablespoon corn starch or flour dissolved in a little water may be added to pot. Stir often during the cooking to make sure the beans do not stick to the pot. When beans are cooked add salt, remove bay leaves, and serve with steamed rice. If there are any left over, navy beans freeze very well. Recipe easily doubled. I usually cook twice the amount, then freeze half of the beans for another meal.

Green Beans and Ham

3 pounds green beans or 2 large cans cut green beans
1 pound ham pieces, cut into small cubes, or ½ pound Canadian bacon, diced
2 tablespoons oil and 2 tablespoon butter, or ⅓ cup Bacon Grease
⅓ cup flour
1 large onion, chopped
2 cloves garlic, minced
Salt to taste
1 teaspoon black pepper
½ teaspoon thyme
4 medium potatoes, peeled and diced
1 tablespoon Worcestershire sauce
2 to 3 cups hot water

Snap ends off beans, break into fourths, wash and set aside. Or drain canned beans and set aside. Melt butter with oil in large pot. Add flour and stir until smooth. Add onions and garlic and sauté until soft. Add ham, stir, and then beans, water, seasonings, and potatoes. Cook about one hour or until beans are tender and potatoes are soft. Add salt to taste. Good served with corn bread or crispy French bread.

Mediterranean Rice Pilaf

2 cups uncooked rice
2 cups chicken broth
4 tablespoons butter or margarine
½ cup seedless golden raisins
½ teaspoon turmeric
½ teaspoon curry powder
1½ teaspoon soy sauce

Mix all ingredients together. Place in pan over hot water and steam until all liquid is absorbed and rice is tender.

Rice Pilaf

2 tablespoons light olive oil
1 carrot, finely chopped
1 stalk celery, finely chopped
2 cloves garlic, minced
1 fresh jalapeño pepper, chopped
1 medium onion, finely chopped
1 small red sweet pepper, chopped
1 bay leaf
1 teaspoon salt
¼ teaspoon black pepper
1 cup white or brown rice
2¼ cups chicken broth
1 tablespoon lemon juice
¼ cup chopped parsley

Heat olive oil in a large skillet. Add garlic, carrot, celery, jalapeño pepper, onion and sweet pepper and cook, stirring, until vegetables soften, about 5 minutes. Add rice and stir well, blending ingredients. Add chicken broth, salt, pepper, and bay leaf. Stir and bring to a boil over high heat, cover and reduce heat to low and simmer 45 to 50 minutes or until rice is tender and all liquid is absorbed. Fluff mixture with fork and sprinkle in lemon juice and chopped parsley. Mix and serve.

Mardi Gras Rice

1 cup raw rice
1 cup chicken broth
½ cup chopped shallots (green onions)
½ cup chopped sweet pepper
4 slices bacon
3 tablespoons diced pimento
¼ cup sliced black olives
¼ cup sliced green olives
Salt to taste

Steam rice in chicken broth until soft. Fry bacon until crisp. Remove, crumble and set aside. Sauté onion and sweet pepper in bacon grease until tender and add remaining ingredients only long enough to heat. Add to rice along with bacon which has been placed in large bowl, and toss lightly.

Calas
(Rice Cakes)
(Belle Calas tout chaud)

Very early in the mornings in nineteenth century New Orleans, cooks would take these rice cakes, piping hot and wrapped in a towel, in a basket, through the streets of the French Quarter, crying "Belle Calas tout chaud." Housewives would come out and buy them to serve for breakfast. They are very seldom sold today but easily prepared for a Creole touch to breakfast. The word "Calas" seems to have originally been an African word for rice.

1½ cups soft cooked rice
1 package dry yeast dissolved in ½ cup warm water*
3 eggs, beaten well
½ cup sugar
½ teaspoon nutmeg
½ teaspoon salt
1¼ cup flour
Oil for deep frying
Powdered sugar

Place rice in a large bowl and mash well. Mix dissolved yeast into it, mixing well. Cover bowl with a cloth and set to rise overnight. In the morning beat in 3 well beaten eggs. Continuing to beat add the sugar, nutmeg, salt, and flour. Beat into a thick smooth batter, cover again, and let rise for about 15 to 20 minutes. If using a deep fryer, heat oil to 375 degrees. Drop by large spoonfuls into hot oil and fry until golden brown. Place on paper towels and serve hot sprinkled with powdered sugar. Serve with café au lait for breakfast.

*1½ cups of self-rising flour may be used in place of yeast and plain flour.

Beans, Rice, and Jambalaya

Riz au Lait
(Rice and Milk. A breakfast dish
from leftover rice)

1 cup cooked rice
2 cups milk
½ cup sugar
½ teaspoon vanilla extract
Nutmeg

Add rice, sugar, and vanilla to milk and heat. When hot, simmer for about 3 minutes. Mix thoroughly and place in dish to cool. Sprinkle with nutmeg and serve.

Riz Persillé
(Parsley Rice)

2 cups raw rice
2 cups chicken broth
3 tablespoons butter
1 bay leaf
1 teaspoon salt
¼ teaspoon black pepper
Few drops Tabasco
3 tablespoons chopped parsley
⅓ cup minced shallots (green onions) green part only

Combine rice, chicken broth, and butter in a large pan. Add bay leaf, salt, pepper and a few drops of Tabasco. Mix well and steam over hot water until rice is tender and liquid is absorbed. When ready, put into serving bowl, discard bay leaf, and mix in shallots and parsley. Cover and keep warm until ready to serve.

Variation: May be cooked on top of stove or in microwave.

Hoppin' John Jambalaya

1 pound dried black-eyed peas, sorted and washed
1 large ham hock
9 cups hot water
½ cup Sautérne or dry Vermouth wine (optional)
1 large onion, chopped
2 cloves garlic, minced
½ cup chopped parsley
1 can (28 oz) tomatoes, undrained and chopped
½ teaspoon cayenne pepper (or to taste)
1 tablespoon Worcestershire sauce
4 chicken bouillon cubes
2 teaspoons salt (or to taste)
2¼ teaspoon oregano
¼ teaspoon thyme
2 bay leaves
2½ cups raw rice

Presoak peas. Drain peas then add peas and rest of ingredients except rice to a large pot. Bring to a boil and immediately lower heat and simmer for about 2 hours. Remove ham hock and cut meat from bone. Return meat to pot along with rice. Cover and simmer for about 20 minutes or until rice and peas are tender. Remove and discard bay leaves. Serve immediately.

Chicken and Sausage Jambalaya L'Acadien
For my Grandson Bobby

As in the preparation of gumbo, chop the vegetables, measure out the seasonings, and cut up the main ingredients before beginning to cook. If you do not have frozen chicken and stock available, prepare chicken according to "Chicken, Cooked in Microwave" recipe the day before cooking Jambalaya. Marinate overnight.

1 chicken, cut up and cooked (Use recipe for Chicken, Cooked in Microwave at page 164)
2 tablespoon cooking oil
1 pound Andouille sausage or Polish Kielbasa sausage, sliced thin
½ pound baked ham, cubed small (optional)
2 medium or 1 very large onion, chopped
¾ cup thinly sliced green shallot (scallion) tops
4 cloves garlic, minced
1 large, sweet pepper, chopped
2 ribs celery, chopped
3 tablespoons finely chopped parsley
3½ teaspoon salt (or to taste)
1 teaspoon black pepper
¼ teaspoon Cayenne pepper (or to taste)
½ teaspoon chili powder
1 teaspoon paprika
2 bay leaves, broken in half
½ teaspoon dried thyme leaves
¼ teaspoon basil
1 tablespoon Worcestershire sauce
3 cups uncooked long grain rice
6 cups chicken stock, or chicken stock with water added to equal 6 cups

In large heavy pot heat oil over high heat. Add sausage and vegetables to pot and reduce heat to medium. If you are including ham, add at this time. Cook, stirring frequently until slightly brown, about 10 minutes. Add seasonings, Worcestershire sauce, and chicken. Stir well and then add chicken stock and rice. Stir gently, raise the heat to high, and bring to a boil. Then turn the heat very low, stir and cover the pot. Cook for about 45 minutes, uncovering from time to time to stir. Remove the cover for the last 10 minutes or so and raise the heat to medium. Stir gently as the rice dries out, checking to make sure the mixture does not stick on the bottom or dry out too much. Serve immediately.

Variation: To make Creole Jambalaya, add 1 large can Italian tomatoes (28 ounce) chopped, along with chicken stock and rice. (Creole Jambalaya is with tomatoes added. Cajun Jambalaya does not use tomatoes.) Jambalaya freezes well.

Seafood

Boiled Crabs 133
Stuffed Crabs 134
Crawfish Etouffee 135
Weldon's Crawfish Etouffee 136
Cajun Crawfish Pie 137
Broiled or Baked Catfish 138
Fish Fillets with Sauce Meuniere (Lemon Butter Sauce) 139
Oven Fried Fish Fillets 139
Fried Fish 140
Red Fish Courtboullion 141
Red Snapper Fillets 142
Oyster Patties 143
Boiled Shrimp 144
New Orleans Barbequed Shrimp 145
Shrimp Sauce Piquant (Shrimp Creole) 146
Shrimp Scampi 147

Seafood

Boiled Crabs

1 dozen live hard shell crabs
6 to 8 quarts cold water
3 lemons, quartered or sliced
1 cup salt
4 tablespoons Yogi or Zatarain's liquid crab boil
10 drops Tabasco sauce
8 small new potatoes (optional)
4 very small ears fresh corn (optional)
4 small onions (optional)

Fill a large (about 10 quart) stockpot one third to one half full of water. Add the lemons, salt, liquid crab boil, Tabasco sauce, and vegetables, if you are using. Cover and bring to a boil. Let mixture boil for 10 minutes. Add the crabs, cover, and return to a boil. Let the crabs boil for 10 to 20 minutes, depending on the size of the crabs. Turn off the heat and let the pot sit, covered, for 10 minutes more. Remove crabs and vegetables and place in a large bowl. Eat either hot or cold. Recipe can be doubled or tripled.

This recipe is very good. But when my Momma, Daughter Laurie, and I (the three in my family most addicted to boiled crabs) would have our mouths set to eat boiled crabs – Right Now! – we would hop in the car and drive to our favorite Seafood House in Bucktown at West End near Lake Pontchartrain and pick up 2 or 3 dozen of their spicy, perfectly seasoned, fat and heavy boiled crabs. Back home, we would cover the table with newspapers, fix some dipping sauce* for the crabs, take the phone off the hook, and with some saltine crackers, cold beer for Mom and I and a Barq's root beer for Laurie, we would sit down and enjoy our most favorite meal in the world.

*Dipping Sauce

1 or 2 tablespoons mayonnaise
1 tablespoon vinegar or lemon juice
Salt and black pepper to taste
8 to 10 drops (or to taste) Tabasco sauce

Stir well and enjoy.

Stuffed Crabs

2 dozen crabs or 1 pound crab meat
1 large onion, chopped fine
4 cloves garlic, minced fine
1 small or ½ large, sweet pepper, chopped fine
2 tablespoons finely chopped parsley
2 eggs, well beaten
Crust from 4 slices day old French bread, crumbled
¾ cup water
2 teaspoons lemon juice
1 tablespoon salt
1 teaspoon black pepper
¼ teaspoon cayenne pepper
1 tablespoon Worcestershire sauce
Italian breadcrumbs

If using fresh crabs, clean crab shells well after removing crab meat. Set aside. Sauté onions, garlic, sweet pepper, and parsley for about 5 minutes. add crab meat and bread moistened with ¾ cup water and mix well. Cook over low heat until water is absorbed. Remove from heat and add beaten eggs, salt, pepper, cayenne, lemon juice, and Worcestershire sauce. Mix thoroughly. Spoon into crab shells or ramekins. Sprinkle with breadcrumbs and put a dot of butter on top of each. Bake at 375 degrees until golden brown. Can be frozen and baked at another time, but do not add breadcrumbs until ready to bake.

Crawfish Etouffee

The word "Etouffee" means smothered. To cook in a tightly covered pot over a low flame. There are many ways to cook Crawfish Etouffee, for every Creole or Cajun cook prepares it their own way. Highly seasoned dishes like Crawfish Etouffee are much better if cooked the day before serving and reheated so the flavors are allowed to blend.

¼ pound (1 stick) butter
¼ cup flour
1 large onion, finely chopped
½ sweet (green bell) pepper, finely chopped
2 ribs celery, finely chopped
3 cloves garlic, minced fine
2 pounds crawfish tails, shelled
1 tablespoon salt
¼ teaspoon black pepper
¼ teaspoon cayenne pepper, or to taste
¼ teaspoon dried thyme
¼ teaspoon chili powder
½ teaspoon basil
1 tablespoon Worcestershire sauce
Tabasco to taste (optional)
1 tablespoon lemon juice
2 tablespoons finely chopped green onions (shallots)
2 tablespoons parsley
2 cups water
Steamed Rice

Sauté the onions, celery, sweet pepper, and garlic in butter. Cook slowly until the vegetables are limp. Stir in the flour, and stirring constantly, cook for a few minutes on low heat. Add crawfish tails, seasonings, lemon juice, shallots tops, and parsley, mixing well. Add water and bring to a boil, then lower heat and simmer for 15 or 20 minutes for flavors to blend, stirring occasionally. Serve over steamed rice. Recipe easily doubled.

Variation: This recipe can also be used for Shrimp Etouffee. Prepare as above, substituting 2 pounds peeled and deveined raw shrimp for crawfish.

Weldon's Crawfish Etouffee
*This recipe was given to me by my brother
Weldon Miscenich*

1 stick butter or margarine
1 onion, diced
2 cloves garlic, minced or ½ teaspoon garlic puree
1 can golden mushroom soup, undiluted (Not cream of mushroom soup)
¼ teaspoon Tony Chachere's Creole seasoning
1 teaspoon Worcestershire sauce
1 pound crawfish tails
Fresh parsley

Heat butter in a medium pot and sauté onions and garlic until soft. Add soup and seasonings and stir in crawfish. Serve over rice with minced parsley on top.

Any left-over Etouffee can be served over boneless sautéed chicken breasts on a bed of rice.

Cajun Crawfish Pie
This rich and delicious pie is a true taste of Acadiana

½ cup unsalted butter
1 medium onion, finely chopped
2 cloves garlic, minced
2 ribs celery, finely chopped
1 sweet pepper, finely chopped
½ cup shallots (green onions) chopped
½ cup chopped parsley
1 pound peeled and boiled crawfish tails, coarsely chopped
1 pound fresh crabmeat, cooked
1 can cream of celery soup, undiluted
1 teaspoon lemon juice
¼ teaspoon liquid crab boil
2 tablespoons dry Vermouth wine (optional)
1 tablespoon grated Parmesan cheese
2 teaspoons salt
¼ teaspoon black pepper
¼ teaspoon cayenne pepper
¼ cup Italian breadcrumbs
1 Package Pillsbury ready to bake pie crusts

Preheat oven to 375 degrees. Remove pie crusts from refrigerator and set aside. Melt butter in heavy saucepan over medium heat. Sauté onion, garlic, celery, sweet pepper, shallots, and parsley until soft, about 10 minutes. Add crawfish and sauté for 5 to 10 minutes more. Add crab and mix well. Add celery soup, lemon juice, crab boil, Vermouth wine, Parmesan cheese, Italian breadcrumbs, salt, black and cayenne pepper. Remove from heat and mix well. Shape one crust in pie plate. Pour seafood filling into crust. Carefully cover with second pie crust and seal the edges. Cut several slashes in top crust to release steam. Bake for 30 to 35 minutes or until golden brown. Remove from oven and let stand for 5 to 10 minutes before serving. Serve pie in slices, spooning any sauce remaining in the pie plate over the crust.

Broiled or Baked Catfish

6 Catfish fillets
Nonstick cooking spray
½ teaspoon salt
¼ teaspoon white pepper
Cayenne pepper to taste
¼ cup olive oil
1 teaspoon fresh thyme leaves (optional)
1 teaspoon garlic powder
Juice of 1 lemon

    Line a baking pan or broiler pan with aluminum foil, spray with cooking spray, and set aside. Adjust the oven rack to about 4 inches from the broiler unit and preheat the broiler Season catfish on both sides with salt, pepper, and cayenne. Place catfish fillets on the baking sheet. Place the olive oil, thyme, and garlic powder in a small bowl and stir to blend. Brush the oil and garlic mixture evenly over the catfish. Sprinkle the lemon juice over the fish. Place the fish under the broiler and broil for 3 minutes. Turn the pan and cook for another 3 minutes or until fish flakes easily. Serve immediately.

    To bake in oven, Preheat oven to 450 degrees. Place prepared fish on pan, as above, and put pan in heated oven and bake uncovered, for 15 minutes, or until fish flakes easily. Serve immediately.

Fish Fillets with Sauce Meuniere
(Lemon Butter Sauce)

4 fish fillets (2 pounds) (trout, bass, red fish, flounder or red snapper)
¼ cup butter
1 tablespoon Worcestershire Sauce
2 teaspoons lemon juice
½ garlic powder
½ teaspoon salt
¼ cayenne pepper

Dry fish on paper towels and place in baking pan. Combine rest of ingredients in a 2 cup Pyrex measuring cup and microwave on high for 1 minute. Pour sauce over fish fillets and bake for 25 minutes in a 350 degree oven until flaky.

Oven Fried Fish Fillets

1 pound catfish, tilapia, or other fish fillets
½ dry Italian breadcrumbs
½ teaspoon dried thyme leaves
½ teaspoon paprika
¼ teaspoon cayenne pepper (or to taste)
¼ cup low fat milk or beer
Olive oil
Salt, black pepper, garlic powder

Preheat oven to 450 degrees. Place breadcrumbs, thyme, paprika and cayenne in a pie plate and mix well. Dip each fillet in milk or beer, then in bread crumb mixture, coating well. Spray a 9 x 13 inch oven proof casserole with cooking spray, and place the coated fillets in it. Brush each fillet with olive oil, lightly sprinkle with salt, pepper, and garlic powder and bake uncovered, about 15 minutes, or until fish flakes with a fork.

Fried Fish
Good for all frying fish and particularly catfish.

4 (6 to 8 ounces each) fish or catfish fillets
1 Can Beer
¾ cup yellow cornmeal
½ cup all-purpose flour
4 teaspoons Creole seasonings*
½ teaspoon paprika
Vegetable oil for frying
Lemon wedges for garnish
Tartar sauce (optional)

Rinse the fillets and pat them dry with paper towels. Place fillets in beer, refrigerate, and marinate in beer for an hour before frying. Mix the cornmeal, flour, Creole seasoning and paprika together in a shallow dish. Remove fish from marinade, drain, and salt and pepper both sides. Dredge each fillet in the cornmeal mixture, coating each side completely. Pour oil into a cast iron or heavy skillet and heat oil until very hot. When the oil is hot, gently lay the fish fillets in the oil, about 2 at a time. Do not crowd them. Fish cooks quickly, so by the time it is golden brown on both sides, or until the fish flakes easily when tested with a fork, (about 2 or 3 minutes each side) it is fully cooked. Drain on paper towels and keep warm. Repeat with remaining fillets. Serve immediately with lemon wedges and tartar sauce.

Variation: Instead of beer, fillets can be marinated in a mixture of 1 cup milk and 1 teaspoon Tabasco sauce whisked together. Proceed as above.

To deep fry fish, heat fryer to 375 degrees. Do not dredge fish in flour or cornmeal ahead of time, otherwise meal or flour will absorb water from the fish and allow grease to go into the fish. Repeat dredging and frying until all fish is cooked.

*Creole Seasoning – See page 337.

Red Fish Courtboullion
(Pronounced Coo-B-Yahn)
The Classic New Orleans Red Fish Dish

4 pounds red fish fillets*
¼ cup bacon drippings or oil
¼ cup flour
1 large onion, chopped
3 cloves garlic, minced
1 large, sweet pepper, chopped
2 tablespoons parsley, chopped
1 large can Italian tomatoes, chopped
1 small can tomato paste
3 bay leaves
2 teaspoons salt
½ teaspoon black pepper
¼ teaspoon (or more) cayenne pepper
½ teaspoon basil
½ teaspoon thyme
1 tablespoon Worcestershire sauce
6 thin lemon slices
2 tablespoons lemon juice
1 cup dry red wine (optional)
2½ cups water

In a large iron or heavy pot make a golden brown roux of the bacon drippings and flour. Add onions, garlic and sweet pepper and sauté until light brown, stirring constantly. Add tomato paste, stirring quickly and then the tomatoes, seasonings, Worcestershire sauce, lemon juice and wine. Mix thoroughly and then slowly add water, continuing to stir. Bring to a boil, uncovered, then lower heat and simmer for about 35 minutes. Put fish in sauce, turning to coat well. Add lemon slices and cover. Simmer over very low heat for 10 minutes, or until fish flakes easily. Remove fish carefully when ready to serve. Goes very well with mashed potatoes.

* For areas where red fish are unavailable, large cod, haddock, or red snapper are good substitutes.

Red Snapper Fillets
In Artichoke and Lemon Butter Sauce
Baked in Microwave Oven

½ cup (1 stick) butter
2 tablespoons chopped parsley
3 cloves garlic, minced
1 (14 ounce) can artichoke hearts, drained and sliced
1 can sliced water chestnuts, drained and each slice cut in half
1 tablespoon lemon juice
¼ cup Sautérne or Dry Vermouth Wine
1 teaspoon salt
½ teaspoon cayenne pepper
6 (2 – 2½ pounds each) Fillets of Red Snapper

In a 4 cup measure heat butter, parsley, and garlic. Microwave on high for 2 minutes. Add Artichoke hearts, water chestnuts, lemon juice, wine, salt, and cayenne pepper. Microwave on high for 3 minutes, or until mixture is well heated. Meanwhile rinse fillets and pat dry with paper towels. Place in microwave safe flat baking dish. When sauce is heated through, pour over fillets. Cover with wax paper and cook on high for 7 to 8* minutes, or until fish flakes easily with a fork. Let stand covered for 4 minutes. Nice served with mashed potatoes or parsley buttered new potatoes.

*Allow 3 minutes cooking time for pound of fish at room temperature.

Seafood

Oyster Patties
This is a classic at New Orleans Cocktail Parties

Can be served in a chafing dish surrounded by small patty shells or as hors d'oeuvres by filling small patty shells with hot oyster mixture. Or fill large patty shells with hot oyster mixture and serve with a green salad for a luncheon or a Sunday night supper.

12 small or 6 large patty shells, reserve tops
2 dozen oysters and liquid
2 tablespoons butter and 2 tablespoons oil
3 tablespoons flour
1 bunch shallots (green onions) chopped
2 cloves garlic, minced fine
2 tablespoons fresh flat leaf parsley, chopped fine
1 teaspoon Worcestershire sauce
½ teaspoon salt
¼ teaspoon black pepper
⅛ teaspoon cayenne pepper (or to taste)
¼ teaspoon thyme leaves
Water

Place patty shells in a shallow baking dish or pan and set aside. Sauté oysters in their own liquid until edges curl. Drain, reserving liquid, and chop oysters into small pieces. Set oysters and liquid aside. Heat oil and butter in a heavy or cast iron skillet or saucepan over medium heat, Add flour and stir until blended and light brown. Add onions and garlic and keep cooking, stirring constantly until roux turns dark brown, being careful not to let it burn. Turn heat to a low simmer and add oyster liquid, parsley, Worcestershire sauce, salt, peppers, and thyme. Continue to stir constantly and add a little water if needed. Add oysters, stir well and remove from heat. Mixture should be thick. Divide the oyster mixture between the patty shells and replace patty shell tops. Bake in a 350 degree oven for about 15 minutes or until they are piping hot. Serve immediately.

Boiled Shrimp

2 pounds whole fresh shrimp
4 quarts water
1½ tablespoons liquid shrimp and crab boil
1 cup salt
Juice of 2 large lemons
4 or 5 drops Tabasco sauce

    Put all ingredients except shrimp in a large pot. Cover and bring to a boil and boil for 10 minutes, then add shrimp to the boiling water. When the water boils again, boil the shrimp for 5 to 7 minutes. (Small shrimp for 5 minutes, very large for 7 minutes). Pour shrimp into colander and drain thoroughly. Cool to room temperature for about 5 minutes then refrigerate.

    If you cannot obtain crab boil, add a mixture of the following ingredients to 4 quarts of water before boiling:

1 cup salt
Juice of 2 large lemons
1 teaspoon allspice
10 whole cloves
4 sprigs fresh thyme or 1 teaspoon dried thyme
5 whole bay leaves, broken in half
1 teaspoon celery seed
½ teaspoon dry mustard
1½ teaspoons freshly ground black pepper

New Orleans Barbequed Shrimp

2 to 3 pounds large raw shrimp, unpeeled
2 sticks (½ pound) butter
½ cup olive oil
3 cloves garlic, minced fine
2½ teaspoons salt
½ teaspoon black pepper
½ teaspoon (or more) cayenne pepper
4 bay leaves
2 teaspoons paprika
1½ teaspoons finely chopped parsley
2 teaspoons oregano
½ teaspoon (or more) Tabasco sauce
½ cup chili sauce
¼ cup Worcestershire sauce
3 tablespoons liquid smoke
2 lemons, sliced
2½ teaspoon salt
3 tablespoons lemon juice
1 cup white wine

Rinse shrimp. Cover with cold water, 2½ teaspoons salt and 1 lemon, sliced. Refrigerate one hour, then drain shrimp and put in shallow baking pan. Combine remaining ingredients in a saucepan over low heat and let simmer for about 10 minutes. Then pour over shrimp, mixing well, and marinate in refrigerator for 3 hours. Baste and turn shrimp every 15 to 20 minutes or so. Bake at 300 degrees for 40 minutes, basting and shaking the pan to turn shrimp several times while baking. Serve shrimp and sauce in soup bowls with French bread.

Shrimp Sauce Piquant
(Shrimp Creole)

3 pounds raw shrimp, peeled and deveined
⅓ cup bacon drippings or oil
⅓ cup flour
1 large onion, chopped
6 shallots (green onions), chopped
1 medium sweet pepper, chopped
4 cloves garlic, minced
3 ribs celery, chopped
¼ cup chopped parsley
1 large can Italian tomatoes, chopped
1 small can tomato paste
1 tablespoon salt
½ teaspoon black pepper
¼ teaspoon cayenne pepper (or to taste)
3 bay leaves
½ teaspoon dried thyme leaves
½ teaspoon chili powder
¼ teaspoon basil
¼ teaspoon sugar
2 tablespoons Worcestershire sauce
¼ cup red wine (optional)
3 cups hot water
4 teaspoons lemon juice

In an iron or heavy pot make a roux by gradually adding flour to the oil, stirring constantly over low heat. When lightly brown add onion, garlic, celery and sweet pepper. Cook over low heat until soft. Add tomato paste and mix well, continuing to stir quickly. Add tomatoes and the rest of the ingredients except shrimp, shallots and parsley. Raise heat and stir until mixture comes to a slow boil. Lower heat and cover. Cook for about 45 minutes, adding shrimp, shallots and parsley after 25 minutes. Remove from heat, adjust seasonings, and let sit for about 15 minutes before serving. Serve over steamed or boiled rice. Also, very good if cooked the day before and reheated as the flavors have a chance to blend better. Recipe easily doubled. Freezes well.

Note To any left over Shrimp Creole, add one can of whole corn and one can of small lima beans (or 2 cans each, depending on the amount of left over Shrimp Creole) and an equal amount of water. Add Tabasco sauce to taste, heat to boiling point, lower heat, simmer for about 5 minutes, and enjoy!

Shrimp Scampi

⅓ cup olive oil
8 to 12 cloves garlic, or to taste, minced fine, or 3 or 4 teaspoons garlic puree
2 pounds raw shrimp, peeled and deveined
½ cup dry white wine
3 tablespoons fresh lemon juice
1 teaspoon salt
½ teaspoon black pepper
3 tablespoons parsley, chopped, plus more for garnish

Heat the olive oil in a large pan. Add garlic and cook for 2 to 3 minutes, just until softened but do not let the garlic brown. Add the shrimp, wine, lemon juice, salt and pepper. Cook over moderate heat for 3 or 4 minutes, until shrimp are cooked through Add the parsley and stir well. Spoon into 4 plates, garnish with additional parsley and serve. May also be served over rice pilaf, plain rice, or 1 pound cooked and drained pasta.

Variation: 1 (11 ounce) package frozen artichokes, thawed and chopped, or 1 (14 ounce) can artichoke hearts, drained and chopped, may be added along with shrimp. Continue as directed.

Poultry

Chicken and Artichoke Hearts ... 151
Chicken and Hash Brown Potatoes ... 152
Mamere's Chicken and Brown Gravy (Chicken Fricassee) ... 153
Chicken and Wine ... 154
Baked Chicken ... 154
Brunswick Stew (Virginia Ambrosia) ... 155
Chicken, Cooked in Microwave ... 156
Chicken Croquettes ... 157
Grilling Chicken ... 158
Chicken Hawaiian Shish Kabobs ... 159
Honey Mustard Chicken ... 160
Chicken in a Bag ... 161
Chicken Marsala ... 162
Chicken with Herbs and Wine ... 163
Chicken Sauce Piquant ... 164
Chicken with Linguine and Marinara Sauce ... 165
Fried Chicken New Orleans Style ... 166
Lemon Chicken Breasts ... 166
Marinated Chicken Breasts Paprika ... 167
Roast Chicken ... 168
Spicy Baked Chicken ... 169
Herbed Roast Cornish Hens ... 170
Herbed Turkey Breast ... 171
Turkey in a Crock Pot ... 171

Chicken and Artichoke Hearts

2 or 3 pound chicken, cut up
2 tablespoons butter, 2 tablespoons oil
3 tablespoons Brandy
2 cloves garlic, minced
2 tablespoon flour
1½ teaspoons salt
¼ teaspoon black pepper
1 cup chicken stock
1 large can artichoke hearts, drained and halved
1 large can sliced mushrooms
2 tablespoons shallots (green onions) chopped fine
¼ cup chopped parsley
¼ cup vermouth
1 cup sour cream

Brown chicken in butter and oil. Transfer to buttered casserole. Add Brandy to skillet in which chicken was browned and scrape to loosen particles left in pan from chicken. Add shallots, garlic, flour, chicken stock and season to taste with salt and pepper, stirring well. Add mushrooms, parsley and vermouth and simmer gently, mixing occasionally, for 10 to 15 minutes. Arrange artichoke hearts over chicken. Pour mixture in skillet over chicken. Cover and bake at 350 degree preheated oven for 1½ hours. Remove chicken pieces and artichokes to a serving platter. Stir sour cream into the sauce. Pour over chicken and artichokes. Serve at once. Nice served with buttered noodles or mashed potatoes, green peas and a salad.

Chicken and Hash Brown Potatoes

1 (30 oz.) package frozen country style hash brown potatoes
¼ teaspoon garlic salt
⅛ teaspoon cayenne pepper
4 cups cooked and diced chicken
1 (4 oz.) can sliced mushrooms, drained (optional)
1 cup sour cream or 1 cup unflavored yogurt
2 cups chicken broth or stock
1 (10 ¾ oz.) can condensed cream of chicken soup, undiluted
2 tablespoons instant chicken bouillon granules
2 tablespoons onions, finely diced (or two tablespoons dried minced onion)
3 tablespoon butter or margarine
Paprika

Thaw hash browns to room temperature. Layer in an ungreased 9 x 13 oven proof casserole and sprinkle with garlic salt and cayenne pepper. Mix chicken and mushrooms with the hash browns. Stir together the rest of the ingredients except paprika and butter. Pour over ingredients in casserole and mix well. Dot with butter and sprinkle with paprika. Bake in 350 degrees preheated oven for about 45 to 60 minutes or until heated through.

Mamere's Chicken and Brown Gravy
(Chicken Fricassee)
For Grand-père Benjamin

⅓ cup bacon dripping or oil
1 (4 to 5 pound) hen, cut up
Salt, black pepper and cayenne pepper to taste
½ cup flour
2 large onions, chopped fine
5 cloves garlic, minced
1 small or ½ large, sweet pepper, chopped
1 rib celery, chopped
6 cups hot water
2 tablespoons chopped parsley
2 bay leaves
½ teaspoon thyme
½ teaspoon basil
1 large can sliced mushrooms
1 small jar stuffed green olives, drained and cut in half (optional)
2 chicken bouillon cubes
1 tablespoon Worcestershire sauce
1 tablespoon Kitchen Bouquet

Place oil in a large heavy pot. Generously sprinkle chicken with salt, black pepper, and cayenne pepper and brown in oil. Remove chicken from pot and make a roux with flour and remaining oil in pot, stirring continuously until golden brown. Add onion, garlic, sweet pepper and celery and sauté until soft. Slowly stir in water, stirring continuously to keep flour from lumping. Add rest of ingredients. Check and adjust seasonings if necessary. Put chicken back into pot; partially cover and simmer until tender and gravy thickens (about 1 to 2 hours). When done, chicken pieces may be served whole, or remove chicken from gravy. Cut chicken from bones. Discard bones and return chicken pieces to pot. Serve over steamed or boiled rice. Dumplings may also be added. For dumpling recipe, see page 255.

Chicken and Wine
For my son Mike

2 chickens, each cut in fourths
Salt, pepper, paprika, and garlic powder
½ cup melted butter or margarine
1 large can sliced B & B Mushrooms, drained
3 tablespoons chopped parsley
Juice of 1 lemon
1 cup Sautérne or Dry Vermouth wine

Sprinkle chicken generously with salt, pepper, paprika and garlic powder. Place in baking pan with skin side down. Pour melted butter over chicken. Put mushrooms, parsley, lemon juice and wine in a bowl, mix well and pour over chicken. Cover pan with foil or plastic wrap and marinate in refrigerator for several hours or preferable overnight. When ready to bake, remove foil or saran wrap and place in a 375 degree preheated oven for 30 minutes. After 30 minutes, turn chicken skin side up and bake an additional 30 minutes, basting occasionally. Goes well with buttered egg noodles, mashed potatoes, or baked potato.

Baked Chicken

2 chickens, halved or cut in fourths
Salt, black pepper, garlic powder and paprika
¼ pound (1 stick) butter or margarine, melted

Preheat oven to 375 degrees. Sprinkle chicken generously with salt, pepper, paprika and garlic powder. Place chicken in baking pan, skin side down, and pour melted butter over chicken. Bake for 1 hour, turning chicken skin side up after 30 minutes.

Brunswick Stew
(Virginia Ambrosia)

In honor of my Virginia friends, this New Orleans woman would like to try to put together her version of a Virginia classic recipe which originated in Brunswick County, Virginia. According to legend, the original Brunswick stew was created in 1828 by a black chef, a camp cook named Jimmy Matthews. A group of friends went on a hunting expedition. While they were gone, the camp cook, Jimmy Matthews, hunted squirrel for the evening meal. Jimmy slowly stewed the squirrels with butter, onions, stale bread and seasoning in a large iron pot. Upon returning, the hunters were reluctant to try the thick concoction, but one taste convinced them to ask for more. This delicious stew has evolved through the years, and there are many ways to prepare it, the squirrel being replaced by chicken or rabbit, and a variety of meats, according to the taste of the one preparing the stew, and vegetables have been added. But the exceptional taste and quality has never been lost. In Virginia Brunswick stew is often served at Barbeque Cookouts, church functions, family reunions, etc., but no matter how or where it is served, it continues to be one of Virginia's most popular dishes. Please accept my version of Brunswick Stew.

1 (3 pound) chicken, cooked in microwave*
6 strips bacon
1 large or 2 medium onions, chopped
3 cloves garlic, minced
2 ribs celery, chopped
1 sweet pepper, chopped
½ pound lean smoked ham, diced (optional)
2 teaspoons salt
½ teaspoons ground pepper
½ teaspoon dried thyme leaves
Bay leaf
2 tablespoons all-purpose flour
⅛ teaspoon (or to taste) cayenne pepper
1 large can (28 ounce) Italian tomatoes, drained and chopped
2 medium potatoes, peeled and diced small
1 package (10 ounce) frozen lima beans, thawed or frozen or 1 can Navy beans, drained and rinsed
1 package frozen okra, thawed (optional)
2 cups corn, fresh or frozen, thawed
1 tablespoon lemon juice
1 teaspoon lemon zest
1 tablespoon Worcestershire sauce

The day before serving, prepare "Chicken, Cooked in Microwave" according to recipe. Marinate overnight in refrigerator. When ready to prepare Brunswick Stew, remove chicken from broth, drain broth into measuring cup, and discard vegetables from broth. Add enough water or extra broth to measuring cup to equal 4 cups and set

(Continued Next Page)

broth aside. Bone chicken and cut up into bite size pieces and set aside. Cut bacon into small pieces and in a heavy Dutch oven fry bacon until crisp. Remove bacon and set aside with chicken. Add chopped onion, garlic, celery and sweet pepper to bacon grease in Dutch oven. Cook over moderate heat, stirring, until soft, about 3 minutes. Add the ham, if using, and the salt, pepper, thyme, cayenne pepper and bay leaf. Cook until lightly browned, about 3 minutes longer. Sprinkle the flour over the mixture in Dutch oven and cook, stirring well, for 30 to 45 seconds. Pour in half the chicken stock. Bring to a boil, scraping bottom of pot and stirring well. Boil, stirring, until slightly thickened. Add the remaining stock, the chicken, and bacon. Add the potatoes, tomatoes, lima beans, and okra, Stir well, bring to a boil, reduce heat to low, and simmer, partially covered and stirring often, for about 2½ hours. Add more broth, if needed. Add corn, lemon juice, lemon zest, and Worcestershire sauce. Stir, and cook, partially covered, for another hour. Remove and discard bay leaf. Taste and adjust seasoning before serving. Brunswick Stew is always more flavorful the next day.

Chicken, Cooked in Microwave

2 to 3 pound chicken, cut up
½ onion, sliced
1 rib celery and leaves, cut into pieces
1½ teaspoons salt
½ teaspoon cayenne pepper
½ cup dry Vermouth or Sauterne wine
2 cups hot water

Place chicken and rest of ingredients in a large, covered, microwave safe, three to five quart casserole. Cook on high for 25 minutes. After cooked, marinate in stock in refrigerator until cool, or overnight. Remove chicken, strain and discard vegetables, and reserve stock. Bone chicken and cut into bite size pieces. Both chicken and stock can be frozen for future use and used for Jambalaya, Gumbo, or any recipe calling for cooked chicken.

Chicken Croquettes

A firm creamy blend of finely chopped chicken and crisp brown crumbs. Traditionally croquettes are shaped like small upside down ice cream cones but other shapes taste just as good. These are shaped like hamburger patties.

2 cups finely diced cooked chicken
½ cup ricotta cheese
2 tablespoons grated Parmesan cheese
½ teaspoon salt
¼ teaspoon ground black pepper
Pinch of cayenne pepper
1 tablespoon lemon juice
1 tablespoon minced parsley
1 teaspoon minced chives (optional)
1 tablespoon finely chopped celery (optional)
½ cup flour
2 eggs, lightly beaten with 1 tablespoon olive oil
2 cups breadcrumbs (Preferably Italian style)
2 tablespoon butter
2 tablespoons olive oil

Combine first 10 ingredients in a bowl and mix thoroughly until well blended. Cover with foil and refrigerate until chilled. Arrange the flour on a plate, the beaten eggs and oil in a bowl next, and the breadcrumbs in a plate next to the eggs. Form the mixture into 6 to 8 croquettes (patties) about the size of small hamburgers. Coat each croquette lightly with flour, dip into egg mixture, then roll them in breadcrumbs. Set them to dry on a dish or piece of wax paper. Heat the butter and oil in a frying pan over medium heat. Add the croquettes and sauté until golden brown, about 2 to 3 minutes on each side. Drain on paper towels and serve at once with tomato sauce. Nice served with potatoes, French fried, or fixed as you desire, and a salad. The patties can also be served on a hamburger bun, dressed according to your taste. Recipe easily doubled.

Variation: Croquettes can be formed into egg shapes and deep fried in hot oil. Drain on paper towels. Place on a warm platter and serve immediately with tomato sauce or a bechamel sauce.

Grilling Chicken
Microwave Before
Grilling on B.B.Q. Pit

    To make chicken ready to eat in about half the time when grilling on the Barbecue pit and to make reasonably sure that it will be cooked inside when it is browned on the outside, try zapping it in the microwave first. If you have ever had a piece of grilled chicken that looked delicious and well done, but oozed blood when you cut or bit into it, you know how important it is to be very sure it is well done.

    Before grilling, arrange chicken pieces on dish in microwave with thicker parts to the outside, and thin or bony parts toward center. Cover for faster cooking. Cook pieces on high 4 to 5 minutes per pound, or until the chicken starts to cook on the outside. Transfer to the hot grill to finish cooking. The chicken skin will be a little more delicate after pre-cooking in microwave, so be sure to oil the grill or spray with non-stick cooking spray before pre-heating. While the chicken is on the grill, baste with a barbecue sauce of your choice.

    Zapping in the microwave before grilling also works with ribs. Don't try it for hamburgers or steak, which cooks quickly on the grill.

Chicken Hawaiian Shish Kabobs

1½ pounds boneless chicken breasts, cut into 1 inch cubes
1 (15 ¼) can unsweetened pineapple chunks, undrained
½ cup soy sauce
¼ cup vegetable oil
1 tablespoon brown sugar
1 teaspoon garlic powder
2 teaspoons ground ginger
¼ teaspoon black pepper
1 teaspoon dry mustard
1 large, sweet pepper (green), cut into I inch pieces
12 medium size fresh mushrooms
18 cherry tomatoes
Hot cooked rice or Mediterranean Rice Pilaf*

    Place chicken pieces in large shallow bowl or container and refrigerate. Drain pineapple, reserving ½ cup of the juice. Combine juice, soy sauce, vegetable oil, brown sugar, garlic powder, ginger, pepper and mustard in a small pot, stir well, and heat to a boil. Reduce heat and simmer for 5 minutes. Pour over chicken, cover and refrigerate for an hour or two, stirring occasionally.

    Remove chicken from marinade, reserving marinade. Place chicken, pineapple, sweet pepper, mushrooms, and tomatoes on skewers, alternating pieces. Broil or grill over hot coals for about 20 minutes, or until chicken is done. Turn and baste frequently with marinade. Serve over hot rice or Mediterranean Rice Pilaf*.

    Variation: 1 pound sirloin steak cut into 1 inch pieces or 1 pound pork tenderloin cut in ½ inch pieces can be substituted for chicken.

*Recipe for Mediterranean Rice Pilaf – see page 124.

Honey Mustard Chicken

2 tablespoon butter or margarine, melted
3 tablespoons honey
1½ tablespoons Dijon mustard
2 garlic cloves, crushed and minced fine
1 teaspoon grated orange peel
2 tablespoons orange or citrus marmalade
2½ pounds chicken thighs or boneless chicken thighs
Salt and pepper to taste

Place melted butter in an ovenproof baking dish or casserole. Stir honey, mustard, garlic, orange peel and marmalade in butter. Sprinkle both sides of chicken with salt and pepper. Add chicken to honey mustard sauce in casserole, turning to coat well. Cover and refrigerate at least 3 hours, turning occasionally. Bake in a 400 degree oven until juices run clear when thickest portion of meat is pierced with a knife, about 30 minutes.

Variation: ¼ cup of lemon or lime juice can be used in place of orange peel and marmalade. Chicken breasts can be used in place of thighs. Broil, turning once, until no longer pink, about 15 minutes.

Chicken in a Bag
Creole "Si Bon" Poulet en Sac

1 large size cooking bag
2 tablespoon flour
2 large chickens, each quartered
Salt and black pepper
Cayenne Pepper or Tony Chachere seasoning
2 cups chopped onion
1 cup chopped celery
1 cup chopped sweet pepper
1 cup chopped parsley
4 cloves garlic, minced fine, or 1 heaping tablespoon garlic puree
1 teaspoon dry crushed thyme
1½ cup Sautérne or dry Vermouth wine
1 tablespoon Soy sauce
1 tablespoon Worcestershire sauce
1 cup water

Preheat oven to 350 degrees. Lightly oil a large baking pan. Spoon flour into extra-large size oven cooking bag and shake, coating bag well. Place bag in baking pan. Generously salt and pepper chicken and put in bag. Add the onion, celery, sweet pepper, parsley, garlic and thyme. Combine the wine, soy sauce, Worchester sauce, and water. Pour over the mixture in the cooking bag and tie bag well. Pierce the bag on top with a large cooking fork about 12 times so the steam can escape. Bake for 1½ hours or until chicken falls off bone. Delicious served with mashed potatoes or small, new potatoes.

Chicken Marsala

4 skinless, boneless chicken breasts (about 1½ pounds)
All-purpose flour
Kosher salt and black pepper
¼ cup extra virgin olive oil
8 ounces mushrooms, stemmed and halved or
1 large jar sliced mushrooms
½ cup sweet Marsala wine
½ cup chicken stock
2 tablespoons unsalted butter
¼ cup chopped flat leaf parsley

Place chicken breasts between pieces of plastic wrap and pound with a flat meat mallet until about ¼ inch thick. Put some flour in a pie plate or a shallow plate and season well with salt and pepper, mixing flour and seasonings well. Dip both sides of the chicken in the seasoned flour, shaking off the excess, and sauté in the oil until golden brown on both sides, about 5 minutes each side. Remove from skillet and set aside. Lower the heat and sauté the mushrooms until they are browned and wilted, about 5 minutes. Season them with salt and pepper. Pour in the Marsala wine and scrape up the bottom bits that are in the bottom of the pan and boil down for a few seconds. Add the chicken stock and stir very well, reducing the liquid in the pan just a little. Stir in the butter, return the chicken to the pan and lower the heat to a very low simmer. Turn chicken over in pan so it has sauce on each side and simmer for a few minutes to heat the chicken through. Adjust seasoning by adding a little more salt and pepper if needed. Garnish with chopped parsley before serving. Serve over steamed rice or noodles.

Variation: To make Veal Marsala, Substitute veal scallops in place of chicken breasts. Proceed as above.

Chicken with Herbs and Wine

6 Chicken boneless breast halves, or equivalent amount of chicken tenders
Salt and pepper
2 tablespoon butter
2 tablespoon oil
1 can (10.5 ounces) cream of chicken soup
¾ cup white wine (preferably Sauterne wine or Gallo Dry Vermouth)
2 tablespoons chopped sweet (green) pepper
¼ teaspoon crushed dry thyme
1 teaspoon dry parsley flakes
¼ teaspoon tarragon or rosemary, crumbled (optional)
¼ teaspoon lemon garlic seasoning

Lightly season chicken with salt and pepper. Heat butter and oil in large skillet, and slowly brown chicken in the butter and oil. When browned, remove chicken from pan and set aside. Add soup to drippings in skillet and stir well. Add wine and stir until smooth. Add remaining ingredients and heat to boiling, continuing to stir well. Return chicken to pan and turn chicken so both sides are covered with sauce. Cover and simmer on low fire for about 3 minutes. Serve chicken with mashed potatoes or noodles, and ladle sauce over chicken.

Chicken Sauce Piquant

2-3 pound fryers, cut up
⅓ cup oil
⅓ cup flour
2 onions, chopped
4 cloves garlic, minced
1 large, sweet pepper, chopped
3 ribs celery, chopped
1 small can tomato paste
1 large (28 ounce) can Italian tomatoes, chopped
½ cup chopped parsley
2 teaspoons salt
½ teaspoon black pepper
¼ teaspoon cayenne pepper
¼ teaspoon basil
½ teaspoon thyme
¼ teaspoon chili powder
2 bay leaves
1 tablespoon Worcestershire sauce
1 tablespoon fresh lemon juice
½ cup dry red wine (optional)
2 or more cups water
Steamed rice

Brown chicken in oil in large iron or heavy pot. Remove when brown to a heated platter and set aside. Add flour to pot and make a golden brown roux. When roux has reached a golden brown, quickly add onions, garlic, sweet pepper and celery. Sauté until soft and transparent. Add tomato paste and about ¼ tomato paste can of water, stirring constantly. Add tomatoes and stir well, then add seasonings, chicken and the rest of the ingredients except rice. Stir well, cover and simmer, stirring often, until chicken is tender (about an hour to an hour and a half). Add more water if needed. When cooked, let it sit for a half hour before serving. Adjust seasoning if needed. Serve over steamed or boiled rice or noodles.

Note: After the chicken is cooked it can be, if you wish, removed from the bone, cut into small pieces, and added to the sauce in the pot.

Variation: To turn the Sauce Piquant into Jambalaya, stir in 4 cups of cooked rice to the deboned chicken and the sauce Taste and season accordingly.

Chicken with Linguine and Marinara Sauce

¼ cup olive oil
6 boneless skinless chicken thighs, sliced into pieces, or equivalent amount of chicken tenders
Salt and pepper
½ cup finely chopped shallots
1 tablespoon minced garlic or garlic puree
⅔ cup Vermouth or Sauterne wine
1 tablespoon finely chopped fresh rosemary leaves
4 cups Marinara sauce (see page 105)
1 pound linguine
Parmesan cheese

Heat oil in heavy skillet over medium heat. Add chicken, season with salt and pepper, and cook until the juices evaporate and the chicken is golden, about 10 minutes. Add the shallots and garlic and cook for about 2 minutes more. Add the wine, scraping the bottom of the pan to scrape up any brown bits on the bottom. Add the rosemary and the marinara sauce and mix well. Bring to a simmer, then reduce heat to medium-low and simmer for about 10 minutes. Pour over cooked linguine and toss to coat, adding about a ½ cup of water the linguine was cooked in if sauce seems too thick. Sprinkle with Parmesan cheese and serve.

Fried Chicken New Orleans Style
For Sam

2 cups self-rising flour
3 tablespoons salt
2 teaspoons each black pepper and paprika
1 heaping teaspoons baking powder
1 to 2 teaspoons cayenne pepper
1 teaspoon garlic powder (optional)
Chicken pieces, amount of your choice

Mix first 6 ingredients well in a large plastic Zip-lock bag. Put chicken pieces in bag, a few pieces at a time, and shake bag to coat well. Fry in deep fryer at 375 degrees for about 15 minutes or until golden brown. Amount of coating easily doubled or tripled depending on the amount of chicken to be fried.

Lemon Chicken Breasts

½ cup butter or margarine
½ teaspoon garlic puree or powder
1 tablespoon Worcestershire sauce
Juice of one lemon (or bottled equivalent)
½ teaspoon salt
⅛ teaspoon cayenne pepper (or to taste)
½ cup grated Parmesan cheese
½ cup Progresso seasoned breadcrumbs
4 boneless, skinless chicken breasts, halved

In a 4 cup Pyrex measuring cup, combine margarine, garlic puree or powder, Worcestershire sauce, lemon juice, salt and pepper. Microwave for one minute or until margarine melts, then stir. In pie plate mix cheese and breadcrumbs. Spray 9 x 13 inch microwave or oven safe casserole with Pam. Dip pieces of chicken in sauce and then roll in cheese and crumb mixture, coating well. Arrange chicken in casserole. Pour remaining sauce over chicken and sprinkle with remaining bread crumb mixture. Bake in conventional oven at 375 degrees for 45 minutes, or cover with saran wrap and bake in microwave oven on high for 9 minutes each side.

Marinated Chicken Breasts Paprika
Cooked in Microwave Oven

4 chicken breasts, skinned, boned and halved
1 (8 oz.) carton plain low fat yogurt
Juice of 1 lemon
1 Tablespoon Worcestershire sauce
1 teaspoon Paprika
¼ teaspoon garlic puree or garlic powder
1 teaspoon salt
¼ teaspoon cayenne pepper
1 cup Progresso Italian breadcrumbs
¼ cup melted margarine

Combine yogurt, lemon juice, Worcestershire sauce, paprika, garlic, salt and pepper in a 2 quart bowl, mixing well. Add chicken, coating each piece well. Cover and refrigerate 8 hours or overnight, turning occasionally. When ready to cook, remove chicken from mixture and dip in breadcrumbs, turning and coating evenly. Arrange chicken in 9"x13" microwave casserole which has been sprayed with Pam. Drizzle melted margarine over chicken. Cover with Saran wrap and microwave on high 9 minutes each side.

Variation: If you prefer bake in conventional oven at 375 degrees for 45 minutes, turning once during cooking time.

Roast Chicken

1 roasting chicken, about 4 to 5 pounds
Salt and freshly ground black pepper to taste
1 lemon, halved
¼ bunch each of thyme and parsley
1 head garlic, halved
8 tablespoons (1 stick) butter
½ cup dry white wine or water

Preheat oven to 425 degrees. Rinse chicken inside and out, then pat dry. Remove the giblets and excess fat from the cavities and season with salt and pepper, Place half of the lemon, the parsley and thyme sprigs, and the two halves of garlic inside. Tie legs together with kitchen string and place, breast side up, in a roasting pan.

In a saucepan, melt the butter over low heat. Squeeze the juice from the remaining lemon half into the butter. Stir well and brush or pour over the chicken. Season with salt and pepper Bake in the center of the oven, basting often with the drippings, and rotate the pan every 20 minutes or so to insure a golden crispy skin, until juices run clear when the thigh is pierced with a sharp knife, about 1½ hours. The chicken should be done when an instant read thermometer says 175 degrees when inserted into the thickest part of the thigh. (The legs of the chicken should wiggle easily from the sockets.)

Remove chicken from the oven and transfer to a carving board or platter, remove the lemon, herbs, and garlic from the cavity, cover loosely, and let rest for 10 minutes. Meanwhile squeeze the lemon and garlic into the pan juices. Stir in the wine or water. Bring the pan juices to a low boil, scraping up the brown bits, and cook until the sauce is reduced, about 2 minutes. Defat the sauce and adjust seasoning. Carve the chicken and arrange on a large platter. Pour the sauce over it. Serve immediately with creamy mashed potatoes, green peas and a salad for a perfect comfort meal.

Variation: Instead of mashed potatoes, tiny red new potatoes can be served with the chicken. Scrub 1½ pounds of peeled or unpeeled small new potatoes, sprinkle well with salt and pepper, and toss around the chicken in the pan. Turn to coat the potatoes in the drippings in the pan. Cook along with the chicken. Serve the roasted potatoes on the side.

Spicy Baked Chicken

1 teaspoon salt
1 teaspoon black pepper
1 cup chicken broth or stock
3 tablespoons olive oil
1 tablespoon lemon juice
1 tablespoon soy sauce
1 tablespoon Italian seasoning
1 teaspoon paprika
1 teaspoon garlic powder
½ teaspoon onion powder
½ teaspoon dry mustard
¼ teaspoon ground ginger
3 pound chicken, cut up

Combine all ingredients except chicken in a bowl and mix well. Season chicken with salt, and pepper and place in a large zip loc bag. Pour mixture in bowl over chicken and shake well, making sure all of the chicken is coated. Marinate in refrigerator for about 2 hours. Preheat oven to 350 degrees. Place chicken and mixture in a baking pan and bake for 1½ hours, basting occasionally. Serve immediately.

Herbed Roast Cornish Hens

6 tablespoons softened butter
4 cloves garlic, minced fine or 2 teaspoons garlic puree
1 tablespoon crumbled dried thyme
1 tablespoons grated lemon zest
1 teaspoon salt
¼ teaspoon black pepper
4 (1½ pound) Cornish hens, rinsed and patted dry
2 tablespoons melted butter

Preheat oven to 450 degrees. Combine the butter, garlic, thyme, lemon zest, salt and pepper. Loosen the skin over the hen's breasts by gently sliding your finger under the skin. Dividing the butter mixture between the four hens, inserting some under the skin and some over the outside of the breasts of the hens. Season the outside of the hens with salt and pepper. Using kitchen string, tie each hen's legs together. Place hens in a roasting pan, breast side up, pour melted butter over them, and roast in the middle of the oven, basting with juices from the pan every 10 minutes. Roast for 30 to 35 minutes or until a thermometer inserted in fleshy thigh registers 180 degrees. Remove hens from pan and let hens rest for 5 to 10 minutes before serving. Gravy can be made with pan drippings if desired.

Herbed Turkey Breast

½ cup butter or margarine, melted
¼ cup lemon juice
1 tablespoon soy sauce
2 tablespoon shallots (Green onions) finely chopped
2 cloves garlic, finely minced
1 teaspoon dried thyme
Salt and pepper to taste
Pinch of cayenne pepper
½ teaspoon bitters (Peychaud or Angostura)
1 tablespoon Worcestershire sauce
½ cup Sautérne or dry Vermouth wine
1 (3 to 5) pound turkey breast

Preheat oven to 325 degrees. In a small saucepan, combine all ingredients except turkey. Bring just to the boiling point and remove from heat. Place turkey in a shallow roasting pan and baste well with butter mixture. Bake, uncovered for 1½ to 2 hours or until meat thermometer reads 170 degrees. Baste every 30 minutes.

Turkey in a Crock Pot

Place all above ingredients above in a crock pot (turkey skin side down) and cook on low 6 to 8 hours, basting turkey occasionally.

Meat

Roasted Beef Brisket	175
Creole Pot Roast	177
Beef and Garlic Brown Gravy	178
Beef Stew in Red Wine (Boeuf a la Bourguignonne)	179
Beef Stew	181
Crock-Pot Beef Stew	182
Grillades and Grits	183
Meat Loaf and Brown Gravy	185
Jonny's "Secret" Recipe	186
Mike's Pork Chops	186
Natchitoches Meat Pies	187
Pepper Steak	188
Pork Chops and Brown Gravy	189
Roasted Pork Tenderloin	189
Shepherd's Pie	190
Beef Stroganoff	191
Panéed Veal (Veal Milanese)	192
Meatballs for Spaghetti Gravy	192
Veal Scaloppine with Wine (Scaloppine di vitello al Vino)	193

Roasted Beef Brisket

Marinade:

½ cup olive oil
1 cup dry red wine
1 tablespoon Worcestershire sauce
½ teaspoon Tabasco sauce (optional)
½ cup chopped shallots (green onions)
½ teaspoon thyme
½ teaspoon garlic powder
⅛ teaspoon cayenne pepper
1 teaspoon dried basil
1 teaspoon coarse or freshly ground black pepper
¼ cup minced parsley
2 bay leaves

Mix all ingredients together in a large bowl, cover with plastic wrap and refrigerate for about 3 hours so flavors will blend.

1 (4 or 5 pound) beef brisket, trimmed
4 cloves garlic, halved

Make several slits in the brisket and insert garlic pieces, pushing down well into the meat.

Place brisket in a large baking dish or large plastic zip lock bag and cover with marinade. Cover, refrigerate and marinate 8 hours or overnight, occasionally turning meat in marinade.

Salt and black pepper
Flour
1 large onion, chopped
2 carrots, cut into 1 inch pieces
2 ribs celery, cut into 1 inch pieces
½ cup beef consommé
¾ cup marinade mix

(Continued Next Page)

When ready to bake preheat oven to 350 degrees. Remove brisket from marinade, reserving marinade. Salt and pepper liberally, rubbing in seasoning into meat with your hands. Then dust the brisket with flour on all sides. Line a large baking pan with heavy aluminum foil. Place brisket in the baking pan. Arrange the onion, carrots and celery around the sides of the meat. Pour the beef consommé and marinade mix over the meat. Cover the pan with a lid or foil and bake for 2½ to 3 hours or until tender. Depending on the grade of meat, it could take a little longer. Allow the meat to cool a bit before slicing across the grain into thin slices. Cover the meat until ready to serve. The gravy is delicious served with the meat. The meat will render a good bit of fat into the gravy. Strain the gravy into a measuring cup and refrigerate for about an hour. When the fat congeals you can lift it off the surface of the gravy, and reheat the gravy. Place the slices of meat into the gravy to reheat it. Serve the brisket hot with the gravy. Creole Tomato Horseradish Sauce can be served on the side. Leftover heated brisket makes great sandwiches the next day.

*Creole Horseradish Sauce – See page 109.

Creole Pot Roast

1 chuck roast, about 4 or 5 pounds
6 cloves garlic or 2 tablespoons garlic puree
Salt, pepper, and cayenne pepper
⅓ cup olive or vegetable oil
½ cup beef stock or water
¼ cup dry red wine
1 tablespoon Worcestershire sauce
1 teaspoon thyme
8 pared small carrots (optional)
6 to 8 pared small red potatoes (optional)
Large jar of sliced mushrooms
1 tablespoon Kitchen Bouquet

Preheat oven to 275 degrees. Either cut slits in roast and insert cloves of garlic deep into roast or spread garlic puree liberally over entire roast making sure you cover both sides. Sprinkle salt and peppers generously on both sides. Heat oil in a heavy Dutch oven and brown the roast over medium high heat on both sides to sear in the juices. When you are sure it is well browned on all sides, remove the beef and set aside. Add the beef stock or water, wine, Worcestershire sauce and thyme to the Dutch oven, scraping the bottom and mixing well. Return the beef to the pot, turning it over in the pot so the liquid covers all of the meat. Place in oven and bake, covered, for 2 to 2½ hours at 275 degrees, Roast until the beef is tender and registers an internal temperature of 130 to 135 degrees. Add water if needed, keeping at least ½ inch of liquid in the Dutch oven. If you are adding carrots and potatoes, place them in a bowl and season with salt and pepper, mixing well. Add to roast about 50 minutes before roast is done.

When meat is done, remove it to a heated platter to keep warm. Skim fat from broth in Dutch oven. Measure broth and add enough water to make 3 cups liquid. One half cup of red wine can be used in place of one half cup of the water. Add 4 tablespoons flour to about 4 to 6 tablespoons water in a bowl and stir until smooth. Stir into liquid in pot. Season with salt and pepper and a dash of cayenne pepper to taste. Add about a tablespoon of Worcestershire and a tablespoon of Kitchen Bouquet browning sauce and stir well. Add drained jar of mushrooms. Cook gravy until thickened. Check seasonings and add salt and pepper, if needed. Place meat sliced on a platter with vegetables and serve gravy in a gravy boat or a bowl. Serve gravy over cooked rice or noodles.

Note: This pot roast can also be cooked on top of the stove covered and at a very low simmer.

Beef and Garlic Brown Gravy
For my Grandson Jonny

2 or 3 pounds beef short ribs or boneless beef stew meat
⅓ cup bacon drippings or oil
½ cup flour
2 quarts boiling water or 1 quart each beef broth and water
2 tablespoons garlic puree
1 tablespoon Kitchen Bouquet
1½ teaspoons salt
½ teaspoon black pepper
½ teaspoon dried thyme
¼ teaspoon cayenne pepper or to taste
2 tablespoons Worcestershire sauce
1 large can sliced B & B mushrooms, drained

In heavy pot, brown meat on all sides in oil. When brown, add flour, stirring quickly. When lightly browned, begin adding water, or water and beef broth, continuing to stir until all water is added. Add garlic puree, Worcestershire sauce, Kitchen Bouquet, seasonings, and mushrooms. Bring to a boil, then lower to simmer, cover and cook until meat is fork tender, about 2½ hours. Serve with steamed rice, mashed potatoes, or egg noodles.

Beef Stew in Red Wine
(Boeuf a la Bourguignonne)
For Daddy

As in most well-known dishes, there are many way to prepare a good Boeuf Bourguignonne. Cooked with care, and well flavored, it is one of the most delicious beef dishes of all. You can prepare it completely the day before serving, and the flavor only improves when reheating. Boiled Parslied potatoes or creamy mashed potatoes are usually served with this dish, but buttered noodles can be served in place of potatoes, along with a green salad and a good wine. As I said, there are many ways to cook this dish. This is our way.

3 cups full bodied red wine (such as Beaujolais, Bordeaux or Burgundy)
2½ cup beef bouillon or stock
1 large or 2 medium onions, chopped
2 carrots, cut in 1 inch chunks
2 ribs celery, cut in 1 inch chunks
4 cloves garlic, mashed or minced well
½ cup chopped parsley
1 teaspoon dried thyme
1 tablespoon whole black peppercorns
1 bay leaf, crumbled
3 pounds boneless beef (rump or chuck) cut into 2 inch cubes
½ pound bacon
1 teaspoon salt
¼ teaspoon pepper
2 tablespoon flour
1 teaspoon paprika
¼ teaspoon cayenne pepper
1 pound fresh mushrooms, cleaned and sliced, or 1 jar sliced mushrooms, drained

In a large, covered bowl or casserole, combine the wine, beef bouillon, onion, carrots, celery, garlic, parsley, thyme, peppercorns, and bay leaf. Add the beef, mixing well to cover all the beef. Cover, refrigerate and marinate overnight. When ready to cook, cut bacon in ½ inch pieces. Place the bacon in a large Dutch oven and fry until crisp. With a slotted spoon transfer bacon bits to paper towels to drain. Remove beef from the marinade, draining well. Reserve the marinade and vegetables separately. Dry the beef well with paper towels and season well with salt and pepper. Then lightly

(Continued Next Page)

sprinkle on the flour and toss to lightly coat the meat with the flour. Turn heat under the Dutch oven to high, and brown the well dried beef in the remaining bacon fat, in batches, adding a little more oil if needed, so the meat browns evenly. When all the meat is browned, return bacon and all the meat back to the pot. Turn the heat to medium, add the reserved vegetable and herb mixture to the meat in pot and cook, stirring, for about 5 minutes. Add the paprika and cayenne pepper and reserved marinade. Stir well and bring to a boil. Taste to check seasoning. Turn heat to low, cover pot with lid and cook on low heat for 1½ to 2 hours. If liquid cooks down, add more wine, bouillon, or water. While meat cooks, sauté fresh mushrooms in 1 tablespoon oil and 2 tablespoons butter until lightly browned, about 3 or 4 minutes. If using mushrooms from a jar or can, drain, and sauté mushrooms in butter and oil for about 2 minutes. Add mushrooms to meat and stir well. When done, the gravy should be thick and the meat tender. You may need to add a little water halfway through the cooking process. If a thicker consistency is desired, stir in 1 tablespoon flour dissolved in 2 tablespoons water and cook until the mixture is thickened. Sprinkle top of finished dish with chopped parsley. Serve with mashed potatoes or noodles.

Beef Stew

¼ cup flour
2 or 3 pounds boneless beef stew meat
⅓ cup vegetable oil
1 large onion, chopped
3 cloves garlic, minced
1 small, sweet pepper, chopped
1 can (14.5 ounce) tomatoes and liquid, chopped
1 tablespoon salt
½ teaspoon black pepper
⅛ teaspoon cayenne pepper (or to taste)
½ teaspoon thyme leaves
2 tablespoons chopped parsley
1 tablespoon Worcestershire sauce
5 cups boiling water
1 large can B & B sliced mushrooms, drained
1 can Petit Pois peas, rinsed and drained (optional)
2 ribs celery, cut in 1½ inch pieces
4 carrots, halved lengthwise and cut in pieces
4 potatoes, peeled and diced

Pout flour in a bowl or plastic bag. Drop in meat, a few pieces at a time and toss until well coated. Reserve leftover flour. Slowly brown meat in hot oil in heavy pot, a few pieces at a time. Remove pieces as they brown. Add onions, garlic, and sweet pepper to pot and sauté until just tender. Stir in reserved flour until well blended. Add tomatoes, salt, pepper, cayenne pepper, thyme, parsley and Worcestershire sauce. Simmer, stirring well. Add boiling water, stir and then add meat, and rest of vegetables. Stir and simmer, partially covered, over low heat for about 2½ hours, or until meat is fork tender. Taste to check seasoning and serve with warm, crusty French bread.

Variation: 1 cup of red wine may be substituted for one cup of water.

Crock-Pot Beef Stew

2 pounds boneless beef stew meat
⅓ cup vegetable oil
⅓ cup flour
1 (14.5 ounce) can diced tomatoes, undrained
1 large onion, chopped
2 cloves garlic, minced
1 small, sweet pepper, chopped
1 large can or jar sliced mushrooms, drained
2 stalks celery, cut in ½ inch pieces
4 carrots, sliced, or 1 (1 pound) package fresh baby carrots
1 pound small (2½ to 3 inch) red potatoes, quartered
1 can Petit Pois peas, drained (optional)
1½ teaspoon salt
½ teaspoon black pepper
½ teaspoon dried thyme leaves
⅛ teaspoon cayenne pepper (or to taste)
1 tablespoons chopped parsley
1 tablespoon Worcestershire sauce
1½ cup water or 1 can beef broth

Brown meat in oil quickly in large pot or skillet and drain well. Place beef cubes in crock-pot. Add flour to meat and mix well to coat thoroughly. Add tomatoes and rest of vegetables, and seasonings to crock-pot. Add beef broth or water, and stir well. Cover and cook on low setting for 10 to 14 hours. (On high setting for 4 to 5 ½ hours.) If gravy seems thin, make a smooth paste of ¼ cup flour and ¼ cup water. Stir into crock-pot, cover and cook until thickened. Taste to check seasoning and serve with warm, crusty French bread.

Grillades and Grits
(Pronounced "Gree-Yads")

    Grillades is a New Orleans creation. It was the ultimate breakfast or brunch dish dating as far back as the mid-19th century, where it was served, along with many other classic Old New Orleans dishes, by the incomparable and unforgettable Madame Begue. Opposite the Famous French Market of old New Orleans is a brick building built in 1826. It still stands on the same downtown corner of Decatur and Madison Streets. It is now the home of the famous Tujague's Restaurant. But shortly before the end of the Civil War it was a distinctive dining place called then, as was the custom, a "Coffee House" owned and operated by a Creole named Louis Dutrey and his German wife, Elizabeth. Twenty-two year old Elizabeth performed such culinary miracles upon the stove that her creative power in the kitchen became well known. After her husband died Elizabeth married Hippolyte Begue, and the Coffee House changed its name to "Begue's." Madame Begue's culinary skills attained her a reputation as the "New Orleans Queen of the Kitchen," for visitors to the Crescent City spread her fame far and wide The butchers, fishermen and farmers, who had worked in the French Market since daybreak, and who were in need of something filling to eat, would go to Madame Begue's for their "Second Breakfast", and she would prepare, among other delicious dishes, these tender little squares or strips of beef or veal known as grillades, swimming in a spicy Creole gravy, over grits. These second breakfasts were gargantuan feasts that began at 11:00 o'clock in the morning and never ended until about 3:00 o'clock in the afternoon. Madame Begue died in 1906 at the age of 75 or 76. These celebrated "breakfasts" of Madame Begue's are now just memories of the past, but they live on in the stories of the thousands who climbed the narrow stairway to the low ceilinged room on the second floor to do homage to the gastronomic fame of Elizabeth Kettering Dutrey Begue, and to eat the meals that could be obtained nowhere else - even in New Orleans. (For those puzzled by names in New Orleans of French flavor; Begue is pronounced "Bay-Gay" and Tujague's may be called "Two Jacks.")

    In New Orleans today Grillades are usually served with grits or steamed or boiled rice as an old fashioned Sunday breakfast or brunch, or an inexpensive Supper. I remember as a child enjoying the Grillades my Mamere, Momma, and my Aunt would cook. There are several ways that Grillades can be prepared, some recipes even calling for mushrooms. But this is the way my Momma, Mamere, and my Aunt cooked it for us. And they would most often prepare it with Veal, not beef, the way Madame Begue did.

(Continued Next Page)

2 large Veal or Beef Round steaks, about ½ in. thick, each cut into 4 pieces
Salt, pepper, and cayenne or Creole seasoning
2 tablespoons plus ½ cup bacon grease or oil
½ cup flour
1 large onion, chopped fine
1 sweet pepper, chopped fine
2 ribs celery, chopped fine
3 or 4 large cloves garlic, minced
1 (16 oz.) can Italian tomatoes, chopped, or (when in season) 3 large Creole tomatoes, peeled and chopped
2 cups water
½ cup red wine (optional)
2 bay leaves
½ teaspoon thyme
⅓ cup chopped parsley
2 tablespoon Worcestershire sauce
Cooked grits, rice, or mashed potatoes

Trim meat of fat and bone and rub the meat with salt, black pepper, and cayenne pepper or Creole seasoning on both sides. Pound with meat mallet to ¼ inch thickness and cut into strips or 2 x 3 inch pieces. In heavy iron pot or Dutch oven heat oil over medium heat and brown meat well. Remove meat to platter and set aside. Add ½ cup oil to pot and slowly stir in flour to make a roux. Stir constantly over medium heat until roux is brown. (Be careful not to burn roux.) When browned, quickly add onions, garlic, celery, and sweet pepper to pot and sauté until limp, stirring constantly. Add tomatoes, water, wine, bay leaves, thyme, parsley, and Worcestershire sauce, continuing to stir. Return meat to pot, cover and simmer over low heat for about 1½ to 2 hours or until the meat is fork tender. Uncover, stir and turn meat several times while cooking. A rich red-brown gravy will form during cooking. If gravy becomes too thick, add a little more water. Meanwhile, prepare grits according to package directions. Reheat meat and gravy if needed. Put meat and grits on plates and spoon gravy over each portion, removing bay leaves before serving.

Use a package of the old-fashioned grits, the kind that takes a ½ hour or so to cook, preferably over a double boiler. After the grits are cooked, add ½ stick butter or margarine, 1 raw egg (this is the old Creole way, but the egg may be omitted) and salt to taste. Beat well and serve.

Meat Loaf and Brown Gravy

2 pounds ground beef or preferably, 1 pound ground beef and ½ pound each ground pork and ground veal
1 onion, chopped
2 cloves garlic, minced
½ sweet pepper, chopped
2 eggs, slightly beaten
1 cup seasoned breadcrumbs
1 cup uncooked oatmeal
1 tablespoons Worcestershire sauce
¾ cup milk or red wine
1½ teaspoon salt
½ teaspoon black pepper
¼ teaspoon cayenne pepper (optional)
1 tablespoon minced parsley
2 tablespoon Parmesan cheese

Preheat oven to 375 degrees. In a large bowl mix all ingredients together thoroughly. Shape into 2 loaves. Both can be cooked at once or freeze one for another time. Place in open shallow baking pan to which ¼ cup bacon drippings have been added. Bake for 1 hour. Remove from pan and let meat loaf sit for about 15 minutes while you make brown gravy from the pan drippings.

Note: Cold leftover meat loaf makes great sandwiches. We use Rye bread for the sandwiches with sweet gherkin pickles on the side.

Brown Gravy

Bacon dripping plus oil from pan to equal ⅓ cup
⅓ cup flour
3 cups boiling water
Salt, black pepper, garlic salt to taste
1 tablespoon Worcestershire sauce
1 tablespoon Kitchen Bouquet
1 large can or jar sliced mushrooms

Make roux with flour and oil. When browned, slowly add water and seasonings. Add mushrooms. Stir slowly and simmer about 10 to 15 minutes. Serve with meat loaf and steamed rice or egg noodles. This gravy also goes well with roast beef.

Jonny's "Secret" Recipe

This recipe was created and given to me by my Grandson Jonny when he was 6 years old. He said I could write it in my cookbook as long as I didn't tell anyone outside the family about it. So, Jonny, Here is your recipe, and I did as you asked. I wrote it in my cookbook but I didn't tell anyone outside the family about it.

1 hamburger bun
Secret Ingredient
A slice of cheese
"Too much ketchup"
Some French fries

I will write the instructions the exact way that Jonny gave them to me. Put a hamburger on the bottom part of the bun. Put on a slice of cheese. Put on "too much ketchup" Lay some French fries on top. And cover it with the top of the bun. Jonny says the "secret ingredient" in the hamburger is meat. Sounds good to me!

(Jonny called Ketchup "Too Much Ketchup" because when he added ketchup to his hamburger, we would all say, "Jonny! That's Too Much Ketchup!!!)

Mike's Pork Chops

8 Bone-in center cut pork chops (about ½ inch thick)
Salt and pepper
2 cups all-purpose flour
2 tablespoons Tony Chachere or other Creole seasoning
About ⅓ cup cooking oil

Season pork chops with salt and pepper. Place flour and Creole seasoning in a zip lock plastic bag and shake well to blend. Place pork chops, two at a time, in bag and shake well to coat. Remove from bag, shaking off excess flour. Fry chops in oil for about 5 minutes each side.

Natchitoches Meat Pies

Natchitoches (pronounced Nack-uh-tish) is a lovely, historic town in North West Louisiana. It is known for the beautiful Christmas festival held yearly along the Cane River that flows through the entire length of the town. It is also famous for its delicious Meat Pies that is sold all over the State of Louisiana.

Filling:
2 tablespoons shortening
2 tablespoons all-purpose flour
1½ pounds ground beef
1½ pounds ground pork
1 large white onion, finely chopped
2 cloves garlic, minced fine
1 cup red or green bell (sweet) pepper, chopped fine
½ cup chopped celery
6 shallots (green onions) green and white parts, chopped
½ cup parsley, chopped
1 tablespoon salt
1 teaspoon black pepper
¼ teaspoon cayenne pepper, or to taste

Over medium heat make a roux in a large Dutch oven of the shortening and flour. Stirring continuously, cook until brown. Quickly add beef, pork and rest of ingredients to the roux, stirring well. When meat mixture has turned brown, remove from heat and skim off any excess fat. Let meat mixture cool to room temperature.

Pastry:
2 cups self-rising flour, sifted
½ teaspoon salt
¾ cup solid Crisco
1 egg, beaten
¾ cup milk

Cut solid shortening into sifted flour and salt. Add egg and milk. Roll the dough into a ball and place on floured surface. Roll the dough out until very thin. Use a saucer to cut circles of the dough into the size of the saucer. Put about 2 tablespoons of the meat mixture on one side of the pastry round. Moisten the edge of the pie with

(*Continued Next Page*)

fingertips dipped in water. Fold the other half of the dough over the filling and crimp the edges together with a fork to seal. Prick the top of the pie twice with a fork. Fry in hot oil in a deep fat fryer at 350 degrees until golden brown. If you wish to fry them at another time, these pies freeze very well. Place pies in a zip lock freezer bag and freeze until ready to use. When frying frozen meat pies, do not thaw before frying. You may also bake these pies in a 375 degree oven until golden brown. Serve hot or at room temperature. Nice served as an evening meal, as snacks, or taken on a picnic.

Variation: Small meat pies served as Hors d'Oeuvres may be made the same way, using a biscuit cutter and 1 teaspoon of filling. Proceed as above.

Pepper Steak

¼ cup cornstarch, divided
½ teaspoon ground ginger
1 cup beef consommé
¼ cup dry sherry (optional)
2 tablespoons Worcestershire sauce
1½ teaspoon crushed dried red pepper flakes
½ teaspoon garlic powder
2 pounds flank, round, boneless top sirloin, or skirt steak, cut into thin strips
2 tablespoon cornstarch
½ teaspoon salt
½ teaspoon black pepper
¼ cup oil
1 medium onion, chopped
2 large, sweet peppers, cut into strips

Whisk together the first seven ingredients in a bowl and set aside. Dredge the meat in remaining 2 tablespoon cornstarch, salt and pepper. In a large, heavy skillet over high heat, add oil to skillet and heat until very hot. Add meat and sear on all sides, browning very well. Remove meat to a plate. Reduce heat and add sweet pepper and onion to the pan and sauté for about 5 minutes, or until tender. Return meat to pan, stir in broth mixture, reduce heat to low and simmer for about 10 minutes. Taste to adjust seasoning. If mixture is too thin, add about 2 tablespoons cornstarch to water and add to sauce. Cook, stirring, until mixture is bubbly. Spoon pepper steak over hot cooked rice, mashed potatoes, noodles, or packaged rice pilaf mix, cooked as directed on package.

Pork Chops and Brown Gravy

6-8 Pork chops
Salt and black pepper
¼ cup oil
¼ cup flour
½ teaspoon garlic puree
1 tablespoon Worcestershire sauce
1 tablespoon Kitchen Bouquet
Salt and pepper to taste
Dash of cayenne pepper
4 cups boiling water (or 2 cups water, 2 cups beef stock)

Season Pork chops with salt and pepper and fry until brown. Remove to heated platter. Measure oil left in pan and add oil to equal ¼ cup. Add flour and make a roux. When brown add water slowly, stirring as you add the water. Add rest of ingredients, bring to a quick boil, stir well and add chops to gravy. Cover and simmer until fork tender, adding more water if needed. Adjust seasoning and serve with steamed rice or mashed potatoes.

Roasted Pork Tenderloin

½ cup soy sauce
¼ cup vegetable oil
2 tablespoons molasses
1 tablespoon ground ginger
2 teaspoons dry mustard
⅛ teaspoon ground cloves
6 cloves garlic, minced fine
1 (4 to 5 pound) boneless rolled tenderloin or pork loin roast

Combine all ingredients except pork loin in a bowl. Whisk well until completely blended. Trim excess fat from pork. Place pork in a large zip-top plastic bag. Pour mixture over pork, turning well to coat. Refrigerate and marinate for 8 hours or overnight, turning occasionally.

When ready to cook preheat oven to 350 degrees. Remove pork, reserving marinade. Place pork in oiled roasting pan. Bake for about 45 to 60 minutes or until meat thermometer registers 160 degrees, brushing occasionally with marinade.

Shepherd's Pie
For Mary

4 tablespoons unsalted butter
2 pounds ground lamb
1 large onion, chopped
2 cloves garlic, minced
2 carrots, sliced
2 teaspoons fresh or dried thyme leaves
2 teaspoons salt
1 teaspoon black pepper
Dash cayenne pepper
1 bay leaf

3 tablespoons chopped parsley
1 tablespoon tomato paste
2 tablespoons flour
1¼ cups beef stock
1 tablespoon Worcestershire sauce
1 large jar sliced mushrooms, drained
1 cup frozen green peas
4 or 5 cups mashed potatoes, recipe follows

Melt the butter in a heavy Dutch oven and add ground lamb. Cook until it begins to lose its red color. Add the onion, garlic, carrots, thyme, salt, black and red pepper, bay leaf, and parsley. Cook, stirring, for about 5 minutes. Add the tomato paste and cook, stirring, for about a minute or so. Add the flour and cook for another minute, stirring well. Slowly stir in the beef stork and Worcestershire sauce, then the mushrooms and green peas. Bring to a boil, then reduce heat to medium-low, and simmer for about 20 to 25 minutes, until gravy thickens.

Meanwhile preheat oven to 400 degrees and prepare mashed potatoes. Lightly grease a 3 quart casserole with butter. Remove bay leaf and pour meat mixture into the casserole. Spread the mashed potatoes on top and cover evenly to the edge of the casserole. Bake for 10 to 15 minutes, or until potatoes are browned on top. Serve immediately.

Mashed Potatoes:

2 pounds potatoes, peeled and cut into 1 inch pieces. Place in a pot, cover with salted water and bring to a boil. Lower heat and cook until fork tender, about ten minutes. Drain potatoes and transfer to a bowl. Mash the potatoes with a potato masher. Add ¼ cup butter, 1½ teaspoon salt, ½ teaspoon black pepper, and ¾ cup heated half and half cream. A dash of grated nutmeg may be added, if desired. Mix well and spread on top of meat mixture.

Variation: Ground, or diced fine, beef, chicken or turkey can be used in place of ground lamb.

Beef Stroganoff

Cut the meat in thin slices diagonally across the grain. If you freeze the meat for an hour or so, just long enough for it to firm up, it will be easier to slice thin.

4 tablespoons butter and 2 tablespoons oil, divided
2 tablespoons finely chopped shallots (green onions)
2 pounds beef tenderloin, sirloin, or top round, cut into thin strips
½ pounds sliced mushrooms
Salt and pepper
¼ teaspoon Tabasco sauce
⅛ teaspoon ground nutmeg
¼ cup dry white wine
1 tablespoon Worcestershire sauce
1 cup sour cream, room temperature
Chopped parsley
Noodles or mashed potatoes

Sauté the shallots in 2 tablespoons melted butter and 1 tablespoon oil in a heavy skillet about 2 minutes. Transfer shallots to a plate and set aside. Turn heat to medium high and add beef to butter in pan and sauté quickly until evenly browned, about 5 minutes. Remove meat and add to shallots on the plate. Add remaining 2 tablespoons butter and 1 tablespoon oil to the pan. Add mushrooms, stir, cover, and cook for 3 minutes. Season well with salt, pepper, Tabasco sauce, and nutmeg. Stir and then add dry white wine and Worcestershire sauce. Whisk well while adding the sour cream, but do not allow it to boil, or it will curdle. Add the beef and onions to the pan and simmer just long enough to heat through. Garnish with chopped parsley. Serve over buttered noodles or mashed potatoes.

Panéed Veal
(Veal Milanese)

2 pounds veal rounds
Salt and pepper
3 eggs, 2 tablespoons milk, beaten well
Italian style breadcrumbs
Lemon

Cut veal rounds into 4 pieces each. Pound with mallet until thin and tender. Salt and pepper well and then dip into egg and milk mixture. Dip into breadcrumbs, coating thoroughly. Refrigerate in single layer for half hour. In heavy pan heat about 2 inches of oil until very hot. Fry meat until brown on both sides. Drain on paper towels. If you would like it extra crusty, coat first with flour, then egg and breadcrumbs as above. Squeeze a little lemon juice over veal before serving, if desired. Any leftovers make delicious sandwiches on crusty French bread or Kaiser rolls heated in oven until warm and crispy.

Meatballs for Spaghetti Gravy

3 pounds ground beef (preferably chuck)
1 large onion, chopped
½ cup chopped shallots (green onions)
1 sweet pepper, chopped
4 cloves garlic, minced
½ cup chopped parsley
3 teaspoons salt
½ teaspoon black pepper
3 eggs, slightly beaten
1 cup Italian breadcrumbs

Preheat oven to 375 degrees. Mix all ingredients together and roll into 1½ to 2 inch diameter balls. Meatballs may be sautéed in 1 cup olive oil in a heavy skillet or placed on baking sheet covered with aluminum foil which has been sprayed with cooking spray and baked for 15 to 20 minutes or until meatballs are brown. Remove meatballs and set aside to be used in spaghetti gravy. Recipe may be doubled and extra meatballs frozen in plastic bag to be used another time.

For a meal in a hurry, amount of meatballs needed for a meal may be removed from freezer and defrosted in microwave. Add purchased bottled tomato gravy, heat, and use over cooked spaghetti with grated Italian cheese.

Veal Scaloppine with Wine
(Scaloppine di vitello al Vino)

4 (5 ounce) thinly sliced veal cutlets (Scaloppine)
3 tablespoons olive or vegetable oil
All-purpose flour, for dredging, spread on a plate or waxed paper
8 sage leaves (optional)
½ teaspoon kosher salt
Freshly ground black pepper (about 4 or 5 twists of the mill)
½ cup dry Marsala or dry white wine
¼ cup chicken broth
2 tablespoons butter
Lemon wedges for serving

Gently flatten the cutlets between sheets of plastic wrap with a meat mallet until the pieces are about ¼ inch thick. Heat the oil over medium high heat in a heavy skillet. Dip the veal cutlets in flour, coating them on both sides and shake off any excess. When the oil is hot slip the cutlets and sage leaves (if using sage) into the pan and quickly brown the cutlets on both sides, which should take only about a minute for each side if the oil is hot enough Transfer the browned cutlets to a warm platter and season with salt and pepper. Tip the pan to draw off most of the fat with a spoon. Turn heat to high, add the wine and chicken broth and boil briskly for a minute or so, scraping and loosening any residue from the cutlets stuck to the pan. Add the butter and any juices that may have been thrown off by the cutlets in the platter. Season with salt and pepper. When the sauce thickens turn the heat to low and add the cutlets back to the pan, turning them and basting them with the sauce once or twice. Transfer the meat and sauce to a warm platter, garnish with sage leaves and lemon wedges, and serve immediately. Serve with buttered noodles.

Vegetables

Microwaved Artichokes	197
Momma's Mayonnaise Pepper Sauce	197
Lemon Herb Butter	197
Brussels Sprouts with Parmesan Cheese	198
Microwaved Cabbage	198
Southern Collard Greens	199
Sunny Carrots	200
French Fried Eggplant	200
Spirited Mushrooms	201
Brabant Potatoes	201
Corn Maque Choux	202
Potato Skin Nachos	203
Cottage Fried Potatoes	204
Microwaved Herbed New Potatoes	204
New Potatoes with Sea Salt and Vinegar	205
Oven Fried French Fries	205
Parmesan Potatoes	206
Potato Mounds (Alsatian Flutters)	207
Turnip Mashed Potatoes	207
Twice Baked Potatoes	208
Momma's Stuffed Sweet Peppers	209
Cherry and Herbed Tomatoes Sauté	210
Tomates Grillées à la Grecque (Broiled Tomatoes with Greek Feta Cheese)	211
Stewed Tomatoes	211
Mixed Roasted Vegetables	212
Eggplant Parmigiana	213
Baked Louisiana Yams	214
Yams, Sweet Potato Pone	215
Golden Louisiana Yam Fries	215
Candied Holiday Yams	216
Sweet Potato Sticks	216
Candied Holiday Yams with Bourbon	217
Praline Yams	218
Yams Hannah	219

Microwaved Artichokes

4 medium artichokes
½ cup water

Wash artichokes by plunging up and down in a large pot or bowl of cold water. Drain upside down in colander. Cut off stem ends and place in a round or oval microwave safe dish. Cover and microwave on high for 10 to 15 minutes or until lower leaves pull out easily, rearranging dish every 5 minutes. Drain, allow to cool and then refrigerate until ready to use. Serve with Mayonnaise pepper sauce or lemon herb butter.

Momma's Mayonnaise Pepper Sauce

2 tablespoons mayonnaise
1 tablespoon vinegar or lemon juice (or more to taste)
Salt, pepper, and cayenne pepper to taste

Combine ingredients and mix well. Good with artichokes or boiled crabs. Recipe easily doubled or tripled.

Lemon Herb Butter

½ cup butter or margarine
3 tablespoons lemon juice
1 teaspoon dried thyme leaves
Dash or Worcestershire sauce (optional)
Salt to taste

Combine all ingredients in a 2 cup Pyrex measure. Microwave uncovered on high for 1 minute or until melted. Stir well to blend.

Brussels Sprouts with Parmesan Cheese

1 quart Brussels sprouts
⅓ cup olive oil
Salt and ground pepper
Lemon juice
Parmesan cheese

If you are using fresh Brussels sprouts trim ends and soak in salted water for 15 minutes. Add to boiling salted water and cook for about 10 minutes or until tender. Drain and toss with a little lemon juice, a sprinkling of salt, freshly ground pepper, olive oil, and Parmesan cheese. If you are using frozen Brussels sprouts, follow package directions for cooking, and then add seasonings as above.

Microwaved Cabbage

½ medium cabbage
½ cup water
Butter
Salt and pepper

Cut cabbage into 4 wedges and core. Place cabbage wedges in a large pot or bowl of cold salted water for about 10 minutes to clean. Drain and place cabbage in round or oval microwave safe dish. Add ½ cup water, cover and microwave on high for 11 to 13 minutes or until tender. Remove from microwave and drain. Chop cabbage into chunks and add butter, salt, and pepper to taste. Recipe easily doubled.

Southern Collard Greens

Collard greens, like any other greens, should be washed thoroughly in several changes of cold water to remove sand and earth. Remove the tough stems by holding the leaf in your left hand and stripping the leaf down with your right hand. Cut up the large leaves into pieces or shred, or stack the leaves on top of each other, roll up, and slice into about ½ inch slices. The long cooking is essential for the unique flavor of collard greens.

1 quart water
2 teaspoons salt
¼ teaspoon black pepper
1 teaspoon garlic powder
1 ham hock, 1 pound pickled pork or ½ pound lean ham pieces
1 tablespoon seasoned salt *
1 large bunch collard greens, washed and prepared for cooking (chopped or sliced)
½ teaspoon hot pepper flakes or 1 tablespoon Louisiana hot sauce
¼ cup butter or margarine (4 tablespoons)

Add water, salt, seasoned salt, pepper, garlic powder and ham hock or seasoning meat of your choice to a large pot and bring to a boil. Lower heat to a simmer and cook, covered, for about 45 minutes. Add the pepper flakes and washed and prepared collard greens to the pot. Stir and simmer, covered tightly, and cook slowly, adding a little hot water if needed to keep them moist, for about an hour, or until tender. Stir occasionally and check for tenderness. When tender add the butter or margarine and cook an additional 45 minutes. Check the seasoning and add a little more salt and pepper if needed. If using a ham hock, remove the meat from the bone and add to the greens. Chop the greens smaller before serving, if desired. Adjust seasoning and serve. The juice left in the pot is called "pot likker." This very nutritious broth is delicious and should be sopped up or eaten with corn bread or crispy French bread.

*Seasoned Salt, see page 341.

Sunny Carrots

8 carrots, sliced on a bias about ½ inch thick (or frozen sliced can be used)
1 tablespoon brown sugar
1 teaspoon cornstarch
¼ teaspoon ginger
¼ teaspoon salt
⅛ teaspoon white pepper
¼ cup orange juice
2 tablespoons butter
Parsley

Cook carrots in boiling salted water 10 to 15 minutes. (If using frozen carrots, cook according to package directions). In a saucepan mix sugar, cornstarch, ginger, salt, pepper and orange juice. Heat, stirring until mixture thickens and comes to a boil. Boil about one minute and then remove from heat and stir in butter. Pour over carrots and mix well. Sprinkle top with chopped parsley before serving.

French Fried Eggplant

1 large eggplant, peeled and cut into circles or size of large French fries
Salted water
2 eggs
1 cup milk
1 teaspoon salt
½ teaspoon pepper
Flour
Hot oil

Soak eggplant slices in salted water for about 30 minutes. Remove and pat dry. Make a batter of eggs, milk, salt, and pepper. Dip eggplant into batter and then into flour, coating well on all sides. Fry in hot oil until golden brown. Drain on paper towels.

Vegetables

Spirited Mushrooms

3 pounds fresh mushrooms, sliced
8 tablespoons (1 stick) butter
Seasoned salt *
⅛ teaspoon garlic powder
¼ cup Worcestershire sauce
½ cup Brandy or Bourbon

Sauté the sliced mushrooms in the butter until brown. Sprinkle well with seasoned salt and garlic powder. Add Worcestershire sauce and simmer until sauce is almost completely absorbed by the mushrooms. Add the Brandy and continue to simmer, stirring, until mushrooms are tender. Delicious served with grilled steak or baked chicken.

*Seasoned Salt, see page 341.

Brabant Potatoes
A New Orleans Favorite

6 steamed or boiled medium potatoes, diced into ¾ inch pieces
4 tablespoons olive or vegetables oil
3 tablespoons butter
Salt and pepper to taste
2 tablespoons minced fresh parsley
1 tablespoon lemon juice

Fry potatoes in oil for a few minutes until lightly browned. Remove from oil and, in another pan, finish browning in butter. Add salt, pepper, parsley, and lemon juice. Serve immediately. Recipe easily doubled.

Corn Maque Choux

Maque Choux (pronounced mock shoo) is a Native American word for smothered corn and tomatoes. It is a popular Cajun dish, probably first learned from the Indians by the early French settlers.

2 tablespoons bacon drippings or oil and 2 tablespoons butter
6 shallots (green onions) with tops, chopped
1 cloves garlic, minced
½ sweet pepper, chopped
About 8 ears fresh corn or 2 (16 oz) cans whole corn, drained, or
4 cups frozen corn kernels, defrosted
1 (10 oz) can Rotel tomatoes with green chilies, chopped and drained
1 teaspoon salt (or to taste)
¼ teaspoon black pepper
1 teaspoon fresh or dried thyme leaves
¼ teaspoon cayenne pepper (if using Hot Rotel tomatoes, omit cayenne)
½ cup half and half cream or heavy cream
½ cup chicken stock or water (or more if needed)
1 tablespoon chopped parsley
2 pounds cooked shrimp, crab meat or crawfish (optional)

If you are using fresh corn, cut and scrape from cob and set aside. Sauté shallots, garlic and sweet pepper in oil and butter until tender, about 3 minutes. Add corn, tomatoes, salt, black pepper, thyme, cream, and water or chicken stock. Stir well, cover and simmer for about one hour on low heat, stirring occasionally. Uncover during the last 5 minutes to allow mixture to thicken slightly. During the last 15 minutes of cooking add parsley and stir well. If you are using seafood, add along with parsley. Adjust seasonings and serve. Freezes well. Recipe easily doubled.

Variation: ½ pound Tasso may also be used in place of shrimp. If using Tasso, dice and sauté with the onions, garlic, and sweet pepper. Proceed as above.

Vegetables

Potato Skin Nachos

4 large baking potatoes, scrubbed
¼ teaspoon each chili powder and salt
1 jar (8 oz.) taco sauce
1½ cup shredded Monterey Jack or cheddar cheese
2 canned jalapeño peppers, seeded and finely chopped
(wash your hands well after handling the peppers)
1 clove garlic, minced
2 tablespoons minced fresh parsley

Preheat oven to 400 degrees. Bake the potatoes for 1 hour. Remove potatoes, leaving the oven on, and let potatoes cool until easy to handle. Halve the potatoes lengthwise and scoop out the pulp, leaving the shells ⅛ in thick. Halve each potato shell lengthwise, and then halve each piece crosswise. Arrange the potato skins, flesh side up, on an ungreased baking sheet. Sprinkle with the chili powder and salt. Bake uncovered, for 10 minutes, or until heated through.

Meanwhile, combine the taco sauce, cheese, peppers, garlic and parsley in a small bowl. Spoon the mixture over the hot potato skins. With the oven rack set 4 inches from the heat, broil the potato skins for 1 to 2 minutes or until the cheese melts. Makes 32 nachos.

Save the scooped out potato from these spicy appetizers to make mashed potatoes for another day.

Cottage Fried Potatoes

4 medium to large potatoes
Salt, pepper, paprika
½ teaspoon Tabasco sauce (optional)
⅓ cup bacon dripping or oil

    Steam or parboil potatoes just until tender. When cool, peel and slice into circles. Sprinkle with salt, pepper and paprika. Stir Tabasco sauce into bacon drippings or oil in heavy frying pan and heat. dd potatoes and fry, turning occasionally until potatoes are golden.

    Variation: Add four or five garlic cloves, mashed and chopped to cold oil in pan. Heat oil and sauté garlic until golden. Meanwhile, sprinkle potato slices with salt and red pepper flakes. Remove garlic from pan and fry potato slices until lightly browned, turning to brown both sides. Remove from pan and place on platter covered with paper towels. A little more salt and red pepper flakes may be sprinkled on potato slices if desired.

Microwaved Herbed New Potatoes

2 pounds small new red potatoes
2 tablespoons water
6 tablespoons butter
2 tablespoons finely chopped parsley
1 tablespoon lemon juice
¼ teaspoon paprika
¼ teaspoon garlic powder
Salt and pepper
⅓ cup grated Parmesan cheese

    Peel a circle around each potato. Wash well and place in cold water in refrigerator for ½ hour. Drain and pat dry. Place potatoes in microwave baking dish in single layer. Add water. Cover and microwave at high 8 to 11 minutes, stirring after 4 minutes. Let stand, covered, for 5 minutes and then drain. Place butter in 2 cup measure and microwave until melted. Stir in parsley, lemon juice, paprika and garlic powder. Salt and pepper potatoes well, then pour butter mixture over potatoes, coating thoroughly. Sprinkle Parmesan cheese over potatoes and then cover and microwave on high for 1 minute. Mix well and serve.

Vegetables

New Potatoes with Sea Salt and Vinegar

3 pounds small (1½ inch) boiling potatoes
2½ tablespoons cider or tarragon vinegar
1½ tablespoons extra-virgin olive oil
Sea salt

Scrub potatoes well, Peel a circle around each potato, leaving the rest of the skin on. Place potatoes in a pot and sprinkle a tablespoon or so of salt over potatoes. Fill pot with water to cover potatoes. Water should be about 1 to 2 inches above potatoes. Bring water to a boil and then lower to simmer. Simmer until tender, about 8 to 10 minutes. Check for tenderness by piercing potato with a fork. Do not overcook or they will break apart. (They will continue to cook after draining) After draining potatoes, rinse them with cold water. While potatoes are still warm, toss with vinegar, olive oil, and sea salt. Potatoes are delicious served hot but may be served also at room temperature. Stir well before serving so potatoes are well covered with seasoning. Nice served with Barbequed steak and chicken or fried chicken.

Oven Fried French Fries

3 pounds large baking potatoes, (about 6 potatoes)
Vegetable cooking spray
½ cup grated Parmesan cheese
½ cup Italian seasoned breadcrumbs
3 egg whites, slightly beaten
1½ tables Creole Seasoning (See page 337)

Preheat oven to 450 degrees. Peel and cut potatoes into long French fry strips. Put in a large bowl and fill with water. Refrigerate for about half an hour. Cover a baking pan with Aluminum foil, crumpling edges around pan. Spray with vegetable spray. Combine Parmesan cheese and breadcrumbs; set aside. Combine egg whites with Creole seasoning. Drain potatoes well and brush with egg white mixture. Coat potatoes with cheese mixture. Place the coated potatoes onto the baking pan, spreading them out to a single layer Bake about 45 minutes, or until the fries are crispy. Turn them with a spatula every 8 to 10 minutes so that they brown evenly. Serve immediately.

Parmesan Potatoes
Oven Fried

4 pounds large russet potatoes, cut lengthwise into eights
¼ cup olive oil
4 cloves garlic, minced fine or 1 teaspoon garlic powder
1 teaspoon dried crushed red pepper
¼ cup minced fresh parsley
2 teaspoons dried oregano, crumbled
2 teaspoon dried basil, crumbled
Salt and pepper to taste
Parmesan cheese

    Place oven rack on lowest third of oven and preheat to 350 degrees. Put potatoes in a large bowl. Add oil, garlic, red pepper, parsley, oregano, basil, and salt and pepper to taste. Toss to coat. Spread potatoes in a single layer on a baking pan. Use a second baking pan if necessary. Bake for about 1 hour, until golden brown and tender on inside and crusty on outside, turning once. Sprinkle with Parmesan cheese. Put back in oven to melt cheese. Season to taste with salt and serve immediately.

    Variation: Instead of cutting potatoes lengthwise, they can be cut into 2 inch cubes. Proceed as above.

    Note: You can omit garlic, red pepper, oregano, basil and salt and pepper. Instead, just add 2 tablespoons Creole seasoning*. Toss and proceed as above.

*Creole Seasoning – See page 337.

Potato Mounds
(Alsatian Flutters)

2 pounds potatoes
2 eggs, slightly beaten
2 tablespoons all-purpose flour
1 teaspoon salt
¼ teaspoon white pepper
2 tablespoons minced parsley
¼ teaspoon garlic puree
Melted butter
Paprika

Steam or boil potatoes until soft, peel and add to large bowl. Add eggs, flour, salt, pepper, parsley, and garlic and mash and beat well until creamy. Form into 12 balls and place in buttered, shallow baking pan. Brush with melted butter, sprinkle with paprika, and bake at 375 degrees for about 25 minutes, or until lightly browned. This dish may be prepared earlier in day and refrigerated until ready to bake.

Variation: After brushing potato balls with melted butter, grated Parmesan cheese may be sprinkled over potatoes, then sprinkle with paprika.

Turnip Mashed Potatoes
For Daddy

6 large potatoes, red or white, peeled
4 or 5 small turnips, peeled
½ cup cream, heated
8 tablespoons (1 stick) butter, melted
½ cup sour cream
Salt and pepper to taste

Cover potatoes and turnips with salted cold water and bring to a boil. Boil for 15 minutes or until fork tender. (Or steam unpeeled potatoes and turnips, then peel when cooked). Drain. Place potatoes and turnips in a large bowl and mash until moderately smooth, (Don't over mash them, a few lumps are nice). Add hot cream, butter, and sour cream. Season with salt and pepper, to taste. Mash and whip again until blended. Adjust thickness by adding more cream if desired. Check seasoning and serve immediately.

Twice Baked Potatoes

4 large baking potatoes
¼ pound (1 stick) butter or margarine, softened
¼ to ½ cup milk or half and half cream, or as needed
½ teaspoon salt
¼ teaspoon black pepper
⅛ teaspoon cayenne pepper
½ to 1 teaspoon garlic salt (optional)
2 eggs yolks, beaten
1 cup shredded cheddar cheese
Paprika

Bake potatoes at 400 degrees for one hour or until soft. Allow to cool slightly. Cut potatoes in half, scoop out the pulp and place in a bowl. Add butter and mash well. Add milk or cream, salt, pepper, cayenne pepper, garlic salt and egg yolks. Mix and mash well. Spoon into potato shells. Top with cheese and sprinkle with paprika. Place on baking sheet and bake at 375 degrees for about 20 minutes or until heated through. These potatoes can be prepared ahead of time, covered and refrigerated. Remove from refrigerator while oven preheats. Bake as directed.

Momma's Stuffed Sweet Peppers

4 large, sweet (green) peppers
⅓ cup bacon drippings
⅓ cup chopped shallots (green onions)
1 large onion, chopped
3 cloves garlic, minced
1 sweet pepper, chopped
1 pound raw shrimp, cleaned and chopped
½ pound slice raw ham, chopped fine
1 cup French bread crust, soaked in water and squeezed dry
1 teaspoon salt
¼ teaspoon black pepper
⅛ teaspoon cayenne pepper (or to taste)
⅛ teaspoon dried thyme
2 tablespoon parsley
1 egg, beaten
Italian cheese and butter

Cut off the top fourth of the sweet peppers and remove the seeds and membranes. Place the peppers upright in ½ inch salted water in a pot. Bring water to a boil, cover, lower flame and cook for 6 minutes. Remove peppers, drain and set aside. Lightly brown onions, garlic, chopped sweet pepper, shrimp and ham in bacon drippings. Add bread and seasonings. Mix well and cook a few minutes longer. Remove from heat and add egg, mixing well. Stuff peppers with the mixture. Sprinkle dry breadcrumbs and Italian cheese on top. Put a little butter on each pepper. Bake at 350 degrees in a preheated oven for 25 to 30 minutes, or until tender and golden brown on top. Recipe easily doubled.

Note: Stuffed peppers freeze very well. Place a few in plastic freezer bags. When ready to use, reheat in microwave until warmed through.

Cherry and Herbed Tomatoes Sauté

3 tablespoon olive oil
2 cloves garlic (2 cloves garlic)
1 pint cherry tomatoes, stemmed and washed
2 tablespoons chopped fresh basil
2 tablespoons chopped fresh parsley
2 tablespoons chopped fresh thyme leaves
¼ teaspoon freshly ground black pepper
½ teaspoon red pepper flakes
1 teaspoon kosher or sea salt

Heat the olive oil in a sauté pan large enough to hold all the tomatoes in one layer. Add the garlic to the oil and cook over medium heat for 30 seconds. Add the tomatoes, basil, parsley, thyme sand and pepper. Reduce the heat to low and cook for 5 to 7 minutes, tossing occasionally, until the tomatoes begin to lose their firm round shape. Add the red pepper flakes, and sprinkle with a little fresh chopped basil and parsley. Serve hot or at room temperature. Recipe easily doubled.

Variation: Cherry tomatoes may be roasted in oven. Preheat oven to 400 degrees. Toss tomatoes lightly with olive oil, garlic and a generous sprinkling of red pepper flakes, kosher or sea salt, and black pepper. Spread into one layer on a sheet pan and roast for 15 or 20 minutes, or until tomatoes are soft. Put tomatoes on a serving platter and sprinkle with chopped basil, parsley, and thyme, and additional salt. Serve hot or at room temperature. Nice served as a side dish or as an appetizer.

Tomates Grillées à la Grecque
(Broiled Tomatoes with Greek Feta Cheese)
This recipe is in memory of my Father's Greek Grandmother

4 firm-ripe tomatoes, sliced ½ inch thick
¼ cup extra virgin olive oil
Salt and black pepper
Finely chopped garlic or garlic salt (optional)
2 tablespoons oregano leaves
1 cup crumbled feta cheese

Preheat broiler. Cover a baking sheet with aluminum foil and lightly oil or spray with cooking spray. Place tomato slices on it and brush or drizzle with olive oil. Season with salt, pepper, and garlic if desired. Add oregano and Feta cheese. Place under broiler and broil until tomato slices soften and cheese is slightly browned, about 3 to 4 minutes. Remove to serving plates. Recipe easily doubled.

Variation: After adding olive oil to tomatoes, lightly sprinkle with seasoned breadcrumbs before adding oregano and feta.

Stewed Tomatoes

1 large can (28 ounce) tomatoes, drained, or
2½ cups quartered, peeled fresh tomatoes
1¼ teaspoon sugar
4 teaspoons flour
¼ teaspoon onion powder
1 teaspoon salt
½ teaspoon black pepper
4 tablespoons butter or margarine

Chop tomatoes in large chunky pieces. Mix sugar and flour. Add to tomatoes and rest of ingredients. Simmer for 10 minutes.

Variation: Stir in 1 cup of heavy cream into tomatoes and cook for 5 minutes more. With a slotted spoon transfer tomatoes to a vegetables dish. Cook sauce over high heat until it is reduced by half. Pour over tomatoes. Check seasoning and add salt and pepper, if needed. Sprinkle with ½ cup seasoned croutons before serving if desired.

Mixed Roasted Vegetables

3 to 4 pounds potatoes, Red, small red new, or russet, cut into 2 inch chunks (red potatoes scrubbed and left unpeeled, small new potatoes, cut in halves
About 6 to 8 carrots, scraped and cut into 1½ to 2 inch chunks
1 large, sweet (green) bell pepper, cut into 1 inch chunks
1 large, sweet (red) bell pepper, cut into 1 inch chunks
1 medium eggplant (about 1½ pound) cut into 1½ inch chunks (optional)
1 medium onion, cut into wedges (optional)
2 medium zucchini, cut into 1 inch chunks (optional)
½ pound whole mushrooms
1 tablespoon salt (or to taste)
½ teaspoon black pepper
2 tablespoons dried basil leaves
4 cloves garlic, minced (or heaping teaspoon garlic powder)
1 teaspoon dried oregano
⅓ cup chopped fresh or dried parsley
1 teaspoon Tony Chachere or other creole seasoning (optional)
⅓ cup olive oil
2 tablespoons red wine vinegar
1 medium or large tomato, cut into pieces
Grated parmesan cheese (optional)

Preheat oven to 375 degrees. Place all vegetables except tomato in a large bowl. (Vegetables in recipe can be added or subtracted, according to your taste). Sprinkle salt, pepper, and rest of seasonings over top. Pour on oil and vinegar and toss well, making sure all vegetables are coated. Spread evenly in large baking pan and bake uncovered for 45 minutes, turning once. Add tomato and mix to coat. Bake for about 15 minutes longer or until vegetables are tender and cooked through. Sprinkle with cheese if desired and serve.

Eggplant Parmigiana

2 large eggplants, about 2 pounds
Salt and pepper
¼ cup extra virgin olive oil
2 cups Marinara Sauce or Creole Tomato Sauce, (see pages 105 or 113 respectively for recipes)
1 bunch fresh basil leaves, chiffonade
1 pound fresh mozzarella, sliced ⅛ inch thick
½ cup freshly grated Parmigiano-Reggiano or Romano cheese
¼ cup Italian breadcrumbs

Prepare the tomato sauce and set aside. Preheat oven to 450 degrees. Peel and slice each eggplant into 6 pieces about ½ to 1 inch thick. Lightly season each eggplant slice with salt and pepper and place on an oiled or sprayed baking sheet Bake for about 12 – 15 minutes, or until the top of slices turn dark brown Do not burn. Remove the eggplant from the oven, and the slices from the baking sheet and place them on a plate to cool.

Lower oven temperature to 350 degrees. In a 9 x 11 inch oven safe casserole place the 4 largest eggplant slices evenly spaced apart. Over each slice, spread ¼ cup of the tomato sauce and sprinkle with a teaspoon of basil. Place one slice of mozzarella oven each and sprinkle with 1 teaspoon grated cheese. Place the smaller slices of eggplant over each of the larger slices and repeat with tomato sauce, basil, and the 2 cheeses. Repeat the layering again until all the ingredients are used.

Sprinkle the breadcrumbs over the top of the eggplant dish, and bake uncovered until the cheese is melted and the tops turn light brown, about 20 minutes. Serve immediately.

Baked Louisiana Yams

Yams are used in many ways in Louisiana, but baking remains one of the most popular ways to prepare them. Baking makes the most of the natural sugar found just under the skin because the sugars caramelize and produce a special flavor.

Preheat oven to 400 degrees. Scrub, dry and oil the yams you are to bake. Place on a cookie sheet and bake at 400 degrees for 15 minutes. Lower temperature to 375 degrees and bake an additional one hour or until yams are soft throughout.

Don't wrap yams in aluminum foil when baking. This steams the yam, and it will not be syrupy or have the flavor of uncovered yams. Baking yams in a microwave will cook them, but they won't have the sweet syrupy taste of oven baked yams. Therefore, a microwave oven is not recommended for baking yams.

Bake a large number of yams at one time to save time and energy. Bake yams in oven. They can be reheated in the microwave or conventional oven and will taste freshly baked. After yams are baked, simply cool them, then wrap individually in aluminum foil, place them wrapped in a large plastic zip-loc bag, and freeze them. When ready to use, remove the number you need from the freezer, thaw them in the wrappings, then unwrap them and heat in the microwave or conventional oven until hot.

You can use canned, leftover baked or boiled yams in recipes that call for cooked yams. Three medium fresh yams equals one (one pound) can, which equals two cups cooked mashed yams.

Vegetables

Yams, Sweet Potato Pone

2 cups peeled, grated raw sweet potatoes
½ cup sugar
1 cup whole milk or half and half
2 eggs, well beaten
½ teaspoon salt
1 tablespoon vanilla extract
¼ cup chopped pecans (optional)
¼ teaspoon grated nutmeg
¼ teaspoon powdered cinnamon
¼ teaspoon ground cloves
2 tablespoons melted butter
Grated peel of 1 lemon
Grated peel of ½ orange

Preheat oven to 350 degrees. Combine all ingredients and mix well. Pour into a buttered baking dish and bake for 50 to 60 minutes or until a knife inserted in the center comes out clean.

Golden Louisiana Yam Fries

2 pounds yams, peeled and cut lengthwise into ¼ inch strips
Oil for frying
Kosher salt and pepper

Heat oil in deep fryer to 325 degrees. Cover baking sheets with several layers of paper towels. Place yams in small batches in fryer basket in hot oil and fry for about 1 minute until yams are almost tender but not limp. (Potatoes will be pale orange and will become limp as they cool). Drain and place on paper towels for at least 10 minutes or up to 2 hours. When ready to serve heat oil to 350 degrees. Fry potatoes in batches for about 1 and a half minutes or until golden brown. Lift basket to drain and place potatoes on paper towels. Sprinkle with salt and pepper and serve immediately.

Candied Holiday Yams

½ pound (2 sticks) butter
2 pounds yams, peeled and coarsely chopped
1 ¾ cup water
¼ cup Bourbon (optional)
1 cup sugar
1 cup packed, dark brown sugar
½ teaspoon salt
1 medium size unpeeled orange, washed, sliced, seeded, and end slices discarded
1 unpeeled lemon, washed, sliced, seeded, and end slices discarded
2 sticks cinnamon
1 tablespoon vanilla extract
½ teaspoon ground mace

 Melt butter in a 5 quart Dutch oven over high heat. Add the rest of the ingredients, stir, cover and bring to a boil. Stir, reduce heat to a simmer, cover and cook for 20 minutes. Remove cover and continue to cook until yams are very tender, about 20 minutes, stirring occasionally. Remove from heat, discard cinnamon sticks and serve immediately.

Sweet Potato Sticks

4 or 5 medium sweet potatoes (about 2 pounds)
1½ tablespoon vegetable oil
½ cup grated Parmesan cheese
Pam vegetable cooking spray

 Peel and cut potatoes into French fry strips. Place potatoes in a large bowl. Drizzle oil over them and sprinkle with cheese. Toss well to coat completely. Proceed with directions for oven French fries. *

*Oven Fried French Fries – see page 215 *

Vegetables

Candied Holiday Yams with Bourbon

8 large yams (about 3 to 4 pounds) or 3 large cans (28 ounces each) yams
½ cup (1 stick) unsalted butter
3 large eggs
½ cup brown sugar
1 cup orange juice
½ cup heavy (whipping) cream or melted vanilla ice cream
¼ cup Bourbon
1 teaspoon cinnamon
½ teaspoon nutmeg
½ teaspoon salt
½ cup chopped pecans (optional)

Preheat oven to 400 degrees. Bake yams until cooked, about an hour. Set aside until cool enough to handle. Lower oven to 360 degrees. Peel yams and place in the bowl of a mixer along with the butter. Beat out all the lumps. Add eggs and the rest of the ingredients. Mix until smooth and re-season to taste. Spoon into a buttered casserole and sprinkle top with chopped pecans. Bake for about 20 minutes until puffed and slightly golden.

Variation: Mixture can be baked in orange cups. Simply cut four large oranges in half, cut around each half of oranges and scoop out the pulp, leaving only the shell. Pulp can be squeezed, and juice used in yams. Spoon mixture into orange cups, mounding and smoothing tops. Bake as above.

Yams may be sliced or cubed instead of mashed. Place sliced or cubed potatoes in bottom of casserole, mix rest of ingredients together and pour over yams. Mix well and bake as above.

Praline Yams

8 large Louisiana yams or 3 large cans (28 ounce each) yams
4 tablespoons butter or margarine
1 cup firmly packed brown sugar
1 teaspoon cinnamon
2 teaspoon vanilla
¼ cup light rum
⅔ cup praline liqueur
1 pint melted vanilla ice cream (optional)
Pecans, chopped fine (optional)

If using fresh yams, preheat oven to 400 degrees. Bake yams until cooked, about an hour. Set aside until cool enough to handle. Peel and slice yams about half an inch thick. If using canned yams, cut yams into small pieces. Place yams in a large oven proof casserole and set aside. In an electric fry pan or large fry pan melt butter. Stir in brown sugar over medium heat and stir continually until a light brown caramel sauce forms. When the sugar has completely dissolved in the margarine, add the cinnamon, vanilla, rum, and liqueur, in that order. Keep stirring as you add the ingredients to liquefy the sauce. When the sauce is thick and syrupy, begin stirring in the melted ice cream. Continue to stir until all the ice cream is in the sauce and it is smooth and creamy.

Pour the sauce over the yams in the casserole. Gently turn yams in the sauce until all are well coated. Add chopped pecans and stir gently. Bake at 350 degrees until hot and bubbly. May be made ahead of time so yams may marinate in sauce. Just reheat in microwave when ready to serve.

If you would prefer making this recipe more of a side dish than a dessert, just leave out the melted ice cream. You may thin it out just a little with a little milk or heavy cream, being careful not to dilute it too much. The sauce should be thick enough to cling to the yams. It is delicious either way, with or without the ice cream. But on special occasions, like Thanksgiving or Christmas, we serve it with the ice cream, and as a side dish!

Yams Hannah

4 tablespoons butter, melted
2 pounds Louisiana yams or sweet potatoes, peeled and cut into rounds
⅓ cup parmesan cheese
¼ teaspoon cumin
¼ teaspoon red pepper flakes
Salt and pepper

Preheat oven to 375 degrees. Use about 1 tablespoon of butter to brush on bottom of baking pan. Toss yam rounds in remaining melted butter in a bowl. Combine cheese, cumin and pepper flakes. Layer potato slices. Sprinkle with ¼ of cheese mixture. Sprinkle with salt and pepper. Repeat layering, top with cheese mixture and salt and pepper. Cover pan with foil and bake for 45 minutes. Uncover pan and bake for 15 to 20 minutes more.

Casseroles

Artichoke Casserole 223
Artichoke, Cheese, and Spinach Casserole 223
Herbed Broccoli Casserole 224
Cauliflower au Gratin 224
Chou Glorioux (Glorified Cabbage) 225
Chicken, Rice, and Water Chestnut Casserole 226
Chili and Macaroni Casserole 227
Pineapple and Cheese Casserole 227
Corn Casserole 228
Crab, Artichoke and Avocado Casserole 228
Oyster and Artichoke Casserole 229
Momma's Stuffed Eggplant Casserole 230
Hominy and Corn Casserole 231
Creole Potato Casserole 231
Rosie's Yam Casserole 232
Potatoes au Gratin 233
Rice Sabrosa Casserole 234
Turnips au Gratin 234
Lagniappe Casserole 235

Artichoke Casserole

This recipe was given to me by my Sister-in-law Barbara Duffy Miscenich, and has become such a family favorite that it is now included in all our holiday meals.

2 cans artichoke hearts, drained and chopped well
1 cup grated parmesan cheese
1 cup Progresso seasoned breadcrumbs
1 teaspoon garlic puree or powder
½ cup olive oil
1 cup water

In a bowl mix Parmesan cheese and breadcrumbs. Add artichoke hearts and rest of ingredients. Mix well and pour into a greased casserole. Sprinkle top with breadcrumbs and paprika and dot with butter. Bake covered at 350 degrees for 30 minutes. Bake uncovered an additional 30 minutes.

Artichoke, Cheese, and Spinach Casserole

4 (10 oz.) packages frozen chopped spinach
½ cup butter or margarine, melted
2 (8 oz.) packages Philadelphia cream cheese, softened
1 can artichoke hearts, drained and chopped fine
1 (8 oz.) can sliced water chestnuts, drained (optional)
1½ teaspoon onion powder
¼ teaspoon garlic powder
¼ teaspoon fresh ground black pepper
Salt to taste
½ cup grated parmesan cheese

Cook spinach according to package directions and drain. In a larger bowl mix together all ingredients except parmesan cheese. Pour mixture into one 9 by 13 inch greased baking dish or two smaller greased baking dishes, reserving one small dish to be frozen for later use. Sprinkle top of dish or dishes with parmesan cheese. Bake in preheated 350 degree oven for 40 minutes.

Herbed Broccoli Casserole

1 (10 ounce) package frozen broccoli florets, cooked and drained
1 cup cooked rice
1 cup shredded sharp cheddar cheese
2 eggs, slightly beaten
2 tablespoons butter or margarine
½ cup milk
1 teaspoon onion powder
1 teaspoon salt
¼ teaspoon black pepper
1½ teaspoon dried thyme flakes
1 teaspoon Worcestershire sauce

    Preheat oven to 350 degrees. Combine all ingredients together and mix well. Put broccoli mixture in a buttered casserole. Bake for 25 minutes. Recipe easily doubled.

Cauliflower au Gratin
*Momma's recipe that has been used
on our Holiday table for as long as I can remember*

2 fresh cauliflower or 3 packs frozen
2 tablespoons butter
2 tablespoons flour
2 cups hot milk or preferably half and half cream
2 cups shredded cheddar cheese
1 teaspoon salt
¼ teaspoon white pepper
¼ teaspoon dried mustard
¼ teaspoon dried thyme
⅛ to ¼ teaspoon cayenne pepper (according to taste)
Paprika and seasoned breadcrumbs for topping

    Preheat oven to 375 degrees. Cook cauliflower and place in oven proof casserole. In double boiler make white roux with butter and flour. Slowly add hot milk, continuing to stir. Add seasonings and cheese, stirring as sauce thickens. Pour over cauliflower and top with seasoned breadcrumbs. Sprinkle with paprika and dot with butter. Bake uncovered for 30 minutes.

Casseroles

Chou Glorioux (Glorified Cabbage)
Cabbage Casserole

1 large head cabbage, cut into fourths, core removed
3 tablespoons vegetable oil
2 onions, chopped fine
1 sweet pepper, chopped
3 ribs celery, chopped
4 slices white bread, toasted, trimmed, moistened with 2 or 3 tablespoons milk
1 cup heavy cream
8 tablespoons (1 stick) butter, room temperature
1 tablespoon minced parsley, or 1 tablespoon dried parsley flakes
3 cloves garlic
Salt and black pepper and cayenne pepper to taste
2 cups shredded cheddar cheese
¾ cups Italian seasoned breadcrumbs
Paprika

Cut the cabbage into 4 wedges and core. Place wedges in a pot or bowl of salted cold water to clean for about 10 minutes. Remove cabbage and drain. Parboil or microwave* cabbage until tender. Drain and finely chop. Heat the oil in a large saucepan or Dutch oven over medium heat. Sauté the onions, sweet pepper, and celery until soft and golden, about 5 to 6 minutes. Add the cabbage, stir well, turn the heat to low, and cook until soft, about 10 minutes, stirring once or twice. Squeeze the milk out of the bread and break into small pieces. Add bread, along with the cream and butter, and stir well until butter is melted. Add the parsley and garlic. Season with salt, pepper, and cayenne and mix well. Pour the mixture into a large oven-proof casserole. Combine the cheese and breadcrumbs and sprinkle evenly over the top. Sprinkle top lightly with paprika Bake in a preheated 350 degree oven for about 30 minutes.

*For Microwaved Cabbage – see page 198.

Chicken, Rice, and Water Chestnut Casserole

2 tablespoons oil
2 tablespoons butter
1 onion, chopped
3 cloves garlic, minced
1 sweet pepper, chopped
2 ribs celery, chopped
2 tablespoons chopped parsley
1 teaspoon salt
½ teaspoon black pepper
½ teaspoon dried thyme flakes
½ teaspoon basil
¼ teaspoon cayenne pepper
1 tablespoon Worcestershire sauce
2 cups chicken broth
1 cup nonfat sour cream or plain yogurt
3 cups diced cooked chicken, turkey, or pork
3 cups cooked rice
8 ounce can sliced water chestnuts, drained
4 ounce jar pimento, drained

Preheat oven to 350 degrees. In a large heavy pot or Dutch oven sauté onions, garlic, sweet pepper, and celery until limp. Add parsley, seasonings and chicken broth, stirring well. Bring just to a boil, lower heat and simmer for 3 minutes. Spoon in sour cream or yogurt. Add chicken, rice, water chestnuts and pimento, mixing well. Pour mixture into large oblong casserole, sprinkle top with paprika and bake for 30 minutes.

Chili and Macaroni Casserole

1 pound lean ground beef or pork, or ½ pound of each
1 medium onion, chopped
½ sweet pepper, chopped
2 cloves garlic, minced
1½ teaspoon salt (or to taste)
¼ teaspoon black pepper
1 tablespoon chili powder
1 tablespoon chopped parsley
1 teaspoon cumin (optional)
1 (15 ounce) can Italian tomatoes, undrained and chopped
1 (16 ounce) can whole corn, drained
1 (16 ounce) can red kidney beans, drained and rinsed (optional)
2 cups cooked elbow macaroni (about 1 cup raw macaroni)
1 cup shredded sharp cheddar cheese

Preheat oven to 350 degrees. Brown ground beef or pork in a Dutch oven over medium heat, stirring well to break up meat. Add onion, sweet pepper, and garlic. Continue to cook, stirring occasionally, until vegetables are tender. Drain fat and return mixture to pot. Add salt, pepper, chili powder, cumin, and parsley and stir well. Add tomatoes, corn, beans, if using, and macaroni. Stir well and cook until well blended and warmed through, continuing to stir, for about 10 minutes. Pour into greased 2 quart casserole dish. Sprinkle top with cheese. Bake until cheese melts, about 15 minutes.

Pineapple and Cheese Casserole

2 (20 oz) cans crushed or pineapple chunks, drained, reserving 6 tablespoons juice
2 cups grated sharp cheddar cheese
6 tablespoons all-purpose flour (preferably Pillsbury Shake and Blend flour)
1 cup sugar
1 cup Ritz cracker crumbs
1 stick (8 tablespoons) butter, melted, plus extra butter for greasing casserole

Preheat oven to 350 degrees. Grease casserole dish with butter and set aside. Combine pineapple and cheese. Mix flour and sugar and stir into pineapple mixture. Put in casserole dish and cover with cracker crumbs mixed with melted butter and reserved pineapple juice. Bake until golden brown, about 25 to 30 minutes.

Corn Casserole

3 cups fresh yellow corn, cut from the cob, or 3 cups frozen corn, defrosted
1 tablespoon flour
½ stick butter or margarine, melted
2 tablespoon brown sugar
1 teaspoon garlic salt
1 tablespoon chopped parsley
1 cup milk
2 eggs, beaten
1 small jar (2 ounces) pimentos, chopped

Preheat oven to 350 degrees. Put the corn into a bowl. Add the flour and mix well. Pour butter over mixture and mix. Add next 6 ingredients and stir until all is well mixed. Pour into a greased baking dish and bake for 1 hour. Recipe easily doubled.

Crab, Artichoke and Avocado Casserole

2 cans cream of mushroom soup
4 tablespoons butter
1 cup half and half milk
1 pound crab meat
1 can artichoke hearts, chopped
½ teaspoon salt (or to taste)
¼ teaspoon white pepper
2 avocados
2 teaspoons Italian seasoned breadcrumbs

Preheat oven to 350 degrees. Add soup to melted butter in a large skillet. Stir and simmer until blended. Add milk, crab meat, chopped artichokes, salt, and pepper and simmer 5 minutes, stirring gently. Peel and slice avocado in an oven proof casserole. Pour crab and soup mixture over avocado. Top with breadcrumbs and dot with butter. Bake until brown, about 15 minutes.

Oyster and Artichoke Casserole

8 tablespoons (1 stick) unsalted butter
2 cups finely chopped shallots (green onions)
1 large clove garlic, minced fine
½ cup finely chopped celery
1 (10 ounce) can cream of mushroom soup
1 tablespoon Worcestershire sauce
1 teaspoon salt
½ teaspoon black pepper
Dash cayenne pepper
½ teaspoon thyme
2 tablespoons finely chopped parsley
1 teaspoon lemon zest
5 dozen oysters, drained and cut in half if they are large
2 cans artichoke hearts, drained and chopped
½ cup Italian breadcrumbs
Parmesan cheese
6 thin lemon slices

Preheat oven to 350 degrees. In a heavy (preferably iron) skillet or pot melt butter. Sauté onions, garlic and celery until soft. Reduce heat; add soup, Worcestershire sauce, salt, pepper, cayenne, thyme, parsley, and lemon zest. Simmer 10 minutes. Add oysters and artichokes and simmer an additional 10 minutes. Pour mixture into a buttered 2 quart casserole. Sprinkle top with breadcrumbs and Parmesan cheese. Arrange lemon slices on top. Place in oven and bake for 30 minutes.

Momma's Stuffed Eggplant Casserole
For my brother Weldon and my sister-in-law Barbara

2 large eggplants, (about 4 pounds) peeled and diced
Water to cover eggplant plus 1 tablespoon salt
8 strips bacon
1 large onion, chopped
2 ribs celery, chopped
1 medium sweet (green) pepper, chopped
½ cup shallots (green onions) chopped
4-5 cloves garlic, minced
½ cup chopped parsley
½ pound slice raw ham, pancetta, or tasso chopped
French bread crust to equal 2 cups after it has been moistened with water and squeezed dry
1 pound raw shrimp or crawfish, peeled and chopped
1 pound crab meat
1 tablespoon Worcestershire sauce
¼ cup grated Parmesan cheese
2 teaspoons salt
½ teaspoon black pepper
¼ teaspoon cayenne pepper (or to taste)
½ teaspoon dried thyme leaves
2 eggs, slightly beaten
¼ cup Italian seasoned breadcrumbs
¼ cup grated Parmesan cheese
2 tablespoons butter

Place diced eggplant in enough water to cover in a large stockpot and bring to a boil. Boil until tender, about 10-12 minutes. Drain and set aside. Chop bacon in very small pieces, place in a large Dutch oven and fry. When crisp, remove from oil and set aside. Add onions, celery, and sweet pepper to pot and sauté until tender. Add shallots, garlic, parsley, and ham and cook for about 5 minutes. Add eggplant, bacon, bread, shrimp or crawfish, crab meat, Worcestershire sauce, parmesan cheese, and seasonings. Mix well and continue to cook over low fire until shrimp or crawfish are cooked, about 10 minutes. Add just a little water if the mixture seems dry. Stir well and remove from heat and add eggs, stirring well. Pour into large oven proof casserole. Sprinkle breadcrumbs and Parmesan cheese on top. Dot with butter. Bake in 350 degree oven for 30 minutes. Serve immediately with a crisp green salad and French bread and butter.

Hominy and Corn Casserole

2 cups canned yellow or white hominy, drained
2 cups fresh or frozen and thawed corn kernels
1 small jar chopped pimento, drained
1 teaspoon garlic puree
1 cup shredded sharp cheddar cheese
2 cups milk
4 eggs, beaten
1 teaspoon salt
¼ teaspoon cayenne pepper

Preheat oven to 350 degrees. Mix together the hominy, corn, pimento, garlic, and cheddar cheese. Pour into a lightly buttered baking casserole. In a separate bowl whisk together the milk, eggs, salt, and cayenne pepper. Pour this mixture over the hominy and corn mixture in the casserole. Bake for 50 to 60 minutes, or until the casserole is set. Remove from oven and let it rest for 5 to 10 minutes before serving.

Creole Potato Casserole

3 cups leftover mashed potatoes
3 tablespoons butter, softened
2 cups small curd cottage cheese
½ cup grated Parmesan cheese
½ cup sour cream
2 eggs, beaten
2 teaspoons salt
¼ cayenne pepper (or to taste)
½ teaspoon garlic powder (optional)
⅛ teaspoon white pepper
Paprika and chopped parsley

Blend together the potatoes and butter. Add cottage cheese, Parmesan cheese, sour cream, eggs, salt, cayenne, garlic powder, and white pepper and beat well. Butter a 2 quart baking dish and fill with mixture. Sprinkle top with parsley and paprika, then bake for 50 minutes in a preheated 425 degree oven.

Rosie's Yam Casserole

*This recipe was given to me by
My Sister-in-law, Barbara Duffy Miscenich*

2 cups mashed yams (1 29 oz. can)
1 cup granulated sugar
2 eggs, beaten
1 teaspoon vanilla
1 cup milk
1 cup flaked coconut
1 stick margarine, melted

Mix all together and pour into 9" x 13" casserole which has been sprayed with Pam.

Topping:

1 stick margarine, melted
1 cup granulated sugar
1 cup self-rising flour
1 cup chopped pecans

Cream butter and sugar together and then add flour and mix well. It will be coarse. Add pecans and sprinkle over yam mixture. Bake at 350 degrees for 45-50 minutes.

Potatoes au Gratin

6 cups peeled and thinly sliced raw potatoes (about 2½ pounds)
2 tablespoons butter
2 tablespoons flour
2½ cups scalded milk or half and half cream
1 teaspoon salt
¼ teaspoon white pepper
¼ teaspoon cayenne pepper
¼ teaspoon paprika
¼ teaspoon garlic salt (optional)
1 tablespoon parsley flakes
1 teaspoon Worcestershire sauce
2 cups shredded cheddar cheese
Italian breadcrumbs
Paprika

Preheat oven to 375 degrees. In a large oval or rectangular oven proof casserole (about 9" by 11") lay potato slices in layers. In double boiler add flour to melted butter. Stir in hot milk. Add salt, white pepper, red pepper, paprika, garlic salt, parsley, and Worcestershire sauce, stirring constantly. Add cheese and stir until melted and slightly thickened. Pour over potatoes, lifting potatoes lightly with a fork so sauce is distributed evenly. Sprinkle liberally with Italian breadcrumbs and paprika. Dot with butter. Put in oven and bake for 45 minutes or until potatoes are tender.

Rice Sabrosa Casserole
For my Grandson Matt

1 pound lean ground beef, pork or turkey
1 large, chopped onion
1 large, chopped sweet pepper
2 teaspoons garlic puree or 2 garlic cloves, minced
1 tablespoon chili powder
2 teaspoons salt
¼ teaspoon black pepper
2 cups (16 oz.) canned tomatoes, chopped
3 cups cooked rice
1 cup grated cheddar cheese

In a large skillet, sauté beef, onion, and sweet pepper with seasonings until meat is lightly browned and vegetables are tender, stirring frequently to crumble meat. Add tomatoes and rice, mixing well. Pour into oven proof casserole. Top with cheese and put into preheated 350 degree oven until cheese melts. Recipe easily doubled.

Turnips au Gratin

2 pounds turnips
4 tablespoons butter
4 shallots, (green onions) chopped fine
½ of a large, sweet pepper, chopped
1 clove garlic, minced
¼ cup celery
4 tablespoons flour
2 or more cups milk
1 cup grated cheddar cheese
1 tablespoon chopped parsley
1 teaspoon salt (or more to taste)
¼ teaspoon black pepper
Italian breadcrumbs and paprika

Peel, slice, and boil turnips until tender. Melt butter and sauté vegetables until soft. Blend in flour and add milk to the desired consistency. Add cheese and seasonings. Cook on low heat until cheese melts and sauce thickens slightly. Put turnips into buttered casserole and cover with sauce. Sprinkle with Italian breadcrumbs and paprika. Dot with butter. Bake at 350 degrees for 20 minutes.

Lagniappe Casserole
Lagniappe is a Creole/Cajun word meaning "A little something extra"

This casserole can be made with almost anything. Prepare with 1 large can tuna or salmon, or a combination of 1 small can of each, 8 hot dogs, sliced or 2 cups diced cooked chicken, turkey or ham.

Choice of the above
4 cups elbow macaroni
1 can cheddar cheese soup
1 can celery or mushroom soup
1 teaspoon Worcestershire sauce
2½ cans milk (3 cups)
1 teaspoon salt
¼ teaspoon black pepper
¼ teaspoon dry mustard
1 teaspoon paprika
¼ teaspoon dried thyme
Dash of cayenne pepper
1 tablespoon parsley
1 small, sweet pepper, chopped
1 small jar stuffed olives, halved (optional)
Progresso seasoned breadcrumbs

Preheat oven to 350 degrees. Boil macaroni in salted water. Meanwhile in a saucepan heat soups, add Worcestershire sauce, milk, and seasonings. Bring to simmer, add sweet pepper and your choice of tuna, etc. and olives. Mix well. Put drained macaroni in large oblong or rectangular oven proof casserole. Pour sauce over macaroni, mixing well. Sprinkle breadcrumbs liberally over top. Sprinkle with paprika and dot with butter. Bake at 350 degrees for 30 minutes.

Pasta

Avocado Pesto with Pasta 239
Chicken and Artichoke Pasta 239
Spaghetti Bordelaise 240
Cauliflower Macaroni 241
Lemon and Artichoke Linguine 242
Macaroni and Artichokes 242
Spaghetti and Creole Meat Gravy 243
Pasta Primavera 244

Avocado Pesto with Pasta

¼ cup pine nuts
2 or 3 plum tomatoes, diced
Avocado Pesto (for recipe see page 25)
½ pound pasta, preferable wheels, shells, or elbow macaroni
1 large avocado, pitted, peeled, and diced

    Preheat oven to 350 degrees and toast pine nuts on a pie plate for about 3 minutes or until lightly browned. Set aside to cool. Cook pasta according to package directions, drain and transfer to serving dish. Add pesto to pasta, folding gently until well blended. If mixture seems too thick, add about a tablespoon of hot water. Add extra salt and pepper if needed and toss well. Add pine nuts, tomatoes and diced avocado and toss again. Serve immediately. Recipe easily doubled.

Chicken and Artichoke Pasta

2 tablespoon olive oil
2 tablespoon butter or margarine
3 cloves garlic, minced
1 small onion, chopped
1 sweet pepper, diced (use half green and half red for color)
1 pound boneless chicken breasts, cubed
1 can artichoke hearts, drained and quartered
Juice of 1 lemon
1 tablespoon basil
1 tablespoon thyme
1 tablespoon parsley
Salt and pepper to taste
¼ teaspoon Tabasco sauce
1 8-oz. container fat-free sour cream
1 pound corkscrew tricolor pasta or pasta of your choice
Italian cheese

    Sauté onions, garlic, and sweet pepper in oil and butter until soft. Add chicken breasts and sauté until meat is opaque. Add artichoke hearts, lemon juice, basil, thyme, parsley, salt, pepper, and Tabasco sauce. Lower heat and stirring gently, cook until warm, about 3 or 4 minutes. Add sour cream and stir until warm. Serve over pasta. Sprinkle lightly with Parmesan or Romano cheese.

Spaghetti Bordelaise
A Favorite Pasta dish served often by New Orleanians

2 tablespoons butter
2 tablespoons olive oil
3 large or 5 small cloves garlic, peeled and crushed or coarsely chopped
½ teaspoon salt
¼ teaspoon white pepper
½ to 1 teaspoon red pepper flakes (optional)
1 tablespoon chopped fresh parsley
1 pound thin spaghetti or linguine
Grated Parmesan or Romano cheese
Freshly ground black pepper

Put salted water for spaghetti on to boil in a large pot. Meanwhile in a small heavy pan melt the butter over low heat. Add olive oil and heat for about 2 minutes. Add garlic, salt, pepper, and red pepper flakes and cook over low heat until garlic turns a light brown. Do not let the garlic burn or it will turn bitter. Turn off heat and remove garlic with a slotted spoon, add parsley, mix, cover and set aside. Cook spaghetti in boiling salted water. Drain thoroughly and return spaghetti to pot. Add sauce to spaghetti and mix well. Cover and let steep for about 7 minutes. Before serving mix well again. Serve in shallow bowls with freshly grated cheese to be added, if desired. Sprinkle with freshly ground black pepper. May be served either as a meatless meal with a vegetable and green salad, or as a side dish with baked chicken or broiled meat.

Cauliflower Macaroni

1 cauliflower or 1 package frozen cauliflower florets
6 quarts water
6 teaspoons salt
1 pound ziti or mostaccioli macaroni or spaghetti
2 tablespoons olive oil
½ stick (¼ cup) margarine
5 cloves of garlic, crushed
¼ to ½ teaspoon crushed red pepper
½ teaspoon salt
¼ teaspoon ground white pepper
1 tablespoon chopped fresh parsley
3 to 4 tablespoons grated Romano cheese (optional)

Bring the 6 quarts of salted water to a boil. Break the cauliflower into flowerets, discarding the core (or defrost frozen cauliflower). Add cauliflower to boiling water. When the water comes back to a boil, add the pasta, and cook at a high boil until macaroni is tender. Meanwhile, add olive and butter to a small pan and heat until butter is melted. Add garlic, red pepper, salt, and white pepper to pan. Cook over low heat for 4 to 5 minutes, until garlic is golden. Remove from heat, remove garlic and red pepper with a slotted spoon then discard them. Drain the pasta and cauliflower, put them in a serving bowl, add the flavored olive oil and margarine, and toss gently. Add freshly ground pepper and parsley. Cover the pot and let contents steep for about 7 minutes. Mix again and serve, adding cheese if desired.

Lemon and Artichoke Linguine

¼ cup butter
2 tablespoons olive oil
1 tablespoon flour
1 cup chicken broth
3 tablespoons lemon juice
1 tablespoon minced parsley
¼ teaspoon garlic puree or 1 clove garlic, crushed
1 teaspoon salt (or to taste)
¼ teaspoon black pepper
¼ teaspoon basil
1 can (14 oz.) artichoke hearts, drained and chopped
3 tablespoons grated parmesan cheese
1 pound linguine pasta

Add flour to oil and melted butter in pan. Stir until smooth. Add broth slowly and stir until thickened. Lower heat to simmer and add lemon juice, parsley, garlic, salt, pepper, basil, artichokes, and cheese. Stir well to blend ingredients, then cover pan and allow to simmer for about seven minutes, stirring occasionally to make sure the sauce doesn't stick. Meanwhile, boil and drain linguine. Place linguine in large serving dish and pour sauce over.

Macaroni and Artichokes

1 pound box ziti macaroni
3 tablespoons olive oil
1 can artichokes hearts, drained and quartered
1 (16 oz.) can tomatoes, drained, and diced
8 ounce can tomato sauce
1 teaspoon basil leaves
Salt and pepper to taste
¼ cup black olives, sliced
2¼ cup Parmesan cheese

Cook pasta in boiling salted water according to package directions. Meanwhile, add olive oil to large skillet and sauté artichokes and tomatoes for 1 minute. Add tomato sauce, basil, salt, and pepper and simmer for 2 minutes. Add olives and keep warm. When pasta is tender, drain well and add to skillet. Mix well. Top with Parmesan cheese and serve.

Spaghetti and Creole Meat Gravy

⅓ cup olive or vegetable oil
1 large onion, chopped
4 cloves garlic, minced
1 large, sweet (green) pepper, chopped
2 lbs. ground beef (preferably chuck) or 1½ lb. ground beef and ½ lb. ground pork
½ cup parsley, chopped fine (or ½ cup dried)
4 teaspoons salt
1 teaspoon black pepper
¼ teaspoon (or to taste) cayenne pepper
½ teaspoon basil
⅛ teaspoon oregano
¼ teaspoon paprika
1 small can tomato paste
1 large can (28 oz.) Progresso Italian tomatoes, chopped
1 large can or jar sliced mushrooms
2 tablespoons Worcestershire sauce
½ cup red wine (optional)
2 or 3 cups hot water
½ cup grated parmesan cheese
2 pounds of spaghetti

Heat oil over medium heat in large iron or heavy pot. Sauté onions, garlic and sweet pepper until soft. Add meat and continue stirring until lightly browned, slowly adding seasonings as meat and vegetables cook. Next add tomato paste, rinsing can with about ¼ can water and add to meat. Brown slightly, stirring quickly and well. Add Worcestershire sauce, tomatoes, mushrooms, wine and water. Stir well and then add ½ cup parmesan cheese. Raise heat, bring to a boil, stir well, then lower heat. Partially cover and simmer slowly for about 2 hours. When ready to serve, pour over cooked spaghetti, topping liberally with parmesan cheese. This recipe will cover 2 pounds of spaghetti. If cooking less spaghetti, remainder of sauce freezes well.

Pasta Primavera

1 pound broccoli or 1 bag frozen florets
1 bag frozen sliced carrots
1 red or yellow sweet pepper, cut into strips
1 cup frozen green peas
1 cup baby corn cobs
1 pound (16 ounce) package linguine

¼ cup olive or vegetable oil
2 large clove garlic, minced
1 tablespoon chopped fresh root ginger
3 chopped shallots (green onions)
1 pound tomatoes, chopped
¼ cup chopped fresh basil

¼ cup chopped fresh parsley
Salt and freshly ground black pepper
Soy sauce to taste (optional)
¼ teaspoon crushed red pepper (optional)
Soy sauce to taste

    If using frozen vegetables, cook according to package directions. If using fresh, cut broccoli into bite-size pieces. Cook fresh vegetables in microwave or steam just until crisp tender, refresh under cold water, place in a large bowl, and set aside Prepare linguini according to package directions. While linguini is boiling, preheat a large skillet or wok, add the oil and sauté garlic, ginger, and shallots for 30 seconds over medium heat. Then add the tomatoes and basil and sauté for 2 to 3 minutes. Add the drained linguine to the tomato mixture in the large skillet or wok and toss over the heat for 3 minutes to heat through. Toss in the vegetables and the parsley. Season with salt, black pepper, soy sauce, and the red pepper Cook, tossing all the time, until dish is piping hot. Pour the mixture into a warmed serving bowl and serve immediately.

A New Orleans Cookbook from Momma's Kitchen

Bread and Sandwiches

Southern Angel Biscuits 249
Creole Fritter Batter
(La Pate a Beignets) 249
Apple Fritters
(Beignets de Pommes) 250
Banana Fritters
(Beignets de Bananes) 250
Orange Fritters
(Beignets d'Oranges) 250
Pineapple Fritters
(Beignets d'Ananas) 250
Banana Nut Bread 251
Banana-Carrot Nut Bread 252
Petit Beignets 252
Beignets 253
Grilled Ciabatta Bread 254
Cinnamon Raisin Bread 255
Southern Dumplings
(Quick Method) 255
New Orleans Skillet Corn Bread
(Pain de Mais) 256
Hushpuppies 257
Cranberry and Nut Muffins 258
French Toast
("Pain Perdu") 259
Garlic Bread
(New Orleans Style) 260
Golden Orange French
Toast 261
Honey and Oatmeal Breakfast
Muffins 262

Momma's Honey or Molasses
Bran Muffins 263
Momma's Molasses Raisin
Bran Muffins 264
Monkey Bread
(Herbed Pull-Apart Bread) 265
Zucchini Muffins 266
Spinach Bread 267
Deep South Spoon Bread
Souffle 268
Creole Spoon Bread with
Sauce 269
Sandwiches 270
New Orleans Famous "Poor Boy"
(Shrimp or Oyster Sandwich on
French Bread) 271
Avocado and Egg Salad
Sandwich 273
Avocado, Chicken and BLT
Sandwiches 273
Tomato Sandwich with Basil
Mayonnaise 274
Olive Pecan Sandwich 274
Cobb Sandwich 275
English Cucumber
Sandwiches 275
Spicy Cheese Toast 276
Muffuletta 277
Seafood Loaf with Creole
Sauce 278

Southern Angel Biscuits

1 package yeast or 1 yeast cake
2 tablespoons warm water
5 cups cake flour
3 teaspoons baking powder
2 teaspoons sugar
1 teaspoon salt
1 cup shortening (2 sticks butter) very cold
2 cups buttermilk, room temperature

Dissolve yeast in warm water and set aside. Sift all dry ingredients together 2 times. Slice shortening into bowl, add dry ingredients and cut, or work flour in with hands until the consistency of corn meal. Pour yeast into buttermilk and add to dry ingredients. Shape dough into a ball and wrap tightly in plastic wrap and refrigerate for at least 2 hours or overnight. When ready to bake bring dough to room temperature and place on floured board. Knead lightly Roll dough to ½ inch thickness and cut with floured cutter. Place on ungreased cookie sheet. Bake in 400 degree oven for 15 to 20 minutes or until golden brown. Nice served with Honey Butter*

* Honey Butter – See page 111.

Creole Fritter Batter
(La Pate a Beignets)

2 egg yolks, beaten well
1 cup flour
¼ teaspoon salt
1 teaspoon baking powder
1 tablespoon butter or margarine, melted
2 tablespoons Brandy, or lemon juice
2 egg whites, beaten to a stiff froth

Add the flour, salt and baking powder to the beaten egg yolks and beat until very light. Add the butter and Brandy or lemon juice, thin with a little water to the consistency of Custard. Fold in the beaten whites of the eggs. You are now ready to dip the fruit of your choice into the batter.

Apple Fritters
(Beignets de Pommes)

3 tart apples, (Granny Smith)
Grated peel of half a lemon
2 tablespoons sugar
½ cup Brandy, whiskey, or rum (optional)
Creole Fritter Batter
Powdered sugar

Peel and thinly slice apples. Place in a bowl and sprinkle grated lemon peel and 2 tablespoons sugar over top. Pour Brandy or rum over top and mix well. Marinate in refrigerator for about 2 hours. Meanwhile prepare Fritter Batter. Preheat oil in a deep fat fryer to 375 degrees. Drain apples and dip one slice at a time into batter. Drop into fryer and fry until golden brown. Drain on paper towels and place in a warmed oven until all apples have been fried. When ready to serve sprinkle with powdered sugar. Place piled high on a serving platter and sprinkle liberally again with powdered sugar before serving. If you prefer not to use the liquor, simply sprinkle the sliced apples with grated lemon peel and the sugar and proceed as above.

Banana Fritters
(Beignets de Bananes)

3 bananas
2 tablespoons sugar
½ cup Cognac or rum – or enough to saturate well (Optional)
Creole Fritter Batter

Peel bananas, cut in half and split lengthwise, or cut into slices. Sprinkle with sugar and liquor, stir gently so all banana pieces are covered and marinate for 30 minutes. Drain and proceed as in apple fritters. If you prefer not to use the liquor, simply slice and proceed as above.

Orange Fritters
(Beignets d'Oranges)

Pineapple Fritters
(Beignets d'Ananas)

For both orange and pineapple fritters, cover with 2 tablespoons sugar, marinate for an hour, then proceed as in Apple Fritters recipe.

Banana Nut Bread

2½ cups all-purpose flour
2 teaspoons baking powder
½ teaspoon salt
½ teaspoon baking soda
1¼ cup sugar
½ cup (1 stick) butter or margarine, room temperature
2 eggs, room temperature
1½ cup mashed ripe bananas (about 2 large bananas)
½ cup whole milk, ½ cup buttermilk, or ½ cup sour cream
1½ teaspoon finely shredded orange peel or ½ teaspoon ground cinnamon
½ to 1 cup chopped pecans

Heat oven to 350 degrees. Lightly spray or grease bottom only of 2 loaf pans, 8 ½ x 4½ x 2 inches or 1 loaf pan, 9x5x3 inches. Sift together in a large bowl the flour, baking powder, salt, and baking soda and set aside. Add the sugar and butter to the bowl of an electric mixer. Mix on medium speed until well blended. Add the eggs, bananas, milk (buttermilk or sour cream), and orange peel. Mix well, scraping down the sides of the bowl, and continue to beat until well incorporated. Pour the mixture into the flour mixture in 3 batches, mixing just until flour is moistened. Fold in pecans. Spoon into loaf pan. Bake 8 inch for 1 hour, 9 inch for about 1 hour and 15 minutes or until toothpick inserted in center comes out clean. Cool in pan for about 5 or 10 minutes. Loosen sides of loaves from pan and remove from pan. Cool completely on wire racks before slicing.

Cool nut breads completely before slicing to prevent crumbling. Preferably wrap tightly in plastic wrap for about 24 hours after cooling. Slice with a thin blade bread knife using a light sawing motion. Bread will last for a week if wrapped tightly and refrigerated.

Banana-Carrot Nut Bread

⅓ cup vegetable oil
1 cup sugar
2 eggs, room temperature
2 cups all-purpose flour
1 teaspoon baking soda
½ teaspoon salt
½ teaspoon cinnamon
½ teaspoon ground cloves (optional)
1 cup mashed ripe bananas (2 to 3 medium)
1½ cup grated carrots (about 3 medium}
½ cup chopped pecans

Preheat oven to 350 degrees. Grease bottom only of a loaf pan 9x5x3. Combine oil and sugar in a large mixing bowl. Add eggs and mix well. In a separate bowl combine flour, baking soda, salt, cinnamon, and cloves. Add flour to the creamed mixture alternately with bananas. Stir in carrots and pecans and pour into pan. Bake for 50 to 60 minutes or until toothpick inserted in the center comes out clean. Cool in pan for 10 minutes. Cool completely on wire rack before slicing. Store tightly wrapped in plastic wrap in refrigerator for one week.

Note: Mix nut breads by hand to avoid over-mixing. A large, lengthwise crack in the thin, tender top is typical.

Petit Beignets

This recipe is a simplified version of the enjoyable and tasty breakfast treats. Served at the French Market Coffee Houses in New Orleans.

2 (or more) rolls of small, plain refrigerated biscuits
Hot oil
Confectioners sugar

If you are using the small cans of biscuits roll flat or with your fingertips flatten and shape into an oval. If you use the larger cans of biscuits (Grands) cut them in half and then flatten and shape the biscuits. Drop into hot grease. Two or three at a time. Turn once. Watch closely, as they brown quickly. Place on paper towels to drain and sprinkle heavily with confectioners sugar. Serve the French Market way – with Café au lait.

Beignets

Beignets are the hot doughnuts covered with powdered sugar and served at all hours of the day and night at the French Market Coffee Houses in New Orleans. They are enjoyed by visitors to the city and natives alike.

1 package dry yeast
¼ cup very warm water
¼ cup granulated sugar
½ teaspoon salt
1 egg beaten well
1 cup canned evaporated milk (no substitute)
2 tablespoons vegetable oil
3 ½ cups all-purpose flour
Oil for deep frying
Powdered confectioners sugar

Dissolve yeast in water in a large glass mixing bowl. When dissolved add sugar, salt, egg, evaporated milk, oil, and flour. Beat well until it becomes too stiff to beat, then mix with your hands until it becomes smooth. Cover with plastic wrap and let rise in a warm place until doubled or refrigerate overnight. When ready to prepare, knead the dough 4 or 5 times and roll out dough on a floured surface to ⅛ inch thickness. Cut into about 2 by 3 inch rectangles, cover lightly with plastic or a clean dish towel, and let rise again for about 20 minutes. Meanwhile heat oil in an electric deep fat fryer or a deep fryer or skillet on the stove to 360 – 365 degrees. Fry 2 or 3 at a time, turning to brown on both sides, until beignets puff and turn golden brown. Remove and drain on paper towels. Serve piping hot, sprinkled liberally with confectioners sugar, and enjoy with a steaming hot cup of café au lait, as the people of New Orleans do.

Grilled Ciabatta Bread

Ciabatta bread is an Italian bread very popular in Italy and around the world. It is gaining popularity in this country and can be found in most bakeries and supermarkets. It's literal meaning is Slipper bread, which identifies its shape. It is a porous bread with a crispy crust, rectangular in shape and is very delicious.

1 loaf ciabatta bread
½ cup olive oil
2 large cloves garlic, peeled and slightly smashed
Salt and black pepper
Parmesan cheese

Bread can be grilled in the oven or on the barbeque pit. If you use the oven, preheat the grill pan to medium high heat. Cut the Ciabatta bread in half lengthwise, then cut halves into ¾ to 1 inch slices. Grill the bread slices until they are golden brown, about 2 minutes. Immediately drizzle or brush the toasted sides with the olive oil. Rub the mashed garlic cloves over the grilled bread. Do this while the bread is still hot so the garlic will melt into the bread. Sprinkle with salt and pepper and lightly sprinkle with parmesan cheese. Serve immediately.

Variation: Cut a tomato in half. Rub the cut side of the tomato over the bread after rubbing with the garlic. Sprinkle with salt, pepper, and parmesan cheese.

Variation:
1½ ounces finely grated Parmigiano-Reggiano cheese
1½ ounces thickly sliced prosciutto, minced
3 tablespoon minced fresh parsley leaves

Mix the cheese, prosciutto, and parsley well in a small bowl. Sprinkle the mixture over each slice of hot grilled bread. Return the bread to the hot grill or oven, cheese side up. Cover the grill or close the oven and heat the bread just long enough to melt the cheese and warm the bread, about 1 minute. Serve hot.

Cinnamon Raisin Bread
Made in the Bread Machine

If you bread machine has a "Fruit and Nut add-in beeper" add raisins when time is indicated. If your bread machine does not have this feature, add all ingredients to bread pan in the order given.

1 ⅛ cup warm water (1 cup and 2 tablespoons)
1 egg
1½ tablespoon vegetable oil or butter
3 ½ cups all-purpose flour (or 3 ½ cups whole wheat flour)
¼ cup dry milk
3 tablespoon sugar or honey
½ to 1 cup raisins
2 teaspoons vanilla
1 teaspoon salt
2 teaspoons dry yeast

Add all ingredients to bread pan in the order given. This will make a 2 pound loaf.

Southern Dumplings
(Quick Method)

2 cups Bisquick baking mix
2 tablespoon dried or fresh chopped parsley
½ teaspoon salt
Dash of cayenne pepper
⅔ cup milk

Mix first four ingredients together. Add milk and stir ingredients until soft dough forms. Drop by spoonfuls into boiling stew. Cover and cook 20 minutes without removing cover. Makes about 10 to 12 dumplings.

New Orleans Skillet Corn Bread
(Pain de Mais)

Corn bread has its own unsurpassed place in the Creole cooking of New Orleans and the Creole cooking of Louisiana. The Creole planters of long ago had their plantations, and also city homes in New Orleans, and their lives were spent between one and the other. And Creole corn bread was enjoyed and graciously placed before guests in both homes as a special morning offering. But it was not only the Creoles of the past that enjoyed this homey, comforting treat. I remember as a child the warm feeling it would give me when Momma would make a pan of cornbread or corn sticks and serve it steaming hot and generously slathered with butter on a cold winter morning. And I also fix the same for my children and grandchildren. Either yellow or white cornmeal can be used, but Momma always used yellow, so to me real cornbread is made with yellow cornmeal. And a little secret - true Southern cornbread is seldom made with sugar.

¼ cup bacon dripping, or oil
1 cup all-purpose flour
1 teaspoon baking soda
½ teaspoon salt
⅛ teaspoon white or cayenne pepper (optional)
1 tablespoon sugar can be added if desired
2 teaspoons baking powder
2 large or 3 medium eggs, lightly beaten
¾ cup buttermilk, whole milk, or 2% milk
1½ cup cornmeal, yellow or white
½ cup cooked crumbled bacon, (optional)

Preheat oven to 450 degrees. Coat bottom and sides of a 10 inch cast-iron skillet with the bacon drippings or oil. Place in oven and heat for 10 minutes. Add cornmeal, flour, baking soda, baking powder, salt, pepper, and sugar, if using, to a large bowl and whisk well to combine. Whisk egg and milk together and add to dry ingredients Add crumbled bacon, Stir until smooth, but do not overbeat. Remove pan from oven (carefully, it will be very hot). Gently swirl the grease around the pan, coating the sides and bottom. Pour batter into the hot skillet. The grease will rise to the top of the batter. Carefully place skillet into the 450 degree oven and bake until brown, about 20 to 25 minutes. Test to see if it is done by piercing with a wooden toothpick. If it comes out clean and dry, it is done. If moist particles cling to the toothpick, return to the oven for

(Continued Next Page)

5 minutes more. Remove skillet from oven and immediately cut into wedges, then cut each wedge horizontally and serve with butter or butter and jam. Cornbread also goes well with corned beef and cabbage, red beans, and rice, etc. Also, a delicious snack can be had any time of the day or evening by reheating leftover cornbread and pouring a generous amount of cane syrup over it.

Cornbread sticks may be made the same way. Use an iron breadstick pan and proceed in the same way as with the iron skillet, being sure to oil each breadstick section as with the pan. Bake 12 to 15 minutes. To make corn muffins, oil each cup of the muffin pan, or line with paper cups, and spoon mixture into muffin cups, bake 12 to 15 minutes.

Hushpuppies

Fried cornmeal fritters. They usually accompany seafood.

1 cup cornmeal
1 cup flour
1 tablespoon baking powder
¼ teaspoon cayenne pepper
½ teaspoon salt
½ teaspoon black pepper
½ teaspoon dried thyme leaves
⅛ teaspoon dried oregano leaves
¼ cup very finely chopped shallots (green onions) tops only
1 teaspoon garlic salt
2 eggs, beaten
1 cup milk (about)

Mix all ingredients with enough milk to make a thick dough. Refrigerate for one hour. Heat oil in a deep fryer to 350 degrees. Wet fingers and roll dough into balls. Drop into hot fat, being sure not to crowd. Cook until golden brown, about 1 to 2 minutes. Remove and drain on paper towels. Serve hot.

Cranberry and Nut Muffins

3 cups all-purpose flour
1 tablespoon baking powder
½ teaspoon baking soda
½ teaspoon salt
1 teaspoon ground cinnamon
1 teaspoon allspice
2 teaspoons ground ginger
1¼ cup whole milk or half and half
2 large eggs
½ pound (2 sticks) unsalted butter, melted and cooled
¾ cup dark brown sugar packed tight, or ¾ cup molasses
¾ cup granulated sugar
1½ cups coarsely chopped fresh Cranberries
½ cup diced Calimyrna or mission figs
¾ cups chopped pecans

    Preheat oven to 375 degrees. Place paper liners in 24 muffin cups and set aside. Sift together the dry ingredients in a large bowl. Add milk, eggs, and melted butter, stirring only long enough to combine. Add rest of ingredients and stir quickly and well. This batter is thick and will not run easily like other muffin batters. Spoon into the muffin cups, filling each cup to the top. Bake for about 22 to 25 minutes until a toothpick inserted in the center comes out clean and the muffins are golden brown on top.

French Toast
("Pain Perdu")

Pain Perdu in French literally means "Lost Bread" which refers to the fact that stale bread might be lost if not made into this delicious breakfast toast.

3 eggs, well beaten
¼ cup sugar or 3 tablespoons honey, warmed for 20 seconds in microwave
1 cup half and half
1 teaspoon vanilla
¼ teaspoon salt
½ teaspoon cinnamon (optional)
8 (½ inch slices) stale bread (French, raisin, country loaf or brioche bread slices)
4 tablespoons butter or margarine
Powdered sugar, syrup, whipped cream or fruit

Preheat oven to 375 degrees. In a medium size bowl whisk together eggs, sugar or honey, half and half cream, vanilla, salt and cinnamon. Continue to beat until well mixed. This may be used immediately or prepared the night before and refrigerated until ready to use. When ready to cook, whisk custard mixture again and pour into a pie pan. Dip bread slices into mixture, coating each side completely. Melt margarine in skillet over medium heat and brown 2 slices of bread at a time until golden, about 2 to 3 minutes each side. Remove bread from pan and place on a cooling rack that is sitting on a cookie sheet. Repeat with all 8 slices. Place rack holding bread into oven and bake for 5 minutes. Serve immediately with powdered sugar sprinkled on top, syrup, cool whip or whipped cream, or fruit.

Variation: To make fluffy French toast, separate eggs. Beat whites with salt and sugar or honey until stiff. Beat yolks with until thick and lemon colored. Add cinnamon, vanilla and half and half. Fold whites into yolks. Dip bread into mixture and fry and bake as above.

Garlic Bread
(New Orleans Style)

8 tablespoons (1 stick) butter, softened
1 tablespoon finely chopped garlic or 1 tablespoon garlic powder
1 tablespoon finely chopped fresh flat leaf parsley
1 tablespoon fresh lemon juice
1 tablespoon Creole Seasoning* or creole seasoning of your choice
½ cup Parmigiano-Reggiano or Parmesan cheese
Salt and white pepper
1 loaf of French bread, split in half lengthwise

Preheat oven to 400 degrees. Combine all ingredients except bread in a bowl. Season with salt and pepper and mix well. Spread mixture over each half of bread. Place on a baking sheet that has been lined with aluminum foil. Bake until bubbly. Cut bread into 2 or 2½ inch wide slices and serve immediately. Bread can also be heated on the grill or on a Barbeque pit.

*Creole Seasoning – See page 337

Variation: 1 cup finely chopped artichoke hearts can be added to the mixture before spreading on bread. Use the artichoke hearts packed in salad oil. Drain before using.

Golden Orange French Toast

12 slices bread
6 eggs yolks, slightly beaten
½ cup half and half cream
⅓ cup orange juice
1 tablespoons grated orange peel or orange zest
¼ teaspoon salt
4 tablespoons margarine

Lay bread slices out overnight to become dry. In a medium size bowl add beaten egg yolks, half and half cream, orange juice, orange peel, or zest, and salt, mixing well. Dip bread in batter, turning to coat. Heat margarine in large pan and cook bread on both sides until brown. May be served with powdered sugar or orange syrup.

Orange Syrup

1 cup brown sugar, firmly packed
½ cup orange juice
2 tablespoons orange zest

Mix all ingredients in a small pot. Simmer over low heat for 5 minutes. Serve warm. May be used over French toast, pancakes or waffles. Any leftover may be refrigerated and reheated in microwave before serving.

Honey and Oatmeal Breakfast Muffins

The sweet smell of hot honey oatmeal muffins wafting through the house is the perfect way to get the heaviest sleeper out of bed on a cold morning. But they are also a healthy snack for any time of the day - tucked into lunch boxes, taken to the office, or for homebodies to take a break during the day, sit and have one of these muffins with a cup of coffee or tea.

1½ cups old fashioned rolled oats
1 cup all-purpose flour
½ cup raisins
½ cup walnuts or pecans
⅓ cup firmly packed brown sugar
1 tablespoon baking powder
¾ teaspoon salt
⅔ cup milk
⅓ cup vegetable oil
1 large egg, beaten
¼ cup honey

Preheat oven to 400 degrees. Grease or line with paper cups the cups of a 12 cup standard size muffin pan. In a large bowl mix together the oats, flour, raisins, nuts, sugar, baking powder, and salt. Set aside. In another bowl stir together the milk, oil, beaten egg, and honey. Stir the milk mixture into the oat mixture just until moistened. Do not over-mix the muffin batter. Fill the muffin cups ⅔ full. Bake in 400 degree oven for 15 to 18 minutes or until the muffins turn golden brown and a toothpick inserted in the center comes out clean. Remove the muffins to a rack. Serve hot. Delicious cut in half and slathered with butter. Freezes easily. Simply take the amount you want out of the freezer, wrap in paper towels and microwave until warm.

Momma's Honey or Molasses Bran Muffins
Split, toasted, and lightly spread with butter, these are homey and good.

1 cup all-bran cereal
1 cup milk, heated until hot
¼ cup butter or margarine, melted
½ cup honey or molasses
2 eggs, well beaten
1½ cup all-purpose flour
3 teaspoons baking powder
½ teaspoon salt
1 teaspoon cinnamon
½ cup raisins

Preheat oven to 400 degrees. Grease bottom only of muffin cups or line with paper baking cups. Place bran in a large bowl and stir in the hot milk. Add butter, molasses, and eggs, mix well and let stand for a minute or so. Mix together the flour, baking powder, salt, cinnamon, and raisins and add. to bran mixture in bowl, mixing just until flour is moistened. Batter should be lumpy. Fill muffin pans ⅔ full. Bake for 20 to 25 minutes or until golden brown. Remove from pan immediately. Recipe can be doubled, and muffins frozen in plastic bag. When ready to use just remove the amount you want from freezer and heat in microwave or warm conventional oven.

Momma's Molasses Raisin Bran Muffins

Split, toasted, and lightly spread with butter, these are homey and good.

1¼ cups all-purpose flour
1 tablespoon baking soda
¼ teaspoon salt
1 teaspoon cinnamon
2 cups all bran cereal
1¼ cups milk, room temperature or slightly heated
¼ cup butter (1 stick) melted
2 eggs, room temperature
½ cup molasses
1 cup raisins

Preheat oven to 400 degrees. Grease muffin pan cups well and set aside. Sift together flour, baking soda, salt, and cinnamon into a bowl and set aside. Place bran and milk in a large mixing bowl, stir, and let sit for about 10 minutes to soften bran. Add butter, eggs, and molasses to bran and milk and mix well. Add flour mixture and raisins to bowl, mixing just until flour is moistened. Fill muffin pans ⅔ full. Bake until a wooden toothpick inserted in center of a muffin comes out clean, about 20 minutes or until golden brown. Serve warm. Recipe can be doubled, and muffins frozen in plastic bag. When ready to use just remove the amount you want from freezer and heat in warm conventional oven or microwave.

Variations: 1 cup chopped dried apricots, blueberries, cranberries, dates, figs, or dried fruit of your choice may be substituted for raisins. Or you can add 1 cup finely chopped apples.

1 teaspoon grated orange zest may be used in place of cinnamon.
1 cup finely chopped pecans or walnuts may be added in place of fruit.

Monkey Bread
(Herbed Pull-Apart Bread)

1 loaf bread dough, 1 loaf frozen dough thawed to room temperature, or Bread Machine Dough (use ingredients for one loaf bread)
¼ pound melted butter or margarine
¼ teaspoon garlic puree or powder, or
1 clove garlic, minced fine
1 tablespoon parsley
½ teaspoon basil
½ teaspoon oregano
1 teaspoon thyme
1 teaspoon caraway seeds (optional)
2 tablespoons grated Parmesan cheese

If you are using a bread machine, set at bread dough cycle. Cut bread dough into 32 pieces. Add melted butter to herbs and cheese, mixing well. Dip each piece of bread in the butter mixture and arrange in a loaf pan, or preferably a 12 cup Bundt pan. Cover with cloth and let rise until doubled in bulk. Bake at 375 degrees for 25 minutes or until golden brown. If using for a large buffet, dinner party or cook-out, recipe may be doubled and baked in 2 loaf pans.

Serve warm or cold. Any leftover bread may be wrapped and frozen. When ready to use, heat in oven.

Variation: Frozen parker house rolls dough may be used in place of loaf bread. When thawed cut each roll in half and proceed as above.

Cinnamon monkey bread may be made by preparing dough the same way, but instead of herbs and cheese, dip each piece of dough into melted butter and then roll into mixture of ½ cup of sugar and two teaspoons cinnamon that has been well blended together. Place bread or roll pieces in 9 inch cake pan or muffin pan cups. Let rise until doubled in bulk. Bake at 375 degrees for 12-15 minutes. After baking remove pan from oven and immediately glaze with mixture of ½ cup powdered sugar and 1 tablespoon water.

Zucchini Muffins

This recipe for zucchini muffins was given to me by my former neighbor and Dear Friend, Iva Morris

¾ cup flour
¼ teaspoon baking powder
¼ teaspoon baking soda
¼ teaspoon salt
¼ teaspoon cinnamon
1 large egg
½ cup sugar
¼ cup oil
1 cup grated medium fine, unpared zucchini, loosely packed
¼ cup raisins
¼ cup chopped walnuts (optional)

Preheat oven to 350 degrees. Stir flour, baking powder, soda, salt, and cinnamon together. In separate bowl beat together egg, sugar, and oil with mixer until blended. Stir in flour mixture, zucchini, raisins, and walnuts. Stir only until dry ingredients are moistened. Fill muffin pans ⅔ full and bake for about 25 minutes. Recipe easily doubled or tripled. Freezes well. Simply remove number of muffins needed from freezer, heat in microwave or oven, and serve plain or split open with butter.

Spinach Bread

This recipe was given to me by my Cousin, Helene Ware Wagner

1 (10 ounce) package frozen chopped spinach
1 (3 ounce) package cream cheese, room temperature
1 long loaf French bread
1 stick (¼ pound) melted butter or margarine
Garlic powder
1 pound Monterey Jack cheese, shredded

 Preheat oven to 400 degrees. Cook spinach according to package directions and drain well. Combine spinach and cream cheese, mixing well. Cut bread in half lengthwise and coat each half with melted butter, spreading on with pastry brush. Sprinkle liberally with garlic powder and one half of shredded Monterey Jack cheese. Carefully spoon on spinach mixture and top with remaining cheese. Place two halves side by side on cookie sheet and bake for 20 minutes. When ready to serve, slice into pieces, preferably with an electric knife, about 2 to 3 inches wide. Freezes well. Wrap in aluminum foil and freeze until ready to serve. Thaw before baking. Serve as appetizers or as a light snack.

 Variation: To make Spinach Crostini, do not cut loaf in half lengthwise. Instead cut bread into ½ inch slices, proceed as above. 2 plum tomatoes, diced small, may be added on top of spinach mixture.

Deep South Spoon Bread Souffle

Spoon Bread is to the South what Johnnycake is to the North. As American as apple pie, and probably much older, there are dozens of "Authentic" recipes for spoon bread. Each area – and each cook – has their own version. Here is our version, with a New Orleans touch by adding ground pecans.

3 cups whole milk or buttermilk
1½ cups stone-ground white cornmeal
3 tablespoon butter, softened to room temperature
1 teaspoon salt
1 teaspoon baking powder
½ teaspoon baking soda
6 eggs, separated
½ cup pecans, ground fine

Generously butter a 1½ or 2 quart baking dish and set aside. Preheat oven to 375 degrees. Heat the milk or buttermilk in a 2 quart heavy saucepan over medium heat until scalded but not boiling. Add the cornmeal in a steady stream, whisking well. Cook, continuing to whisk, until thick, about 2 minutes. Transfer to a large bowl and stir in the butter, salt, baking powder, baking soda, beaten egg yolks, and ground pecans. Cool to lukewarm. Using an electric mixer, beat the egg whites until stiff but not dry. Fold into the cornmeal mixture gently but thoroughly. Pour batter into the prepared baking dish and bake for 45 to 50 minutes, or until golden brown and puffed and cake tester comes out clean. Serve immediately.

Creole Spoon Bread with Sauce

3 cups milk
1 cup cornmeal, enriched self-rising
1 pound cooked shrimp, coarse chopped
⅓ cup sweet pepper chopped fine
⅓ cup onion, chopped fine
⅓ cup parsley, chopped fine
2 tablespoons vegetable oil
¼ teaspoon Tabasco sauce
¾ teaspoon baking powder
1 teaspoon salt
6 egg yolks, beaten well
6 egg whites

Sauce:
2 tablespoons butter
2 tablespoons self-rising, enriched flour
1¼ cup milk
½ cup catsup
1 tablespoon Worcestershire sauce

Heat milk in a large saucepan until almost simmering. Slowly add cornmeal, and cook, whisking until thick and smooth, about 2 minutes. Add next six ingredients, stirring constantly, and over medium heat bring to a boil. Continue to stir for a minute longer, then remove from heat, transfer mixture to a large bowl stir in baking powder, salt and egg yolks. Cool to lukewarm. Beat egg whites with a pinch of salt in a clean bowl using an electric mixer just until they hold stiff peaks. Fold egg whites into cornmeal mixture gently but thoroughly. Spoon batter into a well-greased 2 quart baking dish and bake in preheated 375 degree oven for 45 to 50 minutes, or until golden brown. Serve immediately with sauce.

While spoon bread is baking, make sauce. Melt butter in saucepan and blend in flour. Gradually stir in milk and stirring constantly, cook over medium heat until thickened. (This is a white roux). Stir in catsup and Worcestershire sauce. Spoon sauce over spoon bread when serving.

Sandwiches

The fourth Earl of Sandwich, John Montagu, was an 18th century gambling man who didn't want to leave the gaming tables. So, he ordered some slices of meat between two pieces of bread to satisfy his hunger pangs.

Since then, sandwiches have evolved into at times "one handed meals" that allow you to do practically anything you want - work, drive the car, drink coffee, watch television, Etc. The variety of sandwiches are endless. From dainty tea sandwiches to the Dagwood Bumstead type filled with everything the imagination has to offer. So, sandwiches are anything but humble. Everyone has their favorites.

Growing up in New Orleans, during those wonderful, peaceful years between the great Depression and World War Two, sandwiches always remind me of summer and our picnics in the park. On a warm summer day Momma would often pack a picnic basket full of sandwiches and her delicious oatmeal cookies, and a couple of thermoses of lemonade and ice cold milk. We didn't have a car then, but the Desire Streetcar passed in front of our home. So, Momma would take her three kids and the picnic basket, and we would all board the Streetcar, transfer to the St. Charles Streetcar at Canal street, and ride up beautiful St. Charles Avenue pass the stately mansions lining the Avenue, and on up to Audubon Park, across from the magnificent Loyola and Tulane Universities. Little Weldon, the youngest, loved to ride on the Swan Boat that glided on the lagoons in the park. But my favorite was the Carousel, or as Gene and I called them, the "Flying Horses". We would be sure to get horses on the outer side of the carousel, and wait for the sound of the clanging bell, which meant the metal arm would come out, holding the brass ring, which we would lean out and try to hook on to our finger. Catching the brass ring meant a free ride on the flying horses, and we would try so hard that we became quite adept at it!

Later, Momma would spread a tablecloth on the ground, and we would have lunch. The boys preferred peanut butter and jam sandwiches, but Mom and I would have my most favorite sandwich in the world (at that time). Pickles and olives, chopped and mixed with a little mayonnaise, and spread on a hamburger bun. (I have always loved olives, and when other children would go to the grocery stores and the grocers would give them candy as lagniappe, I would ask for olives instead of candy. Even to this day, every now and then I will fix myself a pickle and olive sandwich and remember Mom and I eating them together.) After lunch, we would walk through the Zoo, which

(Continued Next Page)

was in the section of the park near the Mississippi River. Then, in late afternoon, Momma would take her 3 tired little ones and again board the Streetcar for our long trip home, to wait for Daddy to get home from work so we could tell him about our day. Little Weldon would fall asleep with his head in Momma's lap, and Gene and I would take turns sitting by the window of the streetcar. Such simple pleasures, but such wonderful memories.

As I said, everyone has their favorite sandwiches. Perhaps one of the following sandwiches will become one of your favorites, also.

New Orleans Famous "Poor Boy"
(Shrimp or Oyster Sandwich on French Bread)

Fried shrimp or oysters are delicious served with French fried potatoes and cole slaw or potato salad. But in New Orleans one of the most popular ways to eat them is on a "Po Boy". It may be called a *Po Boy*, but the king of New Orleans sandwiches is a two-fisted feast on crispy French bread piled high and messy with anything from fried oysters or shrimp to roast beef and gravy.

The Po Boy was created during a 1920s streetcar strike by former conductors Bennie and Clovis Martin, owners of the popular Martin Brothers Restaurants, who promised to feed all union members for free. Whenever a striker entered their sandwich shop, Bennie would yell to Clovis, "Here comes another Po boy!"

In New Orleans today, almost every neighborhood has its own po-boy shop. To reproduce this local favorite at home, cut a loaf of French bread into 12 inch lengths, then split the sections in half lengthwise. Scoop out the center of the bread, leaving a hollowed out cavity. Warm it briefly in the oven, then spread a thin layer of either mayonnaise or butter on the inside of both pieces of bread. In New Orleans lingo, you can have them with either just butter or "my-nez" (mayonnaise) or "dressed" (with lettuce, tomato, pickle and my-nez). Heap the fried shrimp or oysters on the bottom half, add catsup and, if desired, a sprinkling of Tabasco sauce and salt, add some pickles and then cover with the top half. Cut the sandwich in half across and enjoy! Incidentally, for couples who can't make up their minds, some restaurants in New Orleans offer seafood po-boys known as Peacemakers, half shrimp and half oysters. One well known use, in the past, of the po-boy earned it the quaint title of "La Mediatrice" as it was known in the Vieux Carre. Every Creole man knew that bringing home his "mediator" to an upset wife, a delicious shrimp or oyster po-boy, bought warm and crusty from the French market just before going home, could win him forgiveness, whatever the sin.

(Continued Next Page)

"Poor boy" sandwiches are also delicious made with hot roast beef and lots of hot beef gravy and piled high with tomatoes and shredded lettuce. A "Ferdi" is a roast beef po-boy with baked ham added. A "Ralph" is a "Ferdi" with Swiss cheese added. Or, how about a meatball po-boy. Mmmmm! My brother Gene's favorite, whenever Momma would make meat balls and gravy. Spread bread with a little mayonnaise, place meatballs on bottom half, cover meatballs with tomato (red) gravy and a sprinkling of Parmesan cheese, and cover with top half. Momma's way was to cut the French bread about 12 inches from the end, and instead of cutting it in half lengthwise, just scooped out the middle of the bread. She would spread a thin layer of mayonnaise on the inside, the meatballs put down into the cavity, and gravy spooned over it. Everything sealed inside the bread – no dripping. And since there were three of us kids, and only two ends to the bread, you can imagine the arguments about who got the ends! You can also simply fix a "poor boy" covered with mayonnaise, French fries, a sprinkling of salt, and catsup with a few drops of Tabasco on top Many days at lunchtime when little Gene and I were in Grammar school we would walk across the park that was in front of our school to a po-boy shop on the corner and get our French fried po-boys, and, with a big bottle of Sarsaparilla (a type of soft drink) between us, would sit on a bench in the park and enjoy our feast….Such a nice memory.

Avocado and Egg Salad Sandwich

4 slices wheat or plain bread
Mayonnaise
Egg salad*
1 avocado, peeled and each half cut into slices
Shredded lettuce

Spread mayonnaise on bread and cover with egg salad. Place Avocado slices on top of egg salad. Sprinkle lightly with salt. Add shredded lettuce and cover with other slice of bread, slice and serve.

* Egg Salad – see page 80.

Avocado, Chicken and BLT Sandwiches
On Pita Bread

12 bacon slices, cooked crisp and crumbled
1 cup cooked and cubed chicken or turkey
10 cherry tomatoes, cut into quarters
2 medium California avocados, seeded, peeled and diced
2 cups shredded lettuce
⅓ mayonnaise
⅓ cup sour cream
½ cup Thousand Island dressing
4 Pita breads, (6 in. size) cut in half

Mix mayonnaise and sour cream together in a bowl. Combine bacon, chicken, tomatoes, avocado, and lettuce in a large bowl. Pour mayonnaise mixture over all, add Thousand Island dressing and toss well to blend all ingredients. Fill each pita half with one half to three quarters cup.

Tomato Sandwich with Basil Mayonnaise

1 cup mayonnaise
10 to 15 basil leaves, chopped
1 teaspoon kosher salt
¼ teaspoon ground black pepper
1 teaspoon freshly squeezed lemon juice
1 tablespoon olive oil
1 teaspoon minced garlic
2 slices country loaf bread
1 large tomato, sliced

Whisk together the mayonnaise, basil, salt, pepper, lemon juice, olive oil and garlic. Spread the mayonnaise mixture on the top of 2 slices of bread. Place the sliced tomato on top of one bread slice. Place the remaining slice of bread, mayonnaise side down, on top of the tomato. Cut the sandwich in half and serve. Recipe easily doubled or tripled.

Olive Pecan Sandwich

8 ounces Philadelphia cream cheese, softened to room temperature
½ cup mayonnaise
½ cup chopped pecans
1 cup chopped salad olives
2 tablespoons olive juice
Dash of black pepper
Lettuce

Mash softened cream cheese with a fork and add mayonnaise. Mix well and add rest of ingredients. Stir well. Put into a bowl or pint size jar, cover and refrigerate for at least 24 to 48 hours. Spread will become thick. Serve on a hamburger bun, thinly sliced toast or plain bread topped with lettuce. Cut sandwiches in half, or if serving at a party or luncheon, cut sandwiches into tiny, fingertip sizes. If this spread is kept in a tightly covered jar it will last weeks in the refrigerator.

Cobb Sandwich

The Cobb sandwich is a takeoff on the Cobb salad, my favorite. The Cobb salad was originally served in the Brown Derby in Hollywood. It's great also as a sandwich.

6 tablespoons mayonnaise
2 tablespoons Dijon mustard
6 Kaiser sandwich rolls, or large rolls of your choice
1 pound turkey, thinly sliced
6 tomatoes slices, sliced thin
2 avocados, peeled and thinly sliced
12 sliced bacon, fried crisp
2 cups shredded lettuce
6 tablespoons crumbled blue or Roquefort cheese

Mix mayonnaise and mustard together in a small bowl. Split rolls and toast under the broiler or heat in oven. Spread the mayonnaise and mustard mixture on bottom half of each roll. Place ingredients on sandwich in this order: Turkey, slice of tomato, a few slices of avocado, bacon, and then the lettuce. Crumble blue or Roquefort cheese over all, spread mayonnaise and mustard on top half and place on sandwich. Cut sandwich in half. Serve a few slices of melon and a couple of strawberries alongside and a drink of your choice and you have a complete meal in itself.

English Cucumber Sandwiches

8 ounces cream cheese, softened
1 envelope dry Italian salad dressing mix
18 slices oatmeal bread (1 loaf)
1 English cucumber, sliced on an angle
Fresh or dried dill weed

Combine the cream cheese and salad dressing mix in a small bowl and mix well. Spread a thin layer of the cream cheese mixture over 9 slices of the oatmeal bread. Top each slice with 4 cucumber slices. Sprinkle with the dill weed and top with the remaining bread slices. Trim the crusts and cut each sandwich into 4 triangles. Makes 3 dozen.

Variation: For open-faced sandwiches, spread slices of the bread with the cream cheese mixture. Cut rounds from each bread slice using a 1¼ to 1½ inch cutter (about 3 per slice). Top each round with a cucumber slice and dill weed.

Spicy Cheese Toast

8 slices bacon, cooked and crumbled
⅓ cup mayonnaise
1 cup shredded sharp cheddar cheese
1 egg, slightly beaten
⅛ teaspoon cracked black pepper
⅛ teaspoon dry mustard
½ teaspoon Worcestershire sauce
¼ teaspoon Tabasco sauce
8 slices day old bread

Preheat oven to 350 degrees. Combine all ingredients except bread in a bowl. Toast and then spread each slice of bread with cheese mixture, slice on a triangle, and bake on baking sheet for about 20 minutes, or until puffy. Delicious served with lettuce and tomato salad for lunch.

Variation: To be used as a party appetizer, remove crust and cut each slice into 3 strips and then bake as above. May be prepared the day before, covered and refrigerated. Bring to room temperature before baking. Recipe easily doubled.

Muffuletta

The Muffuletta is an Italian sandwich which first appeared at two crowded and picturesque Sicilian markets on the same block of Decatur Street in the French Quarter, the Central Grocery and the Progress Grocery, around the turn of the twentieth century. Both stores still make these massive sandwiches, and the locals still go there to enjoy them. The Muffuletta takes its name from Sicily's round seeded loaf that was brought to New Orleans by Italian settlers. It is made on a round loaf of Italian or sourdough bread about 10 inches in diameter. The spicy aromatic olive salad is the key ingredient of this very colorful and flavorful sandwich, and which sets it apart from all other sandwiches. The Muffuletta is also prepared by several local bakeries and grocery stores in New Orleans, but by following the recipe below, may be prepared at home, and will closely resemble the original. A filled New Orleans Muffuletta sandwich, almost the size of a frisbee in diameter, and 3 inches high at the center, is a meal in itself, or is easily divided.

Round loaf of Italian bread about 10 inches across
Freshly minced garlic (optional)
Olive Salad *
½ pound thinly sliced Italian Salami
6 ounces thinly sliced provolone cheese
¼ pound thinly sliced Italian ham

Cut the bread horizontally in half and scoop out some of the soft inner side of the bread. Brush the inside of the bread with juice from the olive salad, and if you wish, some minced garlic. Layer the Italian salami on the bottom half. Cover the salami with half of the olive salad. Next layer the provolone cheese and cover the cheese with the Italian ham. Sprinkle with more minced garlic and remaining olive salad. Cover with top half of the Muffuletta loaf.

Cut sandwich into quarters

Tourists eat one-fourth
Natives eat half
Cajuns eat the whole thing

*Olive Salad – see page 84.

Seafood Loaf with Creole Sauce

2 pounds shrimp, oysters or filet of catfish
Salt, black and cayenne pepper
Cornmeal
Butter or margarine
Shortening
1 long loaf French bread, unsliced
Pickle slices
1 small jar stuffed olives, sliced in half (optional)
1 red onion, sliced (optional)

Sauce:
Mix following ingredients together in a small bowl and set aside

½ teaspoon Tabasco sauce (more if desired)
Juice of ½ lemon
2 tablespoons Worcestershire sauce
2 cups tomato catsup

Sprinkle seafood well with salt, pepper, and cayenne. (Catfish can be left in filets or sliced in 1½ inch cubes). Dredge in cornmeal and fry in deep fat until golden brown. Drain on paper towels and set aside in a warm place. Cut loaf of French bread in half lengthwise and scoop out the dough in the middle of bread. Butter both sides of bread. Place bread in a 350 degree oven for a few minutes until warm and slightly toasted. Remove bread from oven and brush sauce liberally on both sides of bread. Arrange layers of seafood on bottom half of bread, more sauce, then pickles, and olives, and onion, if using. Brush top half of bread with sauce and replace top over seafood. Wrap loaf in heavy aluminum foil and bake in oven at 300 degrees for ten minutes. Remove from foil and serve hot.

Cakes, Cookies and Desserts

Chocolate Cake ... 283
Fig Cake ... 284
Golden Sherry or Rum Cake ... 285
Hummingbird Cake ... 286
Hummingbird Cake
(Made from a Cake Mix) ... 287
Lane Cake ... 288
Strawberry Shortcake Cake ... 289
Lemon and Cherry Upside
Down Cake ... 290
Cherry Sauce ... 290
Lemon Fleck Frosting Cake ... 291
Lemon Meringue Cake ... 292
Old Fashioned Southern
Pound Cake ... 293
Praline Pecan Cake ... 294
Creole Red Velvet Cake ... 295
Cuban Tres Leches Cake
(Three Milk Cake) ... 296
Tangy Sunshine Cake ... 296
Chocolate Fudge Pecan
Layer Cake ... 297
Carrot and Pineapple Cake ... 298
Angel Food Cake with
Berry Compote ... 299
Whipped Cream ... 299
Cookies ... 300
Bourbon Balls ... 300
Chocolate Chip Cake
Mix Cookies ... 301
Fudge Cookies ... 301
Gingersnap Cookies ... 302
Hermits ... 303
Lemon Sugar Cookies ... 304
Coconut Macaroons ... 304
Madeleines ... 305
Momma's Molasses
Oatmeal Cookies ... 306
Orange Carrot Cookies ... 307
Peanut Butter Cookies ... 307

Pfeffernusse Christmas Cookies
(German Peppernuts) ... 308
Praline Snickerdoodles ... 309
Sandstone Health Cookies ... 309
Snickerdoodles ... 310
Glazes ... 311
Pie Pastry ... 312
Basic Pie Pastry ... 313
Tropical Custard Pie ... 313
Deep Dish Country Apple Pie ... 314
Lemon Meringue Pie ... 315
Jo's Pecan Pie ... 316
Cherry Pie ... 317
Pumpkin Pie ... 318
Southern Yam (or Sweet
Potato) Pie ... 319
Bananas Foster ... 320
Blueberry Custard ... 320
Creole Cream Cheese Ice
Cream ... 321
Lemon Ice Dessert ... 321
Cream Puffs
(Profiteroles) ... 322
Creole Caramel Cup Custard ... 323
Pecan Pralines
(Pralines aux Pacanes) ... 324
Sabayon ... 325
Sabayon a la Creole ... 325
Sabayon with Fruit ... 326
Ruby Pears ... 326
Vanilla Cream Filling ... 327
Bread Pudding ... 328
Chocolate Pudding ... 328
Creole Rice Pudding ... 329
Mixed Fruit Pudding ... 329
Hawaiian Delight Rice
Pudding ... 330
Praline Bread Pudding ... 331

Chocolate Cake
Single Layer, Sinfully Rich, With A Ganache Frosting

1 cup (2 sticks) butter, room temperature
9 ounces semisweet chocolate
6 eggs, room temperature
¾ cup granulated sugar
¾ cup brown sugar
¾ cup cake flour
3 tablespoons finely grated almonds
½ teaspoon cream of tartar

Preheat oven to 375 degrees. Grease sides and bottom of an 8 or 9 inch springform pan. Line bottom of pan with wax or parchment paper. Grease the top of the parchment paper and flour pan. Set aside. Put the butter and chocolate in a small microwave safe bowl, and microwave on high for 2 to 3 minutes. When ingredients are completely melted, stir and set aside.

Separate eggs, placing yolks in the large bowl. Put egg whites in another bowl. Beat the white and brown sugars into the egg yolks just until blended. Whisk the still warm chocolate into the yolks. Add the flour and almonds, mixing well. Add the cream of tartar to the egg whites and beat until creamy and peaks form. Gently fold the egg whites into the chocolate mixture without deflating the whites. Pour into cake pan. Bake for about 30 minutes, or until cake is completely set around the sides but still has a soft and creamy circle in the center. If you want a cake-crumb consistency, bake about 40 minutes. Leave cake in the pan until it is thoroughly cool. When the cake is cool, lift off the side of the pan and turn the cake over onto a cake plate. Peel paper off bottom (which is now the top). Frost cake with the Ganache frosting.

Ganache frosting:

1 cup heavy (whipping cream
1½ cups (10 ounces) semisweet chocolate chips, finely chopped

In a small pot, scald the cream until bubbles appear around the edge and it's just about to boil. Remove from heat and stir in the chopped chocolate. Mix until frosting is smooth and starts to thicken. Transfer to a small bowl and frost cake.

Fig Cake

As spring turns into summer, the people in New Orleans and south Louisiana, who are lucky enough to have a fig tree in their back yard, await eagerly to pick this special fruit, to make jams, jellies, or simply to pick them and pop them into their mouth. Figs are easily and successfully flash frozen. Wash them and then lay them on cookie sheets in the freezer. Freeze and then place in plastic bags to be eaten at a later date. They are also delicious made into a cakes. If no figs are available, you can still get the distinctive flavor of figs by using preserves.

2 cups all-purpose flour
1 teaspoon baking powder
1 teaspoon baking soda
1 teaspoon salt
1 teaspoon ground cinnamon
1 teaspoon ground nutmeg
½ teaspoon ground cloves
1 cup butter or margarine (2 sticks) room temperature
1½ cup sugar
3 eggs, room temperature
1 cup whole milk or buttermilk
1 teaspoon vanilla extract
2 cups fig preserves (homemade or store bought)
1 cup chopped pecans

Preheat oven to 350 degrees. Spray or oil and flour a 12 cup Bundt pan or a well-greased 12x9x2 inch baking pan and set aside. In a separate bowl, combine flour, baking powder, soda, salt, and spices and set aside.

In an electric mixer, cream butter. Gradually add sugar while continuing to beat. Add eggs, one at a time, beating after each addition. While mixer is running, slowly add buttermilk and vanilla and beat until smooth. Remove bowl from mixer and stir in flour mixture a little at a time and stirring after each addition, fig preserves and pecans. Stir well to mix all ingredients into a smooth batter. Pour batter into prepared Bundt pan or rectangular baking pan.

Bake at 350 degrees for about an hour, or until a toothpick inserted in center comes out clean. Remove and cool before serving. Serve plain or sift some confectioners sugar over top of cake. Nice served with ice cream or spoon some whipping cream on each slice.

Golden Sherry or Rum Cake

Grease and flour Bundt or angel food pan. Line bottom of pan with ½ cup chopped pecans.

Mix until well blended:
1 pkg. yellow cake mix
1 pkg. instant vanilla pudding
½ cup cooking oil
½ cup milk
4 eggs
1 tsp. vanilla
½ cup golden Sherry or Rum

Pour mixture in pan over pecans and bake at 325° for about 45 minutes or until done when tested with toothpick.

Icing Mix:

1 cup sugar
½ stick butter or margarine, room temperature
⅓ cup water
Cook together until melted, then add:
¼ cup golden Sherry or Rum

About 10 minutes after removing the cake from oven, and while still in pan, punch holes in cake with long tined serving fork and pour icing mix over cake. Allow cake to sit for 15 minutes before removing from pan. When inverted, pecans will be on top.

Hummingbird Cake

This delicious Southern cake is a very dense and moist cake made with pineapple and banana, and usually topped with a cream cheese frosting.

3 cups all-purpose flour
1 teaspoon baking soda
½ teaspoon salt
2 cups sugar
1 teaspoon cinnamon
3 eggs, beaten
¾ cup vegetable oil
1½ teaspoons vanilla
1 (8 oz.) can crushed pineapple, undrained
1 cup chopped pecans
1 ¾ cups mashed bananas
½ cup chopped pecans
Cream cheese frosting

Preheat oven to 350 degrees. Combine first 5 ingredients in a large bowl. Add eggs and oil, stirring until dry ingredients are moistened. Do not beat. Stir in vanilla, pineapple, 1 cup pecans, and bananas. Pour batter into 3 greased and floured 9 inch round cake pans. Bake for 23 to 28 minutes or until a wooden pick inserted in center comes out clean. Cool in pans 10 minutes. Remove from pans and let cool completely on wire racks. Stir the ½ cup chopped pecans into the cream cheese frosting, if desired, or reserve them to sprinkle over top of frosted cake. Spread frosting between layers and on top and sides of cake.

Cream Cheese Frosting

½ cup butter or margarine, softened
1 (8 oz.) package cream cheese, softened
1 (16 oz.) package powdered sugar, sifted
1 teaspoon vanilla

Cream butter and softened cream cheese. Gradually add powdered sugar, then beat until light and fluffy. Stir in vanilla. Yield: Enough for one 3 layer cake.

Hummingbird Cake
(Made from a Cake Mix)

1 package yellow cake mix
1 package (4 serving size) vanilla instant pudding mix
½ cup vegetable oil
1 can (8 ounce) crushed pineapple, well drained with juice reserved
4 eggs, room temperature
1 teaspoon cinnamon
1 medium size fresh or frozen banana, cut up
½ cup finely chopped pecans
¼ cup chopped maraschino cherries, well drained

⅓ cup frosting from a can of prepared cream cheese frosting

Preheat oven to 350 degrees. Coat a 10 inch Bundt pan with nonstick cooking spray. In the bowl of an electric mixer, combine the cake and pudding mixes, the oil, pineapple, eggs, and the cinnamon. Add enough water to the reserved pineapple juice to make 1 cup. Add to the bowl and beat until mixture is thoroughly combined. Add the banana and pecans and continue to beat until well combined. Stir in the cherries, mix well then pour into the Bundt pan. Bake for 55 to 60 minutes or until a wooden toothpick inserted in the center comes out clean. Let the cake cool in the pan for 20 to 25 minutes then invert onto a serving plate. Let cool completely.

In a microwave safe bowl, remove ⅓ cup frosting from a can of prepared cream cheese frosting and heat for 10 to 15 seconds. Stir until smooth and pourable then drizzle over the cooled cake before slicing. The rest of the cream cheese frosting can be refrigerated and used at another time.

Lane Cake

Several Southern States claim this cake as their own, but no matter where it originated, it is one of the South's most outstanding cakes. Like most well-known cakes, there are several versions of this beautiful cake.

3 ½ cups sifted cake flour
2 teaspoons baking powder
¼ teaspoon salt
1 cup butter, room temperature
2 cups sugar
1 cup milk, room temperature
2 teaspoons vanilla extract
8 egg whites, room temperature, reserve yolks

Preheat oven to 375 degrees. Grease and flour 3 round 9-inch cake pans and set aside. Sift flour, baking powder, and salt three times and set aside. In an electric mixer, cream the butter. Gradually add the sugar, beating until light and fluffy. Add the flour mixture to the creamed mixture alternately with the milk, beginning and ending with dry ingredients and beat until light and smooth. Blend in vanilla. In a separate bowl, beat egg whites until stiff peaks form, and carefully fold into batter. Pour batter into prepared cake pans. Bake for 25 to 30 minutes, or until toothpick inserted in center comes out clean. Cool in cake pan for 5 minutes. Turn out on cooling racks and let cool completely. Spread filling between layers of cake. Spread top and sides of cake with frosting.

Filling:

8 egg yolks
1 cup sugar
½ cup butter, room temperature
1 cup maraschino cherries, chopped
1 to 1½ cups finely chopped pecans
¾ cup shredded coconut (optional)
1 cup chopped golden raisins
½ cup Bourbon or Brandy

Cream butter and sugar. Beat egg yolks until thick and light. Add to butter and sugar mixture. Cook, preferably in a double boiler, over medium heat, stirring constantly, until mixture thickens, about 15 to 20 minutes. Remove from heat and stir in the cherries, pecans, coconut, if using, and raisins. Cool thoroughly, and then add Bourbon or Brandy. Spread between layers of cake.

(Continued Next Page)

Frosting:

¾ cup sugar
¼ cup light corn syrup
¼ teaspoon salt
¼ cup water
2 egg whites (room temperature)
½ teaspoon vanilla

In a saucepan over medium heat combine sugar, syrup, salt, and water. Cook, stirring constantly until mixture registers 240 °F on a candy thermometer, the firm ball stage. In the small bowl of an electric mixer beat egg whites on high until stiff peaks form. Continue beating egg whites while slowly adding syrup mixture. Add vanilla and continue beating until spreading consistency is reached. Frost cake.

Strawberry Shortcake Cake
For my daughter Laurie

1 (2 layer) package white cake mix
½ quart strawberries, chopped
½ cup sugar
1 cup whipping cream
2 to 3 tablespoons sugar
1 quart strawberries, cut into halves or quarters

Prepare and bake the cake according to package directions for two 9-inch round cake pans or two 9x9 inch cake pans. Combine ½ quart strawberries and ½ cup sugar in a bowl and mix well. Mash the strawberries in the sugar if desired. Combine the cream and 2 or 3 tablespoons sugar in a mixing bowl and beat until soft peaks form.

To assemble, place 1 cake layer on a serving plate. Spread ½ of the whipped cream over the top. Top with a layer of strawberry halves. Repeat the layers. Store the cake in the refrigerator. Top the individual servings with the sweetened strawberries.

Lemon and Cherry Upside Down Cake
With Cherry Sauce

1 package plain lemon cake mix
8 tablespoons (1 stick) butter, melted
1 cup milk
3 large eggs
1 or 2 cans (14½ ounces) pitted tart red cherries, packed in water, drain and reserve liquid

Preheat oven to 350 degrees. Lightly spray a 13 by 9 inch baking pan or dish with vegetable spray and set aside. Place cake mix, melted butter, milk and eggs in mixing bowl or electric mixer. Blend on low speed for 1 minute. Stop machine and scrape down sides of bowl. Increase the speed to medium and beat for 2 minutes longer. Pour the batter into the prepared pan, smoothing it out with a spatula. Drain cherries, reserving the water. Place cherries on top of the cake mixture, spreading them out evenly. Bake for 40 to 45 minutes, or until it is golden brown and springs back when lightly pressed with your finger. Remove from oven and place on wire rack to cool.

Cherry Sauce

Cherry water (reserved after draining cherries)
½ cup water
2 teaspoons lemon juice
¼ cup sugar
1 tablespoon cornstarch
1 teaspoon almond extract

Place all of the ingredients in a small pot over low heat, whisking constantly, until mixture comes to a boil and thickens, about 3 to 4 minutes. Remove pot from heat. When ready to serve, cut the cake into squares and serve them upside down on a plate. Pour cherry sauce over the squares and serve.

Cake may be kept, unsauced, and covered with plastic wrap or aluminum foil at room temperature for up to 3 days or in the refrigerator for up to 1 week. Prepare the cherry sauce right before serving. The cherry water will keep, covered, in the refrigerator for up to 1 week.

Note: For cherry lovers, add 2 cans of cherries. Double the portions for the cherry sauce.

Lemon Fleck Frosting Cake
For Momma

2¼ cups sifted cake flour
2¼ teaspoons baking powder
¼ teaspoon salt
½ cup butter
1 cup sugar
2 eggs, well beaten
¾ cup milk
1 teaspoon vanilla

Preheat oven to 375 degrees. Sift flour once, measure, add baking powder and salt, and sift together 3 times. Cream butter thoroughly, add sugar gradually, and cream together until light and fluffy. Add eggs and beat well. Add flour, alternately with milk, a small amount at a time, beating after each addition until smooth. Add vanilla. Pour into 2 greased 8 inch layer pans and bake for 25 to 30 minutes. Spread lemon fleck frosting between layers and on top and sides of cake.

For cupcakes bake in cup cake pans at 375 degrees for 20 to 25 minutes.

Lemon Fleck Frosting

2 teaspoons grated orange rind
4 tablespoons butter
Dash of salt
3 cups sifted confectioners sugar
3 tablespoons lemon juice

Cream together orange rind and butter. Add salt and part of sugar gradually, blending well. Add remaining sugar, alternately with lemon juice, until of right consistency to spread. Beat until very smooth. Makes enough frosting to cover tops and sides of 2 8-inch layers, or tops of about 3 ½ dozen medium cupcakes.

Lemon Meringue Cake

Cake:
1 package (18 ¼ ounces) lemon or yellow cake mix
3 eggs
1 cup water
⅓ cup vegetable oil

Filling:
1 cup sugar
3 tablespoons cornstarch
¼ teaspoon salt
½ cup water
¼ cup lemon juice
4 egg yolks, beaten
4 tablespoons butter
1 teaspoon grated lemon peel

Meringue:
4 egg whites
¼ teaspoon cream of tartar
¾ cup sugar

In mixing bowl, combine cake mix, eggs. water and oil. Beat on low until moistened. Beat on high for 2 minutes or until blended. Pour into 2 greased and floured 9 inch round baking pans. Bake at 350 degrees for 25 to 30 minutes or until a toothpick comes out clean. Cool for 10 minutes; remove from pans to wire racks. For filling, combine sugar, cornstarch, and salt in a saucepan. Stir in water and juice until smooth. Bring to a boil over medium heat; cook and stir 1-2 minutes or until thickened. Remove from heat. Stir a small amount of hot filling into egg yolks; return all to pan, stirring constantly. Bring to a gentle boil; cook and stir for 2 minutes. Remove from heat; stir in butter and lemon peel. Cool completely. For meringue, in a mixing bowl, beat egg whites and cream of tartar until foamy. Gradually beat in sugar on high until stiff peaks form. To assemble, split each cake into two layers. Place bottom layer on an ovenproof serving plate; spread with a third of the filling. Repeat layers twice. Top with fourth cake layer. Spread meringue over top and sides. Bake at 350 degrees for 10 to 15 minutes or until meringue is lightly browned.

Old Fashioned Southern Pound Cake
For Momma

1 cup (2 sticks) butter, room temperature
2 cups sugar
1 cup sour cream
6 eggs, room temperature
2 cups all-purpose flour
½ teaspoon baking soda
¼ teaspoon salt
2 tablespoon freshly squeezed lemon juice
1 tablespoon lemon zest
1 teaspoon vanilla
2 tablespoons Brandy (optional)

For Glaze:
½ cup plus 1 tablespoon powdered sugar
1 tablespoon lemon juice

Preheat oven to 325 degrees. Grease and flour a 10 inch tube pan and set aside. Cream butter; gradually add sugar, beating at least 5 minutes, until light and fluffy. Add the sour cream and mix well. Sift the flour, salt and baking soda together. Add eggs, one at a time, alternately with flour, beating well after each addition. Add lemon juice, lemon zest, and vanilla, beating well. If using Brandy, stir in now. Pour into tube pan and bake for 1 and ¼ hours, or until a wooden pick inserted in center comes out clean. Cool thoroughly before removing from pan. Drizzle with glaze, if desired.

Make glaze while cake is cooling. In a small bowl whisk powdered sugar, a little at a time, into lemon juice until smooth and thick. When cake is completely cooled, drizzle glaze over cake and let it drip down sides. If cake is made the day before serving, chill cake, covered, until ready to serve. Serve at room temperature.

Variation: Delicious served with Lemon, Mango, or Orange Sauce; or Raspberry and Blueberry Sauce. Cake may also be served with just blueberries or sliced strawberries. See Pages 104-107.

Praline Pecan Cake

1 Box Duncan Hines deluxe yellow cake mix
1 Box vanilla instant pudding (3 ¾ ounce size)
4 large eggs, room temperature
½ cup Crisco oil
¼ cup Domino liquid brown sugar
¾ cup Praline liqueur
¾ cup chopped pecans

    Preheat oven to 350 degrees. Coat the bottom and sides of a 10 inch Bundt pan with the 2 tablespoons butter or margarine. Sprinkle the ¾ cup of chopped pecans over the bottom and insides of the pan, spreading completely and evenly. Set Bundt pan aside. Pour the cake mix and pudding mix into the bowl of an electric mixer. Add the next four ingredients and with the mixer at low speed mix until thoroughly incorporated, about 2 minutes. Scrape down the sides of the bowl as the mix blends. Turn the mixer to medium speed and blend for 3 to 4 minutes, until mix is at the proper consistency. Remove the bowl from the mixer and fold in the chopped pecans. Pour batter into the Bundt pan and place on the middle rack of the oven. Bake for 45 to 50 minutes or until a toothpick inserted into cake comes out clean. Remove cake from oven and place on a rack for about 20 minutes. Gently remove cake from the pan and cool for another 15 minutes before glazing.

Glaze:
2 cups confectioners sugar
2 tablespoons butter, room temperature
¼ cup Praline liqueur
½ cup pecan halves

    Combine sugar and butter in a small bowl. Whisk or beat with an electric mixer until smooth, adding Praline Liqueur slowly to reach the right consistency. Pierce the top of the cake with a large serving fork, going around the whole top, so the glaze will go into the cake. Drizzle the glaze over the cake slowly and completely, allowing the glaze to run down the sides. Garnish the top of the cake with the pecan halves, making a nice pattern.

Creole Red Velvet Cake

½ cup unsalted butter, room temperature
1½ cups sugar
2 eggs. Room temperature
2 teaspoons cocoa powder
2 tablespoons red food coloring
1 teaspoon salt
1 teaspoon vanilla
1 cup buttermilk
2½ cups sifted cake flour
1½ teaspoons white vinegar
1 teaspoon baking soda

Creamy Frosting, recipe follows
Finely chopped pecans or flaked coconut (optional)

Spray or lightly flour and butter 2 (9-inch) round cake pans and set aside. Preheat oven to 350 degrees. In an electric mixer cream the butter and sugar, adding eggs, one at a time until the mixture is fluffy, about 1 minute. Add the cocoa and food coloring, salt and vanilla to the mixture. Add the buttermilk alternating with the flour. Remove bowl from beaters. Mix the vinegar and baking soda in a small bowl. Gently fold this into the batter. Do not beat. Divide the batter between the 2 cake pans. Put the cake pans in the oven evenly spaced apart. Bake for 25 to 30 minutes, or until an inserted cake tester comes out clean. Remove the cake pans from the oven to a rack and cool for 5 minutes. Remove cake layers from the pans and place on cooling racks, rounded sides up. Let layers cool completely before frosting.

Creamy Frosting
3 tablespoons flour
1 cup milk
1 cup (2 sticks) butter, room temperature
1 cup sifted confectioners sugar
1 teaspoon vanilla
1 cup finely chopped pecans or flaked coconut (optional)

Mix flour and milk until it becomes smooth. Pour into a small saucepan and cook over low heat until thick, stirring constantly. Bring mixture to room temperature. Meanwhile cream butter, sugar, and vanilla. Add flour mixture, a little at a time, beating constantly, until smooth enough to spread. Place one cake layer, rounded side down on a plate. Spread with frosting, spreading enough frosting to make a ¼ to ½ inch layer. Top with remaining layer and cover the top and sides of the cake with the remaining frosting. Sprinkle with chopped pecans or flaked coconut, if desired.

Cuban Tres Leches Cake
(Three Milk Cake)
This recipe was sent to me by my Brother

1 box white cake mix with pudding (made according to package directions)
1 cup whipping cream
1 (14 ounce) can condensed milk
1 can evaporated milk
2 tablespoons white cacao-flavored liquor

Heat oven to 350 degrees. Spray a 9 x 13 in baking pan. Prepare cake mix according to package directions. Pour into pan and bake as directed. Cool 10 minutes. Meanwhile, combine whipping cream, evaporated milk, condensed milk and liquor in large bowl with mixer. Mix well. Poke holes with fork and slowly pour milk mixture over cake until completely soaked. Refrigerate 3 hours.

Tangy Sunshine Cake

1 (8.25 ounce) box yellow cake mix
1 (3.4 ounce) box vanilla flavored instant
Pudding mix
1 (11 ounce) can mandarin oranges, undrained
1 (8.25 ounce) can crushed pineapple, undrained
3 eggs
Vanilla Pineapple Topping (recipe follows)
Garnish: mandarin oranges

Frosting:
1 container (12 ounce) light whipped topping, thawed
1 (3.4 ounce) package instant vanilla pudding mix
1 can (8 ounce) crushed pineapple in juice

Preheat oven to 375 degrees. Grease and flour a 13" x 9" cake pan or coat it with cooking spray. In a large bowl mix together all the cake ingredients until well blended. Beat at medium speed in an electric mixer until combined. Pour the batter into the pan and bake for 30 to 40 minutes, or until a toothpick inserted in the center comes out clean. Cool completely.

Evenly spread Vanilla Pineapple topping over cake. Garnish with mandarin oranges. Store in refrigerator.

Variation: To bake a multi-layer cake, bake the batter in two 9" cake pans for about 25 minutes, or until a toothpick inserted in the center comes out clean. Split the cooled layers in half horizontally. Spread frosting between layers. Stack and then spread frosting on the top and sides of cake.

Chocolate Fudge Pecan Layer Cake

¾ cup (1½ stick) butter
2 squares unsweetened chocolate
2¼ cups all-purpose flour
2 cups sugar
¼ cup unsweetened cocoa powder
2 teaspoons baking soda
1 teaspoon salt
1 ¾ cup buttermilk
2 eggs, room temperature
1 teaspoon vanilla extract
1 cup chopped pecans (optional)

Preheat oven to 350 degrees. Butter and flour two 9-inch round cake pans and set aside. Melt butter and chocolate in a small glass bowl and microwave on high for one to two minutes. Combine the dry ingredients, the flour, sugar, cocoa, baking soda, and salt in the large bowl of an electric mixer. Add the butter and chocolate mixture, buttermilk, eggs, vanilla extract, and pecans, if using. Beat on low for about a minute, scrape down the sides of the bowl, then beat on high for about 2 minutes, until light and fluffy. Pour batter evenly between the two cake pans, and bake for 25 to 30 minutes, or until layers spring back when lightly pressed. Cool in pans for about 5 minutes, then turn out onto cooling racks.

Chocolate frosting

¾ cup whipping cream
1½ cups semisweet chocolate chips

For the frosting: In a small pot scald the cream until bubbles appear around the edge, and it is just about to boil. Stir in the chocolate and mix until frosting is smooth and begins to thicken. Pour into a small bowl and frost layers, sides and top of cake.

Variation: To make a white chocolate frosting, use 9 squares of white chocolate in place of the chocolate chips in the frosting.

Carrot and Pineapple Cake

2 cups all-purpose flour
1 teaspoon baking soda
½ teaspoon salt
¼ teaspoon ground nutmeg
1½ teaspoon cinnamon
3 eggs

¾ cup vegetable oil or margarine
1½ cups sugar
1 teaspoon vanilla
1 (8 oz) can crushed pineapple, drained
3 cups grated carrots (about 5 medium)
½ cup chopped pecans

Preheat oven to 350 degrees. Generously grease two 9 inch cake pans or rectangular pan, 13 x 9 x 2 inches, lightly flour and set aside. Sift flour, baking soda, salt, nutmeg, and cinnamon together and set aside. In a large bowl beat eggs. Add oil, sugar and vanilla and mix well. Add flour mixture, pineapple, carrots, and pecans. Stir well and pour into cake pans. Bake rectangle 40 to 45 minutes, round pans 30 to 35 minutes, or until toothpick inserted in center comes out clean. Cool in pan on wire rack for 10 minutes. Remove from pans and cool completely and frost rectangle or fill and frost layers with cream cheese frosting.

Cream cheese frosting
½ cup margarine or butter, room temperature
1 box (1 pound) sifted confectioners sugar
1 package (8 ounces) cream cheese
1 teaspoon vanilla extract
1 tablespoon orange juice
1 teaspoon grated orange peel

Cream margarine and cream cheese until fluffy. Add vanilla, powdered sugar, orange juice, and orange peel. Beat until of spreading consistency. Spread between and over layers of cake. If baking a rectangular sheet cake, spread over top of cake.

Variation: Chocolate cream cheese frosting: Omit orange juice and orange peel. Add 2 teaspoons milk and 3 ounces unsweetened baking chocolate, melted and cooled, with butter or margarine. Proceed with recipe.

Angel Food Cake with Berry Compote
To be used with Angel Food Cake, but also with Pound Cake or any unfrosted Cake

Angel Food Cake, Homemade, From cake mix, or Store bought

½ cup water
⅓ cup sugar
1 tablespoon fresh lemon juice
3 whole allspice
3 cups fresh or frozen berries, blueberries, blackberries, raspberries, strawberries or mixture
Whipped cream

Bring water, sugar, lemon juice, and allspice to a boil in a small pot over moderate heat, stirring until sugar is dissolved. Boil to reduce to about ¼ cup. Remove allspice and stir in berries. Cook, mixing gently until berries are warm and began to release juice, about 3 minutes. Serve over sliced of angel food cake and top with whipped cream.

Whipped Cream

1 cup heavy cream, well chilled
2 tablespoon sugar
½ teaspoon vanilla

Whip in chilled bowl until soft peaks form. Serve.

COOKIES

Be Sorry for People
Whoever they are,
Who live in a house
Where there's no cookie Jar.

Anon

Bourbon Balls

1 cup finely crushed vanilla wafers
2 tablespoons cocoa, sifted
1 cup powdered (confectioners) sugar, sifted
1 cup finely chopped pecans
¼ cup Bourbon
1½ tablespoons light corn syrup
Sifted confectioners sugar

Add first four ingredients to a bowl and mix well. Add Bourbon and corn syrup and mix well again. Make sure the mixture is moist enough to form a ball. It if is not add a little more Bourbon. Roll into small balls ¾ to 1 inch in diameter. Roll in the sifted confections sugar, making sure all are well coated. Refrigerate, tightly covered, for at least 3 or 4 days before serving so flavors will blend. Recipe easily doubled or tripled, and extra balls may be frozen to be used at a future time.

Rum balls: Substitute ¼ cup rum for the Bourbon
Brandy balls: Substitute ¼ cup Brandy for the Bourbon.
Your food processor can be used to mix ingredients. First crush the cookies and finely chop the pecans. Add rest of ingredients and pulse off and on until mixture is blended well. Remove and roll into balls.

Chocolate Chip Cake Mix Cookies

1 stick (¼ pound) butter or margarine, softened
1 (8 ounce) package cream cheese, softened
1 egg
1 teaspoon vanilla
1 box yellow cake mix
1 (12 ounce) package chocolate chips

Preheat oven to 375 degrees. Grease baking sheets and set aside. Cream butter and cream cheese. Add egg and vanilla. Stir in cake mix and chocolate chips. Mix well and drop by teaspoonfuls onto baking sheet. Bake 8 to 10 minutes. Cool on cake racks.

Fudge Cookies

2 squares Baker's chocolate
½ cup butter (1 stick)
3 eggs, beaten
1 cup sugar
¾ cup flour
½ teaspoon baking powder
½ teaspoon salt
1 teaspoon vanilla
1 cup chopped pecans

Preheat oven to 350 degrees. Melt chocolate and butter together. Add eggs and sugar and beat well. Mix flour, baking powder, and salt and blend well into chocolate mixture. Add vanilla and pecans. Pour into a square baking pan. Bake in moderate oven 45 to 50 minutes. Remove from oven and immediately cut into squares.

Gingersnap Cookies

Gingersnaps have been popular with children for many generations, and today's children also enjoy them. This old fashioned recipe makes cookies that really snap.

1 cup butter or margarine
1 cup sugar
1 cup molasses
1 tablespoon vinegar
4 to 5 cups sifted flour
¼ teaspoon cinnamon
¼ teaspoon cloves
1 teaspoon ginger
2 teaspoon baking soda
1 large egg

Preheat oven to 350 degrees. Place the butter or margarine, sugar, molasses, and vinegar in a saucepan and heat just until the butter is melted and all the ingredients are well blended. Remove from heat and set aside until mixture is lukewarm. While this mixture is cooling, sift the flour, the spices, and the baking soda together in a bowl and set aside. Pour cooled butter mixture into a large mixing bowl. Beat in the egg and then slowly add the sifted flour mixture, a little at a time, adding enough to make a dough that can be rolled out. Roll dough out on a lightly floured board. Cut with a 2 inch round cookie cutter or into any shape you desire. Place on a greased cookie sheet or a cookie sheet lined with parchment paper. Bake for about 10 minutes. Cool on cookie sheet for about 5 minutes. Remove to wire racks, using a spatula, and cool completely.

Hermits
An old fashioned Southern Christmas Cookies

3 cups sifted flour
1 teaspoon baking soda
¼ teaspoon ground cloves
½ teaspoon cinnamon
½ teaspoon allspice
¼ teaspoon nutmeg
¼ teaspoon salt
1 cup butter or margarine, room temperature
1 cup brown sugar
½ cup molasses
2 large eggs, room temperature, beaten
1 tablespoon grated lemon zest
1 cup each: chopped pecans, raisins, and pitted dates or
Snipped dried apricots (the large soft kind are best)
Apricot glaze (optional)*

Preheat oven to 350 degrees. Sift first seven ingredients together. Cream the butter or margarine until smooth. Add the sugar, molasses, and eggs and beat thoroughly. Add the lemon rind, mix, and then the dry ingredients and mix well together. Add nuts and fruit, mixing well. Drop by tablespoons onto oiled cookie sheet. Bake 8 to 10 minutes, until lightly browned. Cool on racks

Bourbon Christmas Hermits: to Recipe add 3 tablespoons Bourbon or Cognac.

Apricot Liquor Glaze:

1 cup apricot preserves
2 tablespoons Bourbon, Cognac, or any desired liquor

Add preserves to a blender and puree. Pour the pureed preserves in a small saucepan and add liquor. Heat, over direct heat to the boiling point. Cool slightly but use while still warm. Drizzle over cookies.

Lemon Sugar Cookies

½ cup butter
½ cup sugar
1 egg
1 tablespoon milk
1 teaspoon lemon juice
2 teaspoon grated lemon rind
1 ¼ cups sifted all-purpose flour
1 teaspoon cream of tartar
½ teaspoon baking soda
½ teaspoon salt

Cream the butter, sugar, and egg thoroughly. Add milk, lemon juice, and lemon rind and mix thoroughly. Sift together and add to mixture the flour, baking powder, cream of tartar, and salt, mixing well. Refrigerate dough until chilled. When ready to bake, heat oven to 425 degrees. Roll dough into walnut size balls, drop on lightly greased cookie sheet, and flatten balls with the bottom of a floured glass. Sprinkle with sugar and bake for 5 to 7 minutes or until delicately browned.

Variation: to make shaped cookies, roll dough lightly with a floured rolling pin. Dip cookie cutter of your choice in flour, shake it and cut cookie dough. For crisp cookies, roll dough very thin.

To make plain sugar cookies, omit lemon juice and rind. Add 1 teaspoon vanilla. 1 cup finely chopped pecans or walnuts may be added.

Coconut Macaroons

14 ounces sweetened shredded coconut
14 ounce can condensed milk
1 teaspoon vanilla extract
2 large egg whites, at room temperature
¼ teaspoon kosher salt

Combine the coconut, condensed milk, and vanilla in a large bowl. Whip egg whites and salt on high speed in the bowl of an electric mixer fitted with the whisk attachment until they make medium firm peaks. Carefully fold the egg whites into the coconut mixture. Drop the batter onto sheet pans lined with parchment paper using either a 1 ¾ inch diameter ice cream scoop or 2 teaspoons. Bake for 25 to 30 minutes, until golden brown. Cool on racks before serving.

Madeleines

Madeleines are delicate little tea cakes that have been popular in France since 1730. They are usually baked in lightly greased and floured scalloped Madeline shells But may also be baked in muffin tins.

2 eggs
½ teaspoon vanilla
1½ teaspoon grated lemon zest
1 cup sifted powdered sugar
¼ teaspoon salt
1 cup sifted cake flour
¾ cup butter, melted and cooled too lukewarm
1 tablespoon rum or Brandy
Powdered sugar

Preheat oven to 350 degrees. Grease and lightly flour 24 Madeline molds or muffin tins and set them aside. In an electric mixer on high speed, beat eggs, vanilla and lemon zest for 5 minutes, to incorporate as much air into the mixture as possible. Slowly beat in the powdered sugar and salt. Beat for 5 to 7 minutes or until thick and creamy, occasionally scraping down sides of mixing bowl. Gradually add sifted cake flour, one fourth at a time, folding in gently. Fold in melted butter and rum or Brandy. Spoon into the prepared molds or muffin tins, filling ¾ full. Bake for 8 to 10 minutes, or until a delicate brown. Cool in molds for 1 minute, and then invert onto rack and cool. When ready to serve sift powdered sugar over tops. Freezes well.

Momma's Molasses Oatmeal Cookies

Momma always made her oatmeal cookies with Blackstrap molasses. The blackstrap gave the cookies a unique flavor, which was delicious.

1 ¾ cups all-purpose flour
1 teaspoon cinnamon
1 teaspoon allspice (optional)
½ teaspoon baking powder
1 teaspoon baking soda
½ teaspoon salt
1 cup (2 sticks butter or margarine, room temperature)
¾ cup sugar
½ cup molasses (preferably blackstrap molasses*)
2 large eggs
1 teaspoon vanilla
3 cups uncooked rolled oats
1 cup raisins

Preheat oven to 350 degrees. Line 2 baking sheets with parchment paper or aluminum foil and set aside. Sift together in a medium bowl the flour, spices, baking soda, baking powder, and salt and set aside. In a large bowl or an electric mixer cream together butter and sugar until light and fluffy, about 3 minutes. Add molasses, egg, and vanilla and beat until well combined, about 1 minute, scraping down sides of bowl as needed. Add the flour mixture in two batches and mix only until well combined. Stir in oatmeal and raisins, mixing well. Drop by teaspoonfuls (or using an ice cream scoop, shape into 1½ in balls). Place about 3 inches apart on cookie sheets. Flatten with the back of a fork. Bake until golden brown, about 15 to 17 minutes for chewy cookies, 3 or 4 minutes more if you like them crispy. Cool cookies on baking sheets for about 5 minutes and then transfer to wire racks to cool completely.

Variation: To make chocolate chip oatmeal cookies, omit raisins. Add one package semi-sweet chocolate pieces (2 cups) along with oatmeal, mixing well.

To make oatmeal spice cookies, decrease allspice to ½ teaspoon and add ½ teaspoon each ground nutmeg, ginger, and cloves.

*Blackstrap is what remains when all the sugar in sugarcane which can profitably be extracted has been taken out. Nevertheless, this molasses, or blackstrap, still contains a good portion of the total sugars in the cane juice, and for being more concentrated it is richer still in vitamins and minerals.

Orange Carrot Cookies

¾ cup butter or margarine
¾ cup sugar
1 cup cooked and mashed carrots
1 egg, slightly beaten
1 teaspoon vanilla
1 teaspoon orange juice
2 cups all-purpose flour
2 teaspoons baking powder
½ teaspoon salt
½ cup raisins
¼ cup chopped pecans (optional)

Preheat oven to 350 degrees and grease cookie sheet. In a mixer, cream butter and sugar. Add carrots, egg, vanilla, and orange juice, beating well. Gradually add flour, salt, and baking powder to bowl. Stir in raisins and pecans. Place a teaspoon full at a time on cookie sheet and bake for 12 to 15 minutes.

Peanut Butter Cookies

2½ cups all-purpose flour
2 teaspoons baking soda
½ teaspoon salt
¾ cup butter, room temperature
1 cup sugar
1 cup dark brown sugar
1 teaspoon vanilla extract
2 large eggs, room temperature
1 cup crunchy peanut butter (or a mixture of half crunchy and half smooth)
¼ cup hot water

Sift together the flour, baking soda, and salt in a bowl and set aside. In an electric mixer, cream butter, sugars, and vanilla until light and fluffy. Add the eggs, one at a time, beating after each addition. Add the peanut butter, blending thoroughly. Stir in the dry ingredients, alternately with the hot water. Refrigerate for at least 30 minutes, or until firm. When ready to bake preheat oven to 350 degrees. Form the dough into small balls and place on cookie sheets. Flatten the balls with a fork into circles about 2 or 2½ inches in diameter, making a crisscross pattern. Bake until lightly browned, about 12 to 15 minutes. Remove from cookie sheets and place on a rack to cool.

Pfeffernusse Christmas Cookies
(German Peppernuts)

German peppernuts are tiny spice cookies which contain pepper as well as several spices. These cookies improve with aging; store them in a cookie tin or tightly covered container. Add a piece of apple to the container before serving to soften them.

¾ cup molasses
¾ cup honey
¾ cup butter or margarine
4 cups sifted all-purpose flour
2 eggs, well beaten
1 teaspoon baking soda
1 teaspoon salt
½ teaspoon freshly ground black pepper
1 teaspoon ground allspice
teaspoon ground mace
¼ teaspoon nutmeg
1 teaspoon cinnamon
¼ teaspoon anise seeds or 1 teaspoon crushed cardamom seeds
¼ cup Brandy
1 teaspoon lemon zest
½ cup candied citron, finely chopped (optional)
¼ cup finely chopped pecans

Combine molasses and honey in a small saucepan and cook over low heat until thoroughly heated, stirring continually. Add butter or margarine, stirring to blend in well, and then remove from heat to cool. Sift flour, baking soda, salt and pepper, and spices into a large bowl. When molasses mixture is completely cooled add eggs and stir well to completely blend. Gradually pour into bowl with flour spice mixture. Add Brandy and lemon zest, stirring just until flour mixture is completely moistened. Stir in citron, if using, and pecans. Mix well, cover and allow to rest for several hours, or overnight.

When ready to bake, preheat oven to 350 degrees. Grease cookie sheets or cover with parchment paper and set aside. Shape dough into 1 inch balls and place on the baking sheets, leaving 2 inches or so between the cookies. Bake for about 10 to 12 minutes or until cookies are firm to the touch and light brown. (Break one in half; if not sticky, the cookies are done). Cookies may be left plain or rolled in powdered sugar and placed on cake racks to cool.

Praline Snickerdoodles

1 cup butter, softened
1 cup sugar
2 egg yolks, room temperature
½ teaspoon vanilla
2 tablespoons Praline liqueur
1 teaspoon orange juice
2 cups all-purpose flour
1 teaspoon baking powder
1 teaspoon cinnamon
½ teaspoon salt
Pecan halves

Cream butter in an electric mixer. Gradually add sugar, beating at medium speed. Add egg yolks, one at a time, beating after each addition. Beat in vanilla, praline liqueur and orange juice. Sift together flour, baking powder, cinnamon and salt. Gradually add to creamed mixture, mixing well. Put mixing bowl into refrigerator for 1 hour. When ready to bake, preheat oven to 300 degrees. Shape dough into one inch balls. Place about 2 inches apart on ungreased baking sheet. Press a pecan half into center of each cookie. Bake for 20 minutes or until lightly browned. Cool on wire racks.

Sandstone Health Cookies

¾ cup whole wheat flour
¼ cup wheat germ
¼ cup non-fat dry milk
¼ teaspoon cinnamon
1 teaspoon salt
¼ baking soda
¼ teaspoon baking powder
¾ cup honey
½ cup butter or margarine

½ cup smooth peanut butter
1 egg, slightly beaten
1 teaspoon vanilla
1 cup raisins
1 cup dried apricots, chopped well
½ cup uncooked rolled oats
⅓ cup sunflower nuts
½ cup chopped pecans

Preheat oven to 350 degrees. Mix together flour, wheat germ, powdered milk, cinnamon, salt, baking soda, and baking powder. In a separate large bowl combine honey, butter, peanut butter, egg, and vanilla. Beat well, then add flour mixture, mixing well. Stir together raisins, apricots, oats, sunflower nuts and pecans. Add to flour mixture and mix well. Drop by teaspoonfuls onto ungreased cookie sheet and bake for 15 minutes. Cool well on wire racks.

Snickerdoodles
Jenny's Southern Tea Cakes

1 tablespoon sugar
1 tablespoon cinnamon
1¼ cup sugar
1 cup butter, room temperature
2 eggs, room temperature
½ teaspoon vanilla
½ teaspoon almond extract
1 teaspoon orange juice
1 teaspoon lemon juice
2 ¾ cups all-purpose flour (measure before sifting)
2 teaspoons cream of tarter
1 teaspoon baking soda
½ teaspoon salt
1 teaspoon grated orange zest

Preheat oven to 350 degrees. Combine sugar and cinnamon in a small mixing bowl and set aside. Beat sugar and butter until light and fluffy. Beat in eggs, one at a time and blending well after each addition. Add vanilla, almond, orange, and lemon juices. Sift dry ingredients together and add to mixture in bowl. Blend in orange zest. Mix well and refrigerate for about 2 hours. When ready to bake roll into small balls between the palms of your hands, about a teaspoonful at a time. Roll each little ball into reserved sugar and cinnamon mixture, coating well. Place on cookie sheets about 2 inches apart. Bake 12 to 14 minutes, or until golden brown. For a chewy cookie, slightly underbake them. Remove immediately from cookie sheet. Place on cake racks to cool, and if you wish, cookies can be frozen for future use. Makes about 7 dozen.

Variation: Colored cake decors can be added to sugar to give a more festive look to cookies.

Glazes

A glaze is a thin icing that is spooned or drizzled over the top of the cake, muffins, or cookies or over a frosting. It is usually made with a cup of sifted powdered sugar blended with 1 or 2 tablespoons melted butter and thinned with fruit juice or liquor until it can be spooned or drizzled from a spoon.

Apricot glaze: 1 cup apricot preserves, 2 tablespoons liquor of your choice. Puree in blender, and then add the liquor and heat, over direct heat, to the boiling point. Cool slightly but use while still warm.

Orange glaze: Thin the powdered sugar with orange juice or a combination of orange juice and orange liquor, and 2 teaspoons orange zest.

Lemon glaze: Same as orange glaze, using lemon juice and zest.

Strawberry glaze: 1 cup powdered sugar, 2 tablespoons melted butter, ½ teaspoon vanilla, and sufficient mashed strawberries to thin the mixture.

Pie Pastry
Delicate and Flavorful

1¼ cups all-purpose flour
¾ cup cake flour
½ teaspoon salt
2 teaspoons sugar
1 cup (2 sticks) butter
3 tablespoons shortening
¼ cup sour cream
2 egg yolks, slightly beaten
Juice of ½ lemon

Place a large stainless steel bowl and beaters in the freezer for 10 minutes. Remove bowl and beaters from freezer and sift the dry ingredients into the cold bowl. Using a pastry blender, cut in butter until the size of small peas. Mix in the shortening, sour cream, egg yolks, and lemon juice. Don't overwork pastry or it will become tough. Form into a ball, wrap in plastic wrap and chill for at least 2 hours. When ready to make pie, crusts remove dough from refrigerator and divide into two balls. Keep one ball wrapped in plastic wrap until ready to use for top pie crust. Roll dough out on a floured board. Using a floured rolling pin, roll from the center out. If dough begins to stick, rub more flour on the board and rolling pin a little at a time. Roll pastry 2 inches larger than inverted pie plate Fold pastry into fourths and ease into pie plate, pressing firmly against bottom and sides. Chill for 15 minutes in the refrigerator.

For one crust pie: Trim overhanging excess of pastry 1 inch from rim of plate. Fold and roll pastry under, even with plate and flatten evenly on edge of plate. Crimp the edge with the tines of a fork or with the fingers. Fill and bake as directed in recipe.

For two crust pie: Place the filling you are using into the pastry lined pie plate. Trim overhanging edge of pastry ½ inch from edge of plate. Place other round of pastry over the top of filling. Trim overhang 1 inch from edge of plate. Roll top edge of pastry over bottom edge, pressing on edge to seal. Flatten pastry evenly on edge of pie plate and crimp with tines of a fork. Brush top of crust with milk for a shiny crust or with a beaten egg yolk mixed with a little water for a glazed crust.

For baked pie shell: Heat oven to 475 degrees. Prick sides and bottom completely with a fork and bake for 7 to 10 minutes or until lightly brown.

Basic Pie Pastry
For a 9 inch two crust pie

2 cups all-purpose flour
1 teaspoon salt
2/3 cup lard or 2/3 cup plus 2 tablespoons butter
4 to 5 tablespoons ice water

Combine flour and salt in a large mixing bowl. Using a pastry blender, cut in lard or butter until particles are the size of small peas. Sprinkle with water, one tablespoon at a time, mixing and tossing with fork until the flour is moistened and pastry almost leaves the sides of the bowl. A little more water may be added if necessary. Shape dough into 2 balls and proceed as in Pie pastry recipe above.

Tropical Custard Pie

1 cup sugar
3 tablespoons all-purpose flour
1 cup light corn syrup
1 cup flaked coconut
1 can (8 ounces) crushed pineapple, undrained
3 eggs, beaten
1 tablespoon fresh lemon juice
1 teaspoon vanilla extract
1 unbaked (9 inch) pie shell
1/4 cup butter or margarine, melted

Preheat oven to 350 degrees. Prepare pie dough or used Pillsbury unbaked pie shell, place in pie pan and set aside. Combine sugar and flour in a bowl. Add the next 6 ingredients, mixing well. Pour into pie shell and drizzle with butter. Bake for 50 to 55 minutes or until knife inserted in center comes out clean. If top seems to be browning too quickly, cover loosely with aluminum foil. Cool on a wire rack and refrigerate before serving. Leftovers are to be refrigerated.

Deep Dish Country Apple Pie

2 (9 or 10 inch) pie shells (See recipe for pie pastry)
8 cups (about 8 medium) peeled and thinly sliced Granny Smith or McIntosh apples, or a combination of both

Sauce
2 tablespoons cornstarch
6 tablespoons sugar
2 teaspoons ground cinnamon
½ teaspoon ground nutmeg
½ teaspoon salt
6 tablespoons butter, melted
⅔ cup light corn syrup
1 teaspoon vanilla
1 tablespoon lemon juice

Topping:
¾ cup brown sugar
3 tablespoons flour
4 tablespoons light corn syrup
4 tablespoons softened butter

Preheat oven to 425 degrees. Prepare pastry. Place bottom crust in large deep dish pie pan. Place sliced apples in a large bowl. Stir ingredients in sauce mixture and pour over apples, mixing well. Pour into pie shell. Mix topping ingredients well and pour about ½ cup of the topping mixture on top of the apples and sauce mixture. Cover with top crust that has slits cut in it, seal and flute. Bake for 45 minutes or until crust is brown and juice begins to bubble through slits in crust. Remove from oven. Spread the rest of the mixture over the warm pie, being careful not to break the crust. Return to oven for about 10 minutes until topping is bubbly. Remove from oven. Pie is good served warm or cold. Especially good served warm with ice cream or a slice of cheddar cheese.

Lemon Meringue Pie

This was Momma's way of making lemon pie
And is now my way.

Recipe for basic pie shell or 1 9-inch Pillsbury unbaked pie crust
1 box lemon Jell-O pie filling
½ cup sugar
2 egg yolks
2¼ cups water

Prepare pastry for a single crust pie or use Pillsbury pie crust, prepared according to package directions. Bake in 450 degree oven for 10 to 12 minutes or until golden. Cool. In a heavy saucepan, mix pie filling with sugar, egg yolks, and water. Mix well and cook on medium heat until mixture come to a full boil; stir and set aside for 5 minutes, Stir well and pour mixture into pie shell.

Meringue:

4 egg whites
½ teaspoon vanilla
½ teaspoon cream of tartar
⅓ cup sugar

In a large glass bowl beat egg whites with vanilla and cream of tartar until soft peaks form. Gradually add the sugar, beating until stiff peaks form. Spread meringue over filling, sealing it very well to the edge of crust. Bake in 350 degree oven for 12 to 15 minutes or until meringue is golden brown. Cool and refrigerate for about 3 hours before serving.

Jo's Pecan Pie
For Daddy

Opulent and absolutely delicious, Pecan Pie has been the "Crème de Crème" of New Orleans Pies since pecans were first grown in Louisiana.

This recipe is for 2 pies. One is never enough. But if you want to make only one pie, divide ingredients in half.

2 (9-inch) pie shells, unbaked, (your favorite homemade or store bought)
1 cup butter or margarine, room temperature
2 cups light brown sugar
2 tablespoons flour
6 large eggs
2 cup light corn syrup
2 tablespoons Bourbon (optional)
½ teaspoon salt
2 teaspoons vanilla
2 tablespoon lemon juice
2 cups chopped pecans
Pecan halves

Preheat oven to 350 degrees. Prepare pie shells and set aside. Cream together butter, brown sugar, and flour. Beat in eggs, one at a time. Add rest of ingredients except pecans and beat until well blended. Fold pecans into blended mixture. Pour into unbaked pie shells and decorate tops with pecan halves. Bake for 45 to 50 minutes or until center is set and knife inserted midway between center and rim comes out clean. Cool on wire rack and serve at room temperature or chilled. Nice served with vanilla ice cream, whipped cream or each slice topped with cool whip.

Chocolate Pecan Pie: Stir in 1 package (6 ounces) semisweet chocolate chips with the pecans. May be added with or without the Bourbon.

Cherry Pie
My Daughter Laurie's favorite pie

Favorite pastry for a 2-crust pie

1 quart fresh sour red cherries, pitted (if fresh cherries are not available, use 2 (2 pound) cans sour red pitted cherries with ¼ cup of the juice)
1 cup sugar
2 tablespoons cornstarch
½ teaspoon grated lemon rind
¼ teaspoon almond extract
1 egg white beaten with 2 teaspoons sugar until frothy, reserve

Combine the cherries with the sugar, cornstarch, lemon rind, and almond extract in a large bowl. Set aside for ½ hour. When ready to bake pie, preheat the oven to 425 degrees. Drain the cherry mixture into a bowl, measure the juices and add water if needed to equal ¼ cup. Mix the filling and pour into the pie shell. Fold remaining pastry in half and place over fruit mixture. Fold edges of pastry just under inside edges of pie pan. Press edges to edges of pan, crimping to form a decorative rim. Brush the top of the pie with the reserved egg white mixture. Cut slits in top to allow steam to escape. Bake on lower third of the oven for 20 minutes. Reduce heat to 375 degrees and bake for 30 minutes more or until lightly browned. Remove pie from oven and let it cool slightly.

Variation: Pie can be made with a lattice top. Leave a 1-inch overhang on lower crust. After rolling pastry for top crust, cut into 10 strips, each about ½ inch wide, with a sharp knife or preferably with a pastry wheel. Moisten the rim of the pie shell with water. Press firmly on the strips, weaving into a lattice pattern. Crimp the overhanging dough into a decorative rim. Brush strips with egg mixture. Proceed as above.

Pumpkin Pie
Rich and delicious with the addition of cheese

Pastry for 9 in. pie crust

1 package (8 ounces) cream cheese, room temperature
¾ cup sugar
½ teaspoon salt
2 tablespoons all-purpose flour
2 cups canned pumpkin
1 teaspoon ground cinnamon
1 teaspoon lemon zest
1 teaspoon orange zest
¼ teaspoon ground nutmeg
¼ teaspoon ginger
¼ teaspoon vanilla
2 eggs, slightly beaten
¼ cup (½ stick) melted butter
1 cup milk or half and half
Ice cream, whipped cream or cool whip, for topping

Preheat oven to 350 degrees. Beat cream cheese, sugar, salt and flour in large mixer bowl until blended. Add rest of ingredients except topping; and beat on medium speed until smooth. Pour into pastry lined pie plate. Bake for 50 minutes or until a knife inserted in the center comes out clean. Place pie on a wire rack and cool to room temperature, then refrigerate for 3 to 4 hours before serving. Cut into slices and top each slice with vanilla ice cream, whipped cream or cool whip.

Southern Yam (or Sweet Potato) Pie

A delicious, old fashioned Pie for the holidays or for any time. Either Yams or Sweet Potatoes can be used, as they are interchangeable. Sweet potatoes are yellowish and flesh toned potatoes, and Louisiana Yams are orangy-Red skinned potatoes with a more distinct flavor, and is what Momma always used. This custard like pie goes back many generations in our family. Either Cane or Maple syrup can be used, but we have always used Louisiana Cane syrup. This is one of the many ways to prepare Sweet Potato Pie.

1 9-inch unbaked pie crust
2 large or 3 medium sweet potatoes or yams, (1½ to 2 cups baked and mashed)
4 tablespoons butter, melted
1 teaspoon vanilla
3 eggs
1 egg yolk
¾ cup half and half cream or evaporated milk

¼ cup plus 2 tablespoons Cane or Maple syrup
¼ cup plus 1 tablespoon brown sugar
¼ cup Bourbon or Brandy (optional)
1 teaspoon grated orange rind
¼ teaspoon salt
¼ teaspoon nutmeg
¼ teaspoon cinnamon
⅛ teaspoon ground cloves
A few grinds black pepper

Preheat oven to 375 degrees. Prepare the pie crust and set aside. Peel the baked sweet potatoes and mash them well with a potato masher. Add the remaining ingredients to the mashed yams and whisk until smooth and well combined. Pour into the pie shell. Place the pie plate on an aluminum foil covered cookie sheet and bake for 30 to 40 minutes, until a knife inserted in the center comes out clean. Do not overcook the filling, checking it frequently near the end of the baking time, as it will set up more as it cools. Serve warm or cool the pie to room temperature. Delicious served with whipped cream or ice cream.

Note: This pie is best with baked and mashed Louisiana yams or sweet potatoes, but for a quicker way, canned yams can be used. Just be sure they are well drained and dried before you use them.

Bananas Foster

1 stick butter
½ cup dark brown sugar
4 bananas, peeled and halved, then cut lengthwise
¼ cup dark rum

    Melt butter in a large fry pan. Add brown sugar and stir until well blended. Add the bananas and cook over medium high heat until caramelized. Pour in the rum and light with a long match. Flambe, being careful to stand back as flame rises from pan. Let the flame die down and serve over vanilla ice cream. Also, nice served over pound cake and vanilla ice cream.

Blueberry Custard

½ cup sugar
2 tablespoons all-purpose flour
⅛ teaspoon salt
1 teaspoon grated lemon peel
1½ cups half and half cream
3 egg yolks, lightly beaten
2 tablespoons butter or margarine
1 tablespoon vanilla extract
1 can (15 ounces) blueberries
1 tablespoon cornstarch

    In a saucepan start custard by combing sugar, flour, salt and lemon peel. Gradually add cream, stirring well until blended. Bring to a boil and stirring constantly, cook for 2 minutes or until thickened. Remove from heat. Stir a small amount of hot mixture into beaten egg yolks. Stir and add to mixture in saucepan. Bring to a slow boil, stirring constantly.

    Remove from heat and add butter and vanilla. Pour into 4 parfait glasses or dessert dishes. Set aside to cool. Drain blueberries, reserving juice. Spoon blueberries evenly over cooled custard. Place blueberry juice and cornstarch in a small saucepan, stirring well until smooth. Bring to a boil over medium heat and boil gently for 1 to 2 minutes until thickened. Spoon sauce over berries.

Creole Cream Cheese Ice Cream
This Recipe Is
From my Great-Grandmother, to Mamere,
to Momma, to Me

4 pints creole cream cheese
1 (16 ounce) can evaporated milk (or 2 cups heavy cream)
1 cup sugar
1 large (16 ounce) can crushed pineapple, drained
Juice of one lemon

Blend all ingredients together until smooth, stirring well. Place in rectangular dish or pan and put in freezer. When it is almost hard - about 1 hour - take it out and stir well. Place back in freezer. Cut into squares with knife.

Lemon Ice Dessert
This delicious recipe was given to me by
My cousin, Vivian Ware Dawkins

9x8 inch square pan
2 cups graham cracker crumbs
¼ cup margarine
½ gallon low fat or regular vanilla ice cream
6 ounce can frozen lemonade

Take 3 tablespoons of graham cracker crumbs and reserve them on the side. Melt the margarine and combine it with the remaining graham cracker crumbs. Press into the bottom and sides of an approximately 9x8 inch square pan to make graham cracker crust. Remove ice cream from freezer and let it soften, then mix together thoroughly with the can of lemonade. Spread into the pan evenly and lightly sprinkle the top with the reserved graham cracker crumbs. Refrigerate a few hours until it is frozen, then serve. Recipe easily doubled.

Cream Puffs
(Profiteroles)
In memory of Momma's wonderful Cream Puffs

1 cup water
½ cup butter or margarine
1 cup all-purpose flour
¼ teaspoon salt
4 eggs
Vanilla cream filling
Chocolate fudge sauce or powdered sugar

    Preheat oven to 400 degrees. Add butter to boiling water in a 1 quart saucepan. Heat until butter melts. Add flour and salt, stirring vigorously, lower heat and continue stirring vigorously until mixture leaves the sides of the pan and forms a ball, about 1 minute. Remove from heat and cool for 10 minutes. Add eggs, one at a time, and continue beating until smooth. Drop by heaping tablespoonfuls (it helps to have the spoon wet) 3 inches apart on greased cookie sheets. Shape with a wet spoon into rounds which point up in the center. Bake for 35 to 40 minutes, or until puffed and golden. Turn off heat, remove from oven and make a tiny incision near the bottom of each puff with the point of a sharp knife to release the steam. Return to oven for a few minutes to dry out Then put them on racks to cool. When ready to serve, cut a slit in one side of each puff, or cut off tops. Fill with vanilla cream filling, ice cream, or whipped cream. If tops are cut off, replace tops and gently press the puff together again. Place on dessert plates and drizzle with Chocolate fudge sauce or dust with Powdered Sugar. Also, very good topped with sweetened crushed strawberries, raspberries, or sliced peaches. 10 to 12 Cream Puffs.

Vanilla Cream Filling – See page 327.
Chocolate Fudge Sauce – See page 101.

Creole Caramel Cup Custard

An elegant, classic French dessert brought
to New Orleans by the original French settlers.

1½ cup sugar, divided
¼ cup water
3 large eggs plus 2 large egg yolks
⅛ teaspoon salt
1 tablespoon vanilla
2 cups milk, heated to scalding
Nutmeg

Preheat oven to 350 degrees. First, caramelize the sugar by mixing ½ cup sugar and ¼ cup water in a small pot. Place overheat and stir until sugar and water caramelizes to a rich golden brown. Remove from heat and continue to stir to keep from burning. Spoon into 6 (4 ounce) custard cups, dividing mixture equally. In a large bowl beat remaining sugar, eggs, salt, and vanilla until well blended. Gradually beat the scalded milk into the egg mixture. Pour equally into the custard cups and sprinkle the tops with nutmeg. Place custard cups in a baking pan. Fill baking pan with water to reach about halfway up the custard cups. Bake for about 45 to 50 minutes. The custard will be set when a knife inserted in center of custards comes out clean. Chill for an hour or two in refrigerator. When ready to serve unmold each cup on a small plate. If necessary, loosen the custard by sliding a thin knife around the custard before inverting on dish.

Variation: Chocolate custard. Melt 12½ ounces of chocolate in the milk while it is being heated to make custard.

Pecan Pralines
(Pralines aux Pacanes)

Pralines have been enjoyed and written of in New Orleans for over 200 years. There was even an old French rhyme that was sung in the banquette (sidewalk) games of the children of New Orleans. Little girls would sing it to the beat of their jump ropes.

"Soeur Rosalie au retour de matines, Plus d'une fois lui porta des Pralines".

Very loosely translated it means something like, "Sister Rosalie returned from the matinee, and took time to sit down to eat Pralines"

There are many New Orleans Creole candies such as pacanes a la crème, la colle, mais tac tac, dragees, guimauves, pastilles, nougates and many others which people have enjoyed for so many years, but the classic Creole candy is still, and I think will always be, the Praline.

1½ cup brown sugar
½ cup granulated sugar
½ teaspoon salt
1 cup half and half cream or 1 cup buttermilk
¼ teaspoon cream of tartar
¼ cup butter, softened
1 teaspoon vanilla
2½ cups pecan, some broken pieces, some halves

Combine the first 5 ingredients in a heavy saucepan. Cook over low fire, stirring all the while, until the sugars dissolve and the mixture comes to a boil. Continue cooking until mixture forms a small ball in cold water, (236 degrees on a candy thermometer). Remove from heat, add butter, vanilla and pecans and continue to beat until creamy and mixture begins to lose its gloss. Drop by spoonfuls onto a piece of buttered wax paper, using a second spoon to push pralines off the first, and working fast before mixture hardens. Wrap each in a piece in wax paper and store in a covered container.

Variation: ½ cup of rum or Brandy may be added and reduce cream or buttermilk to ⅔ cup.

Sabayon

Sabayon is a sort of cream mousse of Italian origin. The word Sabayon in French is a corruption of the Italian word, Zabaglione (Zabaione) Sabayon must not cook over direct heat. It is necessary to have a double boiler. It is best that the upper part have a heavy bottom so you might use an enameled cast iron saucepan or other heavy pot and hold it over water simmering in any other kind of pot. Do not let the water in the bottom pot touch the bottom of the upper pot. Be sure to use a large enough pot as the mixture increases greatly in volume as you beat.

6 egg yolks
1 cup sugar
⅛ teaspoon salt
¾ cup dry Marsala, cream sherry, or white wine, sweet or dry
1 cup heavy cream
1 teaspoon vanilla

In a metal bowl or the top of a double boiler beat egg yolks, sugar, salt and wine with a handheld electric mixer until well combined. Set bowl over a saucepan of barely simmering water and beat mixture vigorously until it becomes frothy and stiff, about 5 to 8 minutes. Remove from heat and set mixture in bowl over a bowl of ice water and continue to beat until chilled. In another bowl beat the heavy cream and vanilla to stiff peaks. In 3 additions fold the whipped cream into the Sabayon. Chill for 2 to 3 hours. When ready to serve, spoon into small ramekins, goblets or Champagne glasses. Serve immediately.

Sabayon a la Creole

Make a sabayon as above with white wine but omit vanilla. Add the peel or zest of an orange, lemon, lime or tangerine. Do not use any of the white part of the fruit. As soon as the sabayon becomes frothy, cool it by sitting the bowl into a bowl of cold water, continuing to beat until cool. Add 4 tablespoons of rum and one cup of stiffly whipped cream. Continue as above.

Variation: Sabayon with Berries or fruit of your choice

Sabayon with Fruit

4 to 5 cups mixed raspberries and quartered strawberries, sliced peaches, pears, or fruit of your choice
¼ cup sugar
2 tablespoons amaretto, or to taste

Place all ingredients in a bowl, mix and set aside to macerate for about an hour at room temperature. When ready to serve, divide the berries or fruit of your choice into small bowls or stemmed glasses and spoon chilled sabayon over the top. Serve. Also, delicious served over pound cake or angel food cake. Spoon fruit and then sabayon over a slice of cake. For Sabayon recipe, see page 325.

Ruby Pears

6 ripe pears, peeled, cored and halved
1 (3 oz.) package cherry flavored gelatin
¾ cup boiling water
1 cup ruby port wine
2 (2 in.) cinnamon sticks
6 whole cloves

Place pears in a 13"x9" baking dish, cut side up. Combine gelatin and water in a bowl. Stir until gelatin is dissolved. Add Port wine, cinnamon sticks and cloves and stir. Pour mixture over pears and cover with aluminum foil. Bake 25 minutes in a preheated 350 degree oven. Uncover and baste well, then bake another 20 minutes or until pears are tender. Take out of oven and let cool in syrup. Remove cinnamon sticks and cloves and serve either warm or cold.

Vanilla Cream Filling

¾ cup sugar
¼ cup all-purpose flour
¼ teaspoon salt
1½ cups milk, very hot but not boiling
5 egg yolks, slightly beaten
2 teaspoons vanilla
1½ cups heavy whipping cream

Combine sugar, flour, and salt in a heavy bottomed 2 quart saucepan. Add the very hot milk and beat until well blended. Continue to stir over medium heat for 4 to 5 minutes, or until very thick and smooth. Pour a little of the mixture into the bowl containing the slightly beaten egg yolks. Beat the mixture into the egg yolks. Slowly pour eggs into milk mixture and cook for about 8 minutes, or until mixture is thick enough to coat mixing spoon. Be careful not to boil. Remove from heat and stir in vanilla. Cover surface with Saran Wrap and chill for about 1½ to 2 hours. In a chilled bowl beat whipping cream until stiff peaks form. Gently fold whipped cream into custard. Makes 4 ⅔ cups.

If cream filling is to be used for cream puffs, place filling in a plastic zip loc bag. Cut one corner of bag off. Pipe filling into cream puff through hole in bag.

Bread Pudding
Another Classic New Orleans Dessert
This was Mamere and Momma's version

5 cups stale French or Italian bread, cubed small (use crust of bread)
4½ cups hot milk
4 eggs, beaten well
1 cup sugar
2 or 3 large green Granny Smith or golden delicious apples, peeled and shredded
1 teaspoon cinnamon
2 teaspoons vanilla
½ teaspoon salt
½ cup butter or margarine, melted
¾ cup raisins

Combine bread and hot milk in a large bowl and set aside. In a separate bowl beat eggs, add sugar and mix well. Stir into bread mixture and add apples, vanilla, cinnamon, salt, butter, and raisins. Pour into buttered 13x9x2 casserole. Bake at 350 degrees in preheated oven for one hour or until knife inserted in the center comes out clean. If you like a more creamy pudding, bake with casserole sitting in a pan of warm water about 1 inch deep. Serve plain or with lemon and/or Brandy sauce.

Chocolate Pudding

1 cup sugar
½ cup baking cocoa
¼ cup cornstarch
¼ teaspoon salt
4 cups milk
2 tablespoons butter or margarine
2 teaspoons vanilla

Combine sugar, cocoa, cornstarch, and salt in a heavy saucepan. Gradually add milk. Bring to a rolling boil over medium heat. Boil and stir for 2 minutes or until thickened. Remove from the heat, stir in butter and vanilla. Spoon into individual serving dishes. Chill well before serving.

Creole Rice Pudding

This was my Mamere's recipe
Given to me by my Momma

3 cups cooked rice (preferably basmati rice)
4 cups milk, hot
¼ cup butter, melted
¾ cup sugar
6 eggs, beaten
1 teaspoon vanilla
4 teaspoons finely chopped orange rind
¾ cup raisins
1 teaspoon cinnamon

Preheat oven to 350 degrees. Combine cooked rice and hot milk. Add butter, sugar, eggs, vanilla, orange rind, and raisins. Pour into a buttered shallow rectangular baking dish and sprinkle with cinnamon. Place baking dish into a larger pan containing about ¼ inch water. Place in the oven and bake about 25 minutes. Allow to cool to room temperature. When cooled, cover dish and refrigerate. Serve cold.

Mixed Fruit Pudding

1 large package vanilla cook and serve pudding
1 (16 ounce) jar maraschino cherries, drained
2 large cans pineapple chunks, reserve juice
2 cans mandarin oranges, reserve juice
3 bananas

Cook pudding according to package directions, using 3 cups juice from canned fruit, pineapple juice first, instead of milk. When pudding has come to a boil and thickened, add all the fruit except the banana to pudding, mixing gently but well. Refrigerate until cold. When ready to serve, add sliced banana and mix gently. May be served plain, over ice cream, or topped with whipped cream or cool whip.

Hawaiian Delight Rice Pudding

4 cups milk, divided
3 cups cooked long grain rice
⅔ cup sugar
½ teaspoon salt
1 package (3 ounce) Philadelphia cream cheese, softened
2 eggs
1 teaspoon vanilla

    Combine 3 ½ cups milk, rice, sugar, and salt in a saucepan; bring to a boil over medium heat. Cook for 15 minutes or until thick and creamy, stirring occasionally. Beat the cream cheese, then the eggs and remaining milk in a mixing bowl. Stir into rice mixture and over medium heat continue to cook, stirring continuously, until mixture reaches 160 degrees on thermometer. Stir in vanilla and spoon into 6 dessert dishes.

Sauce

1 can (20 ounce) pineapple chunks
¼ cup brown sugar, packed tight
1 tablespoon cornstarch
1 tablespoon butter or margarine
⅛ teaspoon salt
½ teaspoon vanilla

    Drain pineapple, reserving the juice; set the pineapple aside. In a pot combine brown sugar, cornstarch, butter, salt, and the pineapple juice. Bring to a boil. Cook, stirring continuously, for about 2 minutes or until thickened. Stir in vanilla and pineapple. Spoon over pudding.

Praline Bread Pudding

4 cups stale French or Italian bread, cubed small (use crust of bread)
4½ cups milk
4 eggs, beaten
1 cup sugar
4 large green Granny Smith or golden delicious apples, peeled and shredded
2 teaspoons vanilla
1 teaspoon cinnamon
½ teaspoon salt
½ cup butter or margarine, melted
1 cup chopped pecans
5 tablespoons praline liqueur

Combine bread and hot milk in a large bowl and set aside. In a separate bowl beat eggs, add sugar and beat well. Stir into bread mixture and add apples, vanilla, cinnamon, salt, butter, chopped pecans, and praline liqueur. Pour into buttered 13"x9" casserole. Bake at 350 degrees in preheated oven for one hour or until knife inserted in the center comes out clean. If you like a more creamy pudding, bake with casserole sitting in a pan of warm water about 1 inch deep. Serve plain or with praline liqueur Sauce.

Praline Sauce

2 cups boiling water
1 cup sugar
2 tablespoons arrowroot
¼ teaspoon salt
¼ cup butter
4 tablespoons praline liqueur
⅓ cup chopped pecans

Gradually stir boiling water into mixture of sugar, arrowroot powder, and salt As water resumes boiling, lower heat to a simmer and cook for 5 minutes, stirring constantly. When sauce is thick, remove from heat and add butter, praline liqueur, and chopped pecans. Stir well to blend and pour over bread pudding.

Lagniappe

(A Creole word for "A Little Something Extra")

Sautéed Spicy Apples 335
Microwaved Applesauce 336
Steak Butter 337
Creole Seasoning 337
One Day Liquid Diet 338
Mojo Topping 339
Popcorn Balls (Mais "Tac Tac") 339
Praline Baked Apples 340
Prunes with Lemon Slices 341
Seasoned Salt 341
Chopped Seasonings for Freezing 342
Shirred Eggs 343
Kitchen Equivalent Chart 344
Cast Iron Skillets 345
Using Leftovers in the South 346

Sautéed Spicy Apples

¼ cup butter
1 cup firmly packed light brown sugar
¼ cup honey
1 teaspoon ground cinnamon
1 teaspoon ground cloves
1 teaspoon ground nutmeg
½ teaspoon salt
4 - 6 Granny Smith apples. Cored and sliced into ¼ inch slices

Heat butter over medium heat in a large skillet until butter is melted. Add brown sugar, honey, spices, and salt, stirring to combine. Add apple slices and toss gently to coat with butter mixture. Cover and cook for 10 minutes, stirring occasionally, until apples begin to get tender. Remove cover and increase heat to medium high. Cook for 15 minutes, stirring frequently, until syrup thickens, and apples are lightly browned.

Variation: Reduce number of apples to 3 and add 3 red cored D'Anjou pears, sliced into ¼ inch thick slices. Continue as above.

Microwaved Applesauce

4 pounds apples, washed, cored and quartered
½ cup water
1 cup honey
¼ teaspoon ground nutmeg
¼ teaspoon ground allspice
2 tablespoons butter
Juice of 1 lemon

Leave the skins on the apples to add fiber and nutrients. Place quartered apples in a large microwave bowl. Add water, cover, and microwave on high for 12 minutes or until apples are soft. After 12 minutes check the apples. If they are not soft enough, cook for a few more minutes. Drain the liquid from the cooked apples and reserve. Place apples in a blender or preferably a food processor. Add rest of ingredients and process on high until smooth. For a thinner consistency, add some of the liquid. Let stand until cool. Store tightly covered and refrigerated, for up to one week. Applesauce may be frozen in serving size portions to be used later. Frozen applesauce will keep up to 9 months.

*Note: McIntosh, Rome Beauty, and Cortland are a few varieties of apple that are good for making applesauce. Avoid using Red Delicious, which cooks down to a sauce that is both poorly flavored and poorly colored. For a well-balanced flavor, mix tart and sweeter varieties.

Variation: Applesauce may be mixed with an equal portion of another fruit sauce such as apple-peach, apple-apricot, apple-plum, or apple-pear.

Steak Butter

4 tablespoons butter
2 cloves garlic
½ teaspoon A1 sauce
½ teaspoon Worcestershire sauce
½ teaspoon salt
½ teaspoon olive oil
1 tablespoon chopped fresh parsley

Allow butter to soften. Mash garlic to paste with salt. Mix everything together. Cook steaks. Spread mixture to both sides and let stand for 2 to 3 minutes. Makes enough for 3 steaks.

Creole Seasoning

2 tablespoons salt
2 tablespoons garlic powder
1 tablespoon ground black pepper
1 tablespoons cayenne pepper
1 tablespoons dried thyme leaves
1 tablespoons dried oregano
2½ tablespoons paprika
1 tablespoon onion powder

Place all ingredients in a sealed jar or container. Shake jar thoroughly to mix. Use to season meats and seafood. Makes ⅔ cup. Keeps indefinitely.

One Day Liquid Diet

This preparatory liquid diet is very good for the beginning of a weight loss diet, or to be used one day a month to tone and rest your stomach. Do not be worried at the prospect of giving up solids for a day as this liquid menu contains a substantial caloric content sufficient to prevent you from feeling wishy-washy. So, using an eight ounce glass per portion, prepare to enjoy this cleansing, healthful day on liquid foods. Although you may pick any day of the week for this one day diet, a Sunday might be the most convenient day.

On Arising .... 1 glass of orange juice
    1 cup coffee, sugar and cream.

Mid-morning .... 1 glass pineapple juice.

At lunch time .... 1 glass grapefruit juice,
    one-half glass prune juice,
    1 cup tea, sugar and lemon.

Two and a half hours
After lunch time .... 1 glass milk.

About 5 P.M. .... 1 glass pineapple and
    grapefruit juice mixed.

At dinner time .... 2 cups hot tomato soup,
    1 glass orange juice.

Shortly before retiring .... 1 glass prune juice
    with the juice of half a lemon.

Mojo Topping
A Healthful addition to a bowl of Soup, especially
If you have a cold or Flu.

1 tablespoon finely minced fresh ginger
1 tablespoon finely minced garlic
1 tablespoon olive oil
1 tablespoon fresh lemon juice
1/8 to 1/4 teaspoon cayenne pepper, according to taste

Combine all ingredients in a small bowl and stir until well blended. Drizzle a teaspoon or so over each bowl of hot soup.

Popcorn Balls
(Mais "Tac Tac")

2 cups Louisiana cane syrup or molasses
1 tablespoon butter or margarine
1/4 teaspoon salt
2 quarts popcorn

Boil syrup over low heat, stirring constantly. When a few drops tested in cold water becomes brittle, add butter and salt. Pour over the popped corn. Mix and shape into large balls.

Praline Baked Apples

4 large apples, (Red or golden delicious, Rome Beauty, Granny Smith)
4 tablespoons light brown sugar
4 tablespoons butter
4 teaspoons finely chopped pecans
4 tablespoons of Praline Liqueur
4 tablespoons of Whipped cream
Nutmeg

Preheat oven to 375 degrees. Remove one inch strip of skin around top and one inch strip around middle of each apple. Core apples to within ½ inch of the bottom. Place apples upright in an ungreased baking dish. Put one tablespoon sugar in each apple. Place 1 tablespoons butter on top of sugar. Sprinkle each apple with 1 teaspoon chopped pecans, as much as possible going into center of apple. Pour 1 tablespoon Praline Liqueur over each apple. Pour water into the bottom of the baking dish to about ¼ inch depth. Bake for 30 to 40 minutes or until the apples are tender when they are pierced with a fork. Spoon syrup in the dish over the apples several times during baking period. Remove apples to serving dishes. Pour a little of the syrup from the baking dish over the apples again and then garnish apples with a tablespoon of whipping cream and a sprinkle of nutmeg on each one.

Note: Apples can also be baked quickly, easily and deliciously in a microwave oven. Follow directions above for peeling and coring apples, place in an 8-inch square microwave safe dish, prepare as above, and cover with vented plastic wrap. Microwave at full power (high) for 7 to 9 minutes, or until almost tender, giving dish a half turn once during cooking time. When cooking time is over, let stand, covered, for 10 minutes. Then proceed as above. Serve warm or cold.

Lagniappe

Prunes with Lemon Slices
Cooked in Microwave

1½ pounds pitted prunes
1 large lemon, washed and very thinly sliced
1 cup sugar
3 cups water

Mix all the ingredients in a large microwave safe bowl. Cover and microwave on high for 11 minutes. Serve cold, adding sliced of lemon to each serving.

Seasoned Salt

2 tablespoons celery salt
2 tablespoons onion salt
2 tablespoons garlic salt
2 tablespoons paprika
1 teaspoon chili powder
¼ teaspoon white pepper
¼ teaspoon black pepper
⅛ teaspoon cayenne pepper

Sift all ingredients together several times. Put in empty spice bottle with shaker insert.

Chopped Seasonings for Freezing

One of my favorite and most used appliance in my kitchen is my food processor. For Louisiana cooks, and for the ones who want to cook like Louisianians, it is almost a necessity. I like the option of having on hand at all times the vegetables I need to make the gumbo, stews, soups, etc. my family likes. So, I buy in bulk, and take a morning, or an evening when the family is busy with other things, and chop and freeze seasonings that not only comes in handy on days when I am rushed, but also saves me money! I like to mix the seasonings I need together in one bag. One cup of mixed vegetables is usually enough for one dish I am preparing - 1 bag for 1 pound of beans, or 1 bag for each pound of meat - but I can add more if needed. But if you prefer, you can put all onion in one bag, all celery, sweet pepper, garlic, etc. in another. Measure it out 1 cup per small freezer bag. Just be sure you mark the bags with a permanent marker saying what is in each bag, and to flatten the seasonings in thin sheets inside the bags. This way, you'll always have fresh onions, garlic, etc. on hand, and all but eliminate the need for dried seasonings. So, pull out your food processor and start saving time, energy and money!

1 stalk celery
2 large red onions
4 heads garlic
2 large, sweet peppers (Green peppers)
2 bunches shallots (green onions)
1 bunch parsley

Clean all vegetables and cut up in large chunks. Mix ingredients evenly in large baking pan and place in food processor a little at a time. Use pulser on processor and continue until all seasonings are chopped. Mix well and measure out 1 cup at a time. Fill small zip-loc freezer bags with 1 cup of the mixture, flatten freezer bag with hand, seal, mark and freeze. Use seasonings frozen. Do not thaw before using. This amount of seasoning should fill about 12 freezer bags. Can easily be doubled.

Lagniappe

Shirred Eggs

8 Eggs
2 tablespoons water
½ teaspoon Tabasco Sauce
¼ teaspoon salt
¼ teaspoon black pepper
Cooked crumbled bacon

    Preheat oven to 325 degrees. For each serving, break two eggs into four small greased, oval shaped gratin dishes In a separate small dish, mix water Tabasco sauce, salt and black pepper. Spoon mixture over eggs in each dish, gently mixing it with the whites of the eggs very carefully so you do not break the yolks. Top with crumbled bacon. Bake until whites are completely set and yolks begin to thicken but are not hard, about 15 minutes. Serve immediately. Makes 4 servings.

    Variation: Shredded cheese may be sprinkled on top before baking and diced ham may be used in place of bacon.

Kitchen Equivalent Chart

A pinch	⅛ teaspoon or less
1 teaspoon	½ tablespoon
3 teaspoons	1 tablespoon
2 tablespoons	⅛ cup
4 tablespoons	¼ cup
16 tablespoons	1 cup
5 tablespoons & 1 teaspoon	⅓ cup
4 ounces	½ cup
8 ounces	1 cup
16 ounces	1 pound
1 ounce	2 tablespoons fat or liquid
1 cup of liquid	½ pint
2 cups	1 pint
2 pints	1 quart
4 cups of liquid	1 quart
4 quarts	1 gallon
8 quarts	1 peck (such as apples, peaches, etc.)
1 jigger	1½ fluid ounce
1 jigger	3 tablespoons

Cast Iron Skillets

To remove the grease build-up on the outside of a black cast iron skillet, place the skillet in a fire. You can either put it in your fireplace or start a fire in your barbecue grill. Place the skillet or pot right in the flames. It should remain in the fire for at least an hour.

After the fire burns down, carefully remove the skillet. Do not cool the skillet with cold water; this could crack it. The fire burns off the build-up so it should be clean and gunk-free.

To re-season the skillet, wash it in sudsy water, rinse well and dry. Put a thick layer of unsalted vegetable shortening on the inside, rubbing it on the sides and inside bottom.

Cover the skillet with an oven-safe lid, place it on a cookie sheet and let it bake ion the oven for 90 minutes at 250 degrees. Swab the grease around periodically with a clean cloth to keep the surface of the skillet evenly coated.

After an hour and a half, allow the skillet to cook and completely wipe out any excess grease. Buff, using a clean, dry cloth.

Using Leftovers in the South

I mentioned in the beginning of this book how Creole cooks never waste any food. Here is a list of ways that leftover food was utilized in the nineteenth and early twentieth centuries. (And still in many households in this day).

Bread: Stale bread or scraps of bread were never thrown away. The broken pieces were browned in the oven and then rolled fine on the bread board. The crumbs were then put in a covered jar and kept for use in cooking, especially for "au Gratin" dishes.

Leftover stale bread was also used (and still is) in making Bread Puddings, Bread Muffins, Queen Puddings, etc. All broken pieces of cake were used in making puddings, such as Banana Souffle, and all Cake Puddings.

I remember when the great hurricane Betsy hit the city of New Orleans in 1965. We were living at that time in an area known as Jackson Barracks, since my husband was a Colonel in the Army. Jackson Barracks was the home of the Louisiana National Guard. Our home was just steps from the high levee that protected the city from the Mississippi River. Much of the city was flooded by the storm, but the section we lived in was spared. It was as if we were on an island in the middle of a lake. We were surrounded by water and without electricity for quite a while. It was in September and the weather was very hot. One day the National Guardsmen came to our home in a big truck. They were passing out ice cream, which had been donated by a local ice cream shop, to everyone in our area. They gave us several gallons of tuti-fruiti ice cream. There were thirteen people in my home at the time, family members from other parts of the city who came to stay with us during the hurricane. Anyway, the ice cream was so welcome, for we hadn't had anything cold for quite a while, so we ate and ate. But we still had some left over. Momma, in the true Creole tradition, could not see that melting ice cream go to waste, so she began wondering what she could do with it. Seeing some left-over stale bread in the kitchen, and luckily some milk and eggs in the large ice chest we had, she decided to make bread pudding with the ice cream. Bread pudding with tuti-fruiti ice cream. And it was delicious! Thank goodness for Momma, and the fact that our gas stove was still operational!

Potatoes: Leftover mashed potatoes were used for making Croquettes or Puffs or Quenelles of Potatoes. Leftover boiled potatoes were used in preparing Lyonnaise Potatoes or Fried Potatoes.

(Continued Next Page)

Greens: Leftover greens were used for salads. Fish or Chicken leftovers were used for Fish or Chicken salad.

Meats: Leftover meats of all types were used in making Hash, Croquettes or Boulettes.

Rice: All leftover Rice was used for Riz au Lait, Griddle Cake, Calas, Jambalaya, etc.

Ham: When they were finished with the ham bone, all the meat was cut off to be used as seasoning meat, and the bone was used with cabbage or turnips or other vegetable greens, or with red or white beans, or to use in soup.

When making Gold Cake, the whites of the eggs were saved for Silver Cakes, or used for making Angel Cake, Apple Snow, or other forms of desserts in which meringues were called for.

In those Creole kitchens, nothing was wasted. And those habits are continued to this day. But of course, now we have it so much easier. We have blenders and food processors for the breadcrumbs, and chopped chicken and meats, etc. We have freezers to save leftover meals. And we have the memory of our Mothers, Grandmothers and Great- Grandmothers who instilled these thrifty ways in our hearts.

Index

Index

A

Apple(s)
    Deep Dish Country, Pie · 314
    Fritters · 250
    Microwaved Applesauce · 336
    Praline Baked · 340
    Sautéed Spicy · 335
Apricot
    Glaze · 311
Artichoke (s)
    Balls · 23
    Butter Sauce · 98
    Casserole · 223
    Cheese, and Spinach Casserole · 223
    Chicken and, Hearts · 151
    Chicken and, Pasta · 239
    Crab, and Avocado Casserole · 228
    Creamy, Soup · 51
    Lemon and, Linguine · 242
    Macaroni and · 242
    Microwaved · 197
    Oyster and, Casserole · 229
    Oyster and, Soup · 61
    Party · 24
Asparagus
    Cream of, Soup · 52
Avocado (s)
    and Cucumber Soup · 50
    and Egg Salad Sandwich · 273
    Chicken and BLT Sandwiches · 273
    Chilled, Soup · 49
    Crab, Artichoke and, Casserole · 228

Avocado (s) (*continued*)
    Dip No. 1 · 24
    Dip No. 2 · 25
    Guacamole · 32
    Pesto · 25
    Pesto with Pasta · 239
    Shrimp Stuffed · 90

B

Banana (s)
    Carrot Nut Bread · 252
    Foster · 320
    Fritters · 250
    Nut Bread · 251
Bean (s)
    Green, and Ham · 124
    Green, Salad · 83
    Kale and, Soup · 57
    Navy, (White Beans) and Rice · 123
    Preparing dried, for cooking · 117
    Red, and Rice · 119
    Salad · 73
    Tuscan White, Soup · 63
Beef
    and Garlic Brown Gravy · 178
    Creole Pot Roast · 177
    Crock-Pot, Stew · 182
    Meatballs for Spaghetti Gravy · 192
    Pepper Steak · 188
    Roasted, Brisket · 175
    Stew · 181
    Stew in Red Wine · 179
    Stroganoff · 191
Beignets · 253
    Petit · 252

Black-Eyed Peas
    and Rice · 121
    Side Dish · 122
    with Wine · 122
Blue Cheese
    Celery Stuffed with · 28
    Classic, and Sautérne Dip · 26
    Dip with Bacon · 27
    Roquefort or, Dressing No. 1 · 72
    Roquefort or, Dressing No. 2 · 72
    Sautérne Dip · 26
Blueberry
    Custard · 320
    Raspberry and, Sauce · 107
Brandy
    Whiskey or, Sauce · 100
Bread
    Banana Nut · 251
    Banana-Carrot Nut · 252
    Cinnamon Raisin · 255
    Creole Spoon, with Sauce · 269
    Deep South Spoon, Souffle · 268
    Garlic · 260
    Grilled Ciabatta · 254
    Monkey · 265
    New Orleans Skillet Corn · 256
    Praline, Pudding · 331
    Pudding · 328
    Southern Angel Biscuits · 249
    Southern Dumplings (Quick Method) · 255
    Spinach · 267
Broccoli
    Cream of Broccoli Soup · 50

Index

Broccoli (*continued*)
    Herbed, Casserole · 224
Brussels Sprouts
    with Parmesan Cheese · 198
Butter
    and Wine Sauce · 101
    Artichoke, Sauce · 98
    Cranberry · 102
    Herb and Seasoned · 112
    Honey · 111
    Lemon Herb · 197
    Parsley or Cilantro-Lime · 112
    Raspberry · 111
    Steak · 337

C

Cabbage
    Chou Glorioux (Glorified Cabbage) · 225
    Microwaved · 198
Cake
    Angel Food, with Berry Compote · 299
    Carrot and Pineapple · 298
    Chocolate · 283
    Chocolate Fudge Pecan Layer · 297
    Creole Red Velvet · 295
    Cuban Tres Leches · 296
    Fig · 284
    Golden Sherry or Rum · 285
    Hummingbird · 286
    Hummingbird (Made from a Cake Mix) · 287
    Lane · 288
    Lemon and Cherry Upside Down · 290
    Lemon Fleck Frosting · 291
    Lemon Meringue · 292
    Old Fashioned Southern Pound · 293
    Praline Pecan · 294
    Strawberry Shortcake · 289
    Tangy Sunshine · 296

Carrot (s)
    and Pineapple Cake · 298
    Banana-, Nut Bread · 252
    Orange, Cookies · 307
    Sunny · 200
Casserole
    Artichoke · 223
    Artichoke, Cheese, and Spinach · 223
    Cauliflower au Gratin · 224
    Chicken, Rice, and Water Chestnut · 226
    Chili and Macaroni · 227
    Chou Glorioux (Glorified Cabbage) · 225
    Corn · 228
    Crab, Artichoke and Avocado · 228
    Creole Potato · 231
    Herbed Broccoli · 224
    Hominy and Corn · 231
    Lagniappe · 235
    Momma's Stuffed Eggplant · 230
    Oyster and Artichoke · 229
    Pineapple and Cheese · 227
    Potatoes au Gratin · 233
    Rice Sabrosa · 234
    Rosie's Yam · 232
    Turnips au Gratin · 234
Cast Iron Skillets
    General Information · 345
Catfish
    Broiled or Baked · 138
Cauliflower
    au Gratin · 224
    Macaroni · 241
Cheese
    Artichoke, and Spinach Casserole · 223
    Ball No. 1 · 28
    Ball No. 2 · 29
    Creole Cream, Ice Cream · 321
    Drops or fingers · 29
    Marinated · 30

Cheese (*continued*)
    Pineapple and, Casserole · 227
    Savory, Rounds · 30
    Welsh Rarebit · 38
Cherry
    Lemon and, Upside Down Cake · 290
    Pie · 317
    Sauce · 290
Chicken
    and Artichoke Hearts · 151
    and Artichoke Pasta · 239
    and Hash Brown Potatoes · 152
    and Sausage Gumbo · 45
    and Sausage Jambalaya L'Acadien · 129
    and Wine · 154
    Avocado, and BLT Sandwiches · 273
    Baked · 154
    Brunswick Stew · 155
    Cooked in Microwave · 156
    Croquettes · 157
    Fingers with Dipping Sauce · 31
    Fried, New Orleans Style · 166
    Grilled, Sauce · 103
    Grilling · 158
    Hawaiian Shish Kabobs · 159
    Herbed Roast Cornish Hens · 170
    Honey Mustard · 160
    in a Bag · 161
    Lemon, Breasts · 166
    Mamere's, and Brown Gravy (Chicken Fricassee) · 153
    Marinated, Breasts Paprika · 167
    Marsala · 162
    Party, and Tomatoes · 33
    Rice, and Water Chestnut Casserole · 226
    Roast · 168
    Salad · 75

Index

Chicken (*continued*)
    Sauce Piquant · 164
    Soup · 53
    Spicy Baked · 169
    with Herbs and Wine · 163
    with Linguine and Marinara Sauce · 165
Chocolate
    Cake · 283
    Chip Cake Mix Cookies · 301
    French Hot · 11
    Fudge Cookies · 301
    Fudge Pecan Layer Cake · 297
    Fudge Sauce · 101
    Hot Cocoa · 10
    Microwaved Hot Fudge Sauce · 102
    Pudding · 328
    Quick, Malt · 7
    Sauce · 8
    Speedy, Fudge Sauce · 101
    Super, Malt · 7
Chopped Seasonings for Freezing · 342
Cocktail (s)
    Creole Mary (The Designated Driver's Drink) · 17
    Mimosa · 17
    Mint Julep · 17
    Ramos Gin Fizz (New Orleans Gin Fizz) · 18
Coffee
    Café au Lait · 4
    Café Brulot · 4
    Café Parfait (Iced Coffee) · 5
    Irish · 5
    New Orleans Chicory · 3
Cognac
    Café Brulot · 4
Cookies
    Bourbon Balls · 300
    Chocolate Chip Cake Mix · 301
    Coconut Macaroons · 304
    Fudge · 301

Cookies (*continued*)
    Gingersnap · 302
    Hermits · 303
    Lemon Sugar · 304
    Madeleines · 305
    Momma's Molasses Oatmeal · 306
    Orange Carrot · 307
    Peanut Butter · 307
    Pfeffernusse Christmas (German Peppernuts) · 308
    Praline Snickerdoodles · 309
    Sandstone Health · 309
    Snickerdoodles · 310
Corn
    and Crab Bisque · 55
    Casserole · 228
    Corn Maque Choux · 202
    Hominy and, Casserole · 231
    New Orleans Skillet, Bread · 256
Crab (s)
    Artichoke and Avocado Casserole · 228
    Boiled · 133
    Corn and, Bisque · 55
    Hot, Dip · 33
    Stuffed · 134
Cranberry
    and Nut Muffins · 258
    Butter · 102
    Molded, Salad · 80
    Punch · 15
    Spiced, Punch · 14
Crawfish
    Cajun, Pie · 137
    Etouffee · 135
    Weldon's, Etouffee · 136
Creole Seasoning · 337
Cucumber
    Avocado and, Soup · 50
    English, Sandwiches · 275
Custard
    Blueberry · 320
    Creole Caramel Cup · 323
    Tropical, Pie · 313

Custard (*continued*)
    Vanilla Cream Filling · 327

D

Dessert (s)
    Bananas Foster · 320
    Cream Puffs · 322
    Ruby Pears · 326
    Sabayon · 325
        a la Creole · 325
        with Fruit · 326
    Spiced Fruit Compote · 72
Dip
    Avocado, No. 1 · 24
    Avocado, No. 2 · 25
    Blue Cheese Sautérne · 26
    Blue Cheese, with Bacon · 27
    Classic Bleu Cheese and Sautérne · 26
    Guacamole · 32
    Hot Crab · 33
    Tapenade · 37
Dressing
    Classic French · 69
    Creamy Fruit Salad · 69
    Honey-Poppy Seed Salad · 70
    Italian · 70
    Lemon and Oil Salad · 71
    Lemon Vinaigrette · 71
    Roquefort or Blue Cheese, No. 1 · 72
    Roquefort or Blue Cheese, No. 2 · 72
    Vinaigrette · 69

E

Egg (s)
    Avocado and, Salad Sandwich · 273
    Deviled · 32
    Salad · 80

Egg (s) (*continued*)
    Shirred · 343
Eggplant
    French Fried · 200
    Momma's Stuffed, Casserole · 230
    Parmigiana · 213
Etouffee
    Crawfish · 135
    Weldon's Crawfish · 136

F

Fish
    Broiled or Baked · 138
    Fillets with Sauce Meuniere (Lemon Butter Sauce) · 139
    Fried · 140
    Oven Fried, Fillets · 139
    Red Snapper Fillets · 142
    Red, Courtboullion · 141
    Seafood Loaf with Creole Sauce · 278
Fritters
    Apple · 250
    Banana · 250
    Creole, Batter · 249
    Orange · 250
    Pineapple · 250

G

Glaze (s) · 311
    Apricot · 311
    Lemon · 311
    Orange · 311
    Strawberry · 311
Gravy
    Red Eye · 109
Grillades and Grits · 183
Gumbo
    Chicken and Sausage, (Gumbo Ya Ya) · 45
    Seafood, Filé · 47

Gumbo (*continued*)
    Turkey and Sausage · 48
    Z'Herbes (Green Gumbo) · 43

H

Honey
    and Oatmeal Breakfast Muffins · 262
    Butter · 111
    Momma's, or Molasses Bran Muffins · 263
    Mustard Chicken · 160
    Poppy Seed Salad Dressing · 70
Hushpuppies · 257

I

Ice Cream
    Black Cow Shake · 8
    Creole Cream Cheese · 321
    Gelatin and, Drink · 8
    Soda · 6
    Strawberry Soda · 6
Ice Cream Soda · 6
    Strawberry, · 6
    Tropical Cooler · 6
Ice Ring Mold · 11

J

Jambalaya
    Chicken and Sausage, L'Acadien · 129
    Hoppin' John · 128
    Jonny's "Secret" Recipe · 186

K

Kitchen Equivalent Chart · 344

L

Lemon
    and Artichoke Linguine · 242
    and Cherry Upside Down Cake · 290
    and Oil Salad Dressing · 71
    Chicken Breasts · 166
    Fish Fillets with Sauce Meuniere (Lemon Butter Sauce) · 139
    Fleck Frosting Cake · 291
    Glaze · 311
    Herb Butter · 197
    Ice Dessert · 321
    Lemonade · 12
    Meringue Cake · 292
    Meringue Pie · 315
    Prunes with, Slices · 341
    Sauce · 104
    Sugar Cookies · 304
    Vinaigrette · 71

M

Malt
    Quick Chocolate · 7
    Super Chocolate · 7
    Vanilla · 7
Mango
    Sauce · 104
Meat
    Loaf and Brown Gravy · 185
    Natchitoches Meat Pies · 187
    Spaghetti and Creole, Gravy · 243
    Vegetable and, Soup · 64
Milkshake
    Black Cow · 8
    Strawberry · 7
Mojo Topping · 339
Muffins
    Cranberry and Nut · 258
    Honey and Oatmeal Breakfast · 262

Index

Muffins (*continued*)
    Momma's Honey or Molasses Bran · 263
    Momma's Molasses Raisin Bran · 264
    Zucchini · 266
Mushroom (s)
    Spirited · 201
    Stuffed, Hors d'Oeuvres · 34

O

Oatmeal
    Honey and, Breakfast Muffins · 262
    Momma's Molasses, Cookies · 306
One Day Liquid Diet · 338
Orange
    Carrot Cookies · 307
    Glaze · 311
    Golden, French Toast · 261
    Orange Fritters · 250
    Sauce · 106
Oyster
    and Artichoke Casserole · 229
    and Artichoke Soup · 61
    Patties · 35, 143
    Soup · 60

P

Pasta
    Avocado Pesto with · 239
    Cauliflower Macaroni · 241
    Chicken and Artichoke · 239
    Lemon and Artichoke Linguine · 242
    Macaroni and Artichokes · 242
    Primavera · 244
    Salad · 85
    Spaghetti and Creole Meat Gravy · 243

Pasta (*continued*)
    Spaghetti Bordelaise · 240
Peach
    and Strawberry Sauce · 106
Pear (s)
    Ruby · 326
Pecan (s)
    Chocolate Fudge, Layer Cake · 297
    Jo's, Pie · 316
    Olive, Sandwich · 274
    Praline, Cake · 294
    Pralines · 324
    Roasted Spiced · 36
Pie
    Basic, Pastry · 313
    Cherry · 317
    Deep Dish Country Apple · 314
    Jo's Pecan · 316
    Lemon Meringue · 315
    Pastry · 312
    Pumpkin · 318
    Shepherd's · 190
    Southern Yam (or Sweet Potato) · 319
    Tropical Custard · 313
Pineapple (s)
    and Cheese Casserole · 227
    Carrot and, Cake · 298
    Fritters · 250
Popcorn Balls · 339
Pork
    Chops and Brown Gravy · 189
    Mike's, Chops · 186
    Roasted, Tenderloin · 189
Potato (es)
    au Gratin · 233
    Brabant · 201
    Chicken and Hash Brown · 152
    Cottage Fried · 204
    Cream of Leek and, Soup · 58
    Creole, Casserole · 231
    German, Salad · 81

Potato (es) (*continued*)
    Microwaved Herbed New · 204
    Momma's, Salad · 86
    Mounds (Alsatian Flutters) · 207
    New, with Sea Salt and Vinegar · 205
    Oven Fried French Fries · 205
    Parmesan · 206
    Skin Nachos · 203
    Soup · 54
    Turnip Mashed · 207
    Twice Baked · 208
    Vichyssoise · 65
Praline (s)
    Baked Apples · 340
    Bread Pudding · 331
    Pecan Cake · 294
    Pecan Pralines · 324
    Snickerdoodles · 309
    Yams · 218
Prune (s)
    with Lemon Slices · 341
Pudding
    Bread · 328
    Chocolate · 328
    Creole Rice · 329
    Hawaiian Delight Rice · 330
    Mixed Fruit · 329
    Praline Bread · 331
Pumpkin
    Pie · 318
Punch
    Champagne, a La Creole · 16
    Cranberry · 15
    Hurricane · 14
    Laurie's Champagne (Wedding Punch) · 16
    Planter's · 15
    Spiced Cranberry · 14

R

Raspberry
  and Blueberry Sauce · 107
  Butter · 111
Rice
  Black-Eyed Peas and · 121
  Calas (Rice Cakes) · 126
  General Information · 118
  Mardi Gras · 125
  Mediterranean, Pilaf · 124
  Navy Beans (White Beans) and · 123
  Pilaf · 125
  Red Beans and · 119
  Riz au Lait (Rice and Milk) · 127
  Riz Persillé (Parsley Rice) · 127
  Sabrosa Casserole · 234
Roux
  Blond (White Roux) · 95
  Microwave · 96
  The French · 95

S

Salad
  Aspic Ring for · 74
  Bean · 73
  Chicken · 75
  Chopped · 77
  Cobb · 78
  Egg · 80
  Five Cup · 81
  German Potato · 81
  Greek · 82
  Green Bean · 83
  Layered Fruit · 76
  Molded Cranberry · 80
  Momma's Cole Slaw · 74
  Momma's Fruit · 75
  Momma's Potato · 86
  Niçoise · 87
  Okra and Tomato · 84
  Olive · 84

Salad (*continued*)
  Pasta · 85
  Shrimp · 85
  Shrimp, with Sea Salt and Dressing · 88
  Sicilian · 89
  Spinach · 78
  Waldorf · 88
Sandwich (es) · 270
  Avocado and Egg Salad · 273
  Avocado, Chicken and BLT · 273
  Cobb · 275
  English Cucumber · 275
  Muffuletta · 277
  New Orleans Famous "Poor Boy" · 271
  Olive Pecan · 274
  Seafood Loaf with Creole Sauce · 278
  Tomato, with Basil Mayonnaise · 274
Sauce
  Artichoke Butter · 98
  Bechamel (White Sauce) · 99
  Bordelaise · 100
  Butter and Wine · 101
  Cherry · 290
  Chocolate Fudge · 101
  Creole Alfredo · 97
  Creole Tomato · 113
  Creole Tomato Horseradish · 109
  Grilled Chicken · 103
  Hollandaise · 103
  Le Salse Alla Puttanesca (Puttanesca Sauce) · 108
  Lemon · 104
  Mango · 104
  Marinade, for Pork or Steak · 98
  Marinara · 105
  Meuniere · 104
  Microwaved Hot Fudge · 102

Sauce (*continued*)
  Momma's Mayonnaise Pepper · 197
  Mornay (Cheese Sauce) · 99
  New Orleans Tartar · 111
  Orange · 106
  Peach and Strawberry · 106
  Pesto · 107
  Raspberry and Blueberry · 107
  Remoulade · 110
  Speedy Chocolate Fudge · 101
  Tapenade · 37
  Whiskey or Brandy · 100
Seasoned Salt · 341
Shellfish
  Boiled Crabs · 133
  Boiled Shrimp · 144
  Cajun Crawfish Pie · 137
  Clam Chowder · 54
  Corn and Crab Bisque · 55
  Crab, Artichoke and Avocado Casserole · 228
  Crawfish Etouffee · 135
  Hot Crab Dip · 33
  New Orleans Barbequed Shrimp · 145
  Oyster and Artichoke Casserole · 229
  Oyster and Artichoke Soup · 61
  Oyster Patties · 35, 143
  Oyster Soup · 60
  Seafood Gumbo Filé · 47
  Seafood Loaf with Creole Sauce · 278
  Shrimp Salad · 85
  Shrimp Salad with Sea Salt and Dressing · 88
  Shrimp Sauce Piquant (Shrimp Creole) · 146
  Shrimp Scampi · 36, 147
  Shrimp Stuffed Avocado · 90
  Stuffed Crabs · 134
  Weldon's Crawfish Etouffee · 136

Index

Shrimp
- Boiled · 144
- New Orleans Barbequed · 145
- Salad · 85
- Salad with Sea Salt and Dressing · 88
- Sauce Piquant (Shrimp Creole) · 146
- Scampi · 36, 147
- Stuffed Avocado · 90

Smoothie
- Breakfast · 9
- Fruit · 9
- Queasy Stomach · 9
- Super · 10

Soup
- a l'Oignon Gratinée (Onion Soup Gratineed with Cheese) · 60
- Avocado and Cucumber · 50
- Chicken · 53
- Chilled Avocado · 49
- Clam Chowder · 54
- Corn and Crab Bisque · 55
- Cream of Asparagus · 52
- Cream of Broccoli · 50
- Cream of Leek and Potato · 58
- Creamy Artichoke · 51
- French Onion (Soupe a L'Oignon) · 59
- Gazpacho · 56
- Kale and Bean · 57
- Oyster · 60
- Oyster and Artichoke · 61
- Potato · 54
- Split Pea · 62
- Tuscan White Bean · 63
- Vegetable and Meat · 64
- Vichyssoise · 65

Southern Collard Greens · 199

Strawberry
- Glaze · 311
- Milkshake · 7
- Peach and, Sauce · 106
- Soda · 6

Sweet Peppers
- Momma's Stuffed · 209

Sweet Potato (es)
- Baked Louisiana Yams · 214
- Candied Holiday Yams · 216
- Candied Holiday Yams with Bourbon · 217
- Golden Louisiana Yam Fries · 215
- Praline Yams · 218
- Rosie's Yam Casserole · 232
- Southern Yam , Pie · 319
- Sticks · 216
- Yams Hannah · 219
- Yams, Pone · 215

T

Tea
- Iced, and Ginger Ale · 13
- Mint Iced · 12
- Pink, Refresher · 13

Toast
- French · 259
- Golden Orange French · 261
- Spicy Cheese · 276

Tomato (es)
- Cherry and Herbed, Sauté · 210
- Creole, Horseradish Sauce · 109
- Creole, Sauce · 113
- Marinated · 83
- Okra and, Salad · 84
- Party Chicken and · 33
- Sandwich with Basil Mayonnaise · 274
- Stewed · 211
- Tomates Grillées à la Grecque (Broiled Tomatoes with Greek Feta Cheese) · 211

Turkey
- Herbed, Breast · 171
- in a Crock Pot · 171

Turkey (*continued*)
- and Sausage Gumbo · 48

Turnip (s)
- au Gratin · 234
- Mashed Potatoes · 207

U

Using Leftovers in the South · 346

V

Veal
- Panéed · 192
- Scaloppine with Wine · 193

Vegetable (s)
- and Meat Soup · 64
- Copper Pennies (Marinated Carrots) · 79
- Crudites and Dip · 27
- Mixed Roasted · 212

W

Whipped Cream · 299

Whiskey
- Irish Coffee · 5
- or Brandy Sauce · 100

Wine
- Beef Stew in Red · 179
- Black-Eyed Peas with · 122
- Blue Cheese Sautérne Dip · 26
- Butter and, Sauce · 101
- Champagne Punch a La Creole · 16
- Chicken and · 154
- Chicken with Herbs and · 163
- Classic Bleu Cheese and Sautérne Dip · 26
- Mulled · 19

Wine (*continued*)
    Spanish Sangria (Wine Punch) · 18
    Veal Scaloppine with · 193

Y

Yam (s)
    Baked Louisiana Yams · 214
    Candied Holiday · 216
    Candied Holiday, with Bourbon · 217
    Golden Louisiana, Fries · 215
    Hannah · 219
    Praline · 218
    Rosie's, Casserole · 232
    Southern, (or Sweet Potato) Pie · 319
    Sweet Potato Pone · 215
    Sweet Potato Sticks · 216

www.ingramcontent.com/pod-product-compliance
Lightning Source LLC
Chambersburg PA
CBHW080437170426
43195CB00017B/2809